HERMENEUTICS

THE ART AND SCIENCE OF INTERPRETING THE

BIBLE

NATHANIEL MCCLAIN

authorHOUSE®

AuthorHouse™
1663 Liberty Drive
Bloomington, IN 47403
www.authorhouse.com
Phone: 833-262-8899

Published by AuthorHouse 02/28/2022

ISBN: 978-1-6655-4882-3 (sc)
ISBN: 978-1-6655-4883-0 (hc)
ISBN: 978-1-6655-4884-7 (e)

Library of Congress Control Number: 2022903882

Print information available on the last page.

OTHER BOOKS BY THIS AUTHOR

›

All human strife is facilitated by spiritual wickedness that goes virtually unseen. This book provides the reader with a real biblical view of the enemy and his plan. It also provides the tools to combat the enemy in accordance with God's plan.

Every tree has a root. This book explains the roots of the Christian faith. It explains salvation, the ordinances and why they exist, stewardship not just as something we do, but why, and the structure and government of the church. It also gives a glimpse of end time prophecy.

This book exposes some of the most-denied realities that have made themselves homes in the Church but have no place in Heaven. It biblically and skillfully addresses subject matter that calls into question many of the unfounded principles practiced in Christendom. It includes many helpful evangelical tools.

OTHER BOOKS BY THIS AUTHOR

The genetic influence of the inherent evil that resides in the flesh of every person is capable of responding to the voice of Satan like a child responds to the voice of its mother. Why? Because, Satan planted his DNA in Eve and then led an angelic revolt to do the same with the antediluvian women. The misconception that God ordered a flood to vindicate the marriage of two brothers' children is absurd. Such considerations are totally void of the presence of angels and their part in the conflict that God has with His creation. Spiritual Ménage a Trois unveils the cause of human evil and offers biblical approaches to the defeat of the same.

John the apostle was given a tour of Heaven and a spiritual journey that took him back in history and forward in the future. The book of Revelation is a perfect treasure of what is, what was, and what will be. It opens the mysteries of life from both physical and spiritual perspectives. The reader joins the apostle during his epic voyage through time. From the first page to the last, the reader is submerged, real time, into the lives and culture of the first century Saints. Imagine being engrossed in a dramatic action-packed story and emerging with a true biblical understanding of world affairs.

HERMENEUTICS

THE ART AND SCIENCE OF

INTERPRETING THE
BIBLE

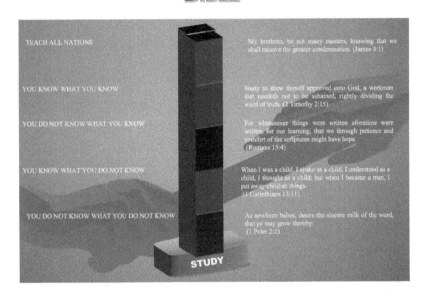

TEACH ALL NATIONS

YOU KNOW WHAT YOU KNOW

YOU DO NOT KNOW WHAT YOU KNOW

YOU KNOW WHAT YOU DO NOT KNOW

YOU DO NOT KNOW WHAT YOU DO NOT KNOW

My brethren, be not many masters, knowing that we shall receive the greater condemnation. (James 3:1)

Study to shew thyself approved unto God, a workman that needeth not to be ashamed, rightly dividing the word of truth. (2 Timothy 2:15)

For whatsoever things were written aforetime were written for our learning, that we through patience and comfort of the scriptures might have hope. (Romans 15:4)

When I was a child, I spake as a child, I understood as a child, I thought as a child: but when I became a man, I put away childish things. (1 Corinthians 13:11)

As newborn babes, desire the sincere milk of the word, that ye may grow thereby: (1 Peter 2:2)

STUDY

CONTENTS

PREFACE

This book was written to assist the student of Bible Study in the art of Spiritual comprehension. Such comprehension is here referred to as an epiphany. Isn't it a great feeling to read a passage of Scripture and come away saying, "Aha! I got it." It is equally discouraging when it seems that The Scripture is beyond comprehension. It might make you feel better to know that at times even the apostles struggled with interpretation. Surely you have heard and probably even said, "Anything worth having is worth fighting for." Well, that's exactly what one must be willing to do to reach discernment with Scriptures. The fight is a Spiritual fight and therefore you will have to employ (PRAY) God's protection and guidance. (Ephesians 6:12, II Peter 3:16)

The Enemy to truth and understanding is doing everything in his power to hinder and discourage. Daniel sought understanding. God dispatched to him an angelic messenger, but the messenger was intercepted by the forces of evil, delaying his arrival. Michael the Archangel was sent to aid the release of The Messenger who finally got to Daniel.[1]

Like Daniel, we must prayerfully seek God's will. God ensures our deliverance and increases our understanding.[2] However, for understanding to take effect, one must apply adequate study.[3] To

---

[1]   Then said he unto me, Fear not, Daniel: for from the first day that thou didst set thine heart to understand, and to chasten thyself before thy God, thy words were heard, and I am come for thy words. (Daniel 10:12) But the prince of the kingdom of Persia withstood me one and twenty days: but, lo, Michael, one of the chief princes, came to help me; and I remained there with the kings of Persia. (Daniel 10:13) Now I am come to make thee understand what shall befall thy people in the latter days: for yet the vision is for many days. (Daniel 10:14)

[2]   So shall my word be that goeth forth out of my mouth: it shall not return unto me void, but it shall accomplish that which I please, and it shall prosper in the thing whereto I sent it. (Isaiah 55:11)

[3]   Study to shew thyself approved unto God, a workman that needeth not to be ashamed, rightly dividing the word of truth. (2 Timothy 2:15)

study is to prayerfully search The Scriptures in search of life changing discoveries. A change of behavior is the evidence of learning.

One may be an avid reader. However, it is not of the norm to engage in the arduous task of reading a reference book or professional journal unless one desires more than entertainment. For many, The Bible belongs solely to pastors/teachers, a condition instituted by the organized system of church most notable in the 16th Century. William Tyndale, theologian and scholar, championed the cause of spreading The Gospel of God by translating and providing bibles to common people in opposition to the established Church. He took his mission seriously enough to risk life and succumb to death.

Born in 1494, Tyndale developed and grew in scholarship, becoming so fluent in eight different languages, one could not be sure which was his native tongue. Taking advantage of Gutenberg's movable-type press, Tyndale published The Scriptures in English and made them available to all who desired to read for themselves God's Word. Such was considered by The Catholic Church and later The Church of England as unacceptable. In 1536, at the instigation of King Henry VIII and The Anglican Church, William Tyndale, was burned at the stake. But of the many heroic feats accomplished by Tyndale, the following speaks volumes of the significance and worthiness of personal bible knowledge:

> "A clergyman hopelessly entrenched in Roman dogma once taunted William Tyndale with the statement, *"We are better to be without God's laws than the Pope's"*. Tyndale was infuriated by such Roman Catholic heresies, and he replied, *"I defy the Pope and all his laws. If God spare my life ere many years, I will cause the boy that drives the plow to know more of the scriptures than you!"*[1]

Due to the obedience of men such as Tyndale, his friend John Rogers, AKA "Thomas Matthew," and countless others, we now hold in our hands the most precious book of all times, "The Bible!" The Author, Jesus, wrote The Bible with His own blood; His couriers, The

---

[1] TYNDALE-BIBLE.com

Prophets and Apostles, sacrificed their lives to further the cause. In 1948, Tyndale's only surviving copy of The English New Testament sold for two million dollars when purchased by the British Museum. Today you can have your own personal copy of God's Word for free.

When confronted by The Spirit of Intimidation, one must rely on a perceivable system of support. Anxiety, confrontations, and opposition are the experiences of every sincere student of God's Word. First and foremost, one must trust that God did not send His Word to confuse, but to conform humanity. Secondly, one must accept that God, by the virtue of The Holy Spirit, is The Teacher. Finally, one must be willing to allow through learning the qualities desired by God to become the Fruit of Life.

There is yet an unseen enemy lurking in The Halls of Bible Study. It is the deception of Satan. Its mission is that of justifying why one should not embark upon the path of Spiritual interpretation and application, resulting in the rewards discovered during those often-grueling sessions which are required to reach a convincing interpretation of a previously perplexing passage of Scripture. This book will help to confirm that The Bible was written to all of humanity, revealing God's love. Do not be afraid to confront those beliefs that you hold without any real biblical proof. But rather, welcome the opportunity to uncover the many unfounded embedded principles possessed solely by our innate human intelligence.

Perception, although sometimes wrong, is always right to him who perceives it as such. To discuss, study, or deliberate a subject unveils countless truths otherwise hidden by lies disguised as truth. A structured Bible Study guide and curriculum is vital to bible understanding. The tendency to misrepresent The Bible by creating confusing concepts is the work of misguided individuals, many of whom do not have a clue of their inadequacies.

> *And I, brethren, could not speak unto you as unto spiritual, but as unto carnal, even as unto babes in Christ. I have fed you with milk, and not with meat: for hitherto ye were not able to bear it, neither yet now are ye able. For ye are yet carnal: for*

whereas there is among you envying, and strife, and divisions,
are ye not carnal, and walk as men?

(1 Corinthians 3:1-3)

The physical world in which we live presents us with an initial carnal interpretation. Carnality is the process of relating to creation from a purely sensuous perspective. Carnal interpretation establishes meaning based only from the values assigned to stimuli received from the eye/sight, ear/sound, mouth/taste, nose/smell, and touch/feel. Spiritual interpretation requires absolute trust in The Spoken Word of God. Such reasoning may contradict an otherwise logical interpretation. Every word spoken to humanity must bear a reasonable sense of interpretation if communication is to be effective. Therefore, God uses The Written Word, which relates to something physical in order to elevate one's understanding of something spiritual (Romans 1:20).

The spirit of every person must accept The Spirit of The Creator or fall to the spirit of His enemy.[1] Because The Bible was written to reveal a very real and formidable foe, Satan does everything in his power to prevent God's people from accomplishing the strength, knowledge, wisdom, and understanding required to resist him.[2]

But if our gospel be hid, it is hid to them that are lost: In whom
the god of this world hath blinded the minds of them which
believe not, lest the light of the glorious gospel of Christ, who
is the image of God, should shine unto them.

(2 Corinthians 4:3, 4)

To you, The Glorious Gospel of our Lord and Saviour shines through the windows of His Word like the sunshine on a cloudless day. However, if one is to enjoy the sunshine, certain efforts must be applied. First, you must get out and into it. Then you must take appropriate precautions to ensure that you are not overly exposed. So, it is with God's Word. You are called from the darkness into the glorious light.

---

[1]   For what man knoweth the things of a man, save the spirit of man which is in him? even so the things of God knoweth no man, but the Spirit of God. (1 Corinthians 2:11)

[2]   Submit yourselves therefore to God. Resist the devil, and he will flee from you. (James 4:7)

For God, who commanded the light to shine out of darkness, hath shined in our hearts, to give the light of the knowledge of the glory of God in the face of Jesus Christ.

(2 Corinthians 4:6)

Ever learning, and never able to come to the knowledge of the truth.

(2 Timothy 3:7

INTRODUCTION

Humanity, through The Arts, has discovered many alternatives to reality. We have our politics, poetry, sports, theaters, movies, and performers to help us escape the crushes of truthfulness. When they alone are not sufficient, we may turn to intoxicants of many different classes for help. You need not survive a drunken stupor to acknowledge that the same problem thought to have been drowned by intemperance only adds to the recovery process in detoxification. When a person's life is conscientiously approaching the end, most will seriously ponder the question of whether there is truly a God. That is because, as real as life is, death, although often denied, is equally as real.

When the question of whether God exists becomes a quest, there are several ways to answer. This book defines the seven general considerations (Atheist, Agnostic, Pantheist, Polytheist, Deist, Dualist, and Theist). But for now, the fact that every human being will naturally consider the question of God's existence makes it reasonable to come up with the answer rationally, logically, and correctly.

Life has taught us that dependence is essential to the health and welfare of every human being. Where would you and I be today if others had not considered it their duty to ensure our well-being? Equally important is the question: What would they think of us if we had not benefitted from their efforts with a proven productive independence?

> *Wherefore seeing we also are compassed about with so great a cloud of witnesses, let us lay aside every weight, and the sin which doth so easily beset us, and let us run with patience the race that is set before us,*
>
> *(Hebrews 12:1)*

To be able to say, "I have made it," is the substance of self-actualization. At the end of life, and for some it comes seemingly too soon, everyone would like to be able to embrace the feeling of having lived usefully.

> *I have fought a good fight, I have finished my course, I have kept the faith:*

> *(2 Timothy 4:7)*

There is a conscious immortality that begins at the end of mortality.[1] The nucleus of every human being existed in the mind of The Creator before the mother was blessed with the knowledge of its existence. As such, the physical world is but transitional to that which preexisted and shall post exist. Logically speaking, if there is "The Creator," He would introduce Himself to His Creatures.

Since communication and its many different channels speak perceptively of our prosperity, why wouldn't it also speak to our posterity? Because reading is truly the key to knowledge, as books are the safes of human discoveries and the plans of human success, only those who endeavor to learn the art of spiritual comprehension shall benefit from the wealth of The Bible.[2] Perpetual ignorance is a condition perpetrated only by those who helplessly refuse to apply their God-given skills to study. Every successful endeavor requires some form of study, documentation, and follow-up. It matters not what degree one holds in theology; what matters is to what degree one's theology holds to God's Word (TRUTH).[3]

We often miss vitally important achievements because of perception. Take the Agnostic for example; he believes that there is not sufficient evidence to validate the existence of God; therefore, he believes it is utterly impossible to know Him. For the Agnostic, I suppose such consideration rates high on the scale of respect and admiration. However, when The Creator has given Himself, His Blood, and His Love to make Himself known, such considerations are violent insults.

---

[1] So then every one of us shall give account of himself to God. (Romans 14:12)

[2] Blessed is he that readeth, and they that hear the words of this prophecy, and keep those things which are written therein: for the time is at hand. (Revelation 1:3)

[3] God is a Spirit: and they that worship him must worship him in spirit and in truth. (John 4:24)

Wherefore I say unto you, All manner of sin and blasphemy shall be forgiven unto men: but the blasphemy against the Holy Ghost shall not be forgiven unto men.

(Matthew 12:31)

Faith is the most important word in The Bible, without which it would be impossible to know The Spirit World. So, God's Word says that we are to be perfect even as The Lord is perfect.[1] Well, for many, their interpretation is no one can be as perfect as The Lord. And to that extent, they are correct. But The Bible does not call on us to be as perfect. It calls on us to seek such perfection. In the process of seeking, we will undoubtedly rise higher than we would have if such were not our quest; and the journey will be endless. If humanity sets its goal to reach the most distant planet and falls short, it will ultimately rest among the stars.

But seek ye first the kingdom of God, and his righteousness; and all these things shall be added unto you.

(Matthew 6:33)

As newborn babes, desire the sincere milk of the word, that ye may grow thereby:

(1 Peter 2:2)

Any journey begins with a first step. If one is to properly interpret God's Word, one must begin by keeping The Scriptures in context. Take, for example, the present-day use of the terms "Apostles, Prophets, Evangelists, and Pastors/Teachers." Although each is a major instrument of God for the spiritual building of humanity, they are grossly misrepresented. As explained in detail in *(Nathaniel McClain (2015), The Great Christian Asleepening, USA, OutskirtsPress)*, the spiritual course, as recorded in Ephesians 4:11, maps the development of humanity from the inaugural "Word-Bible" of God to the present.[2]

---

[1] Be ye therefore perfect, even as your Father which is in heaven is perfect. (Matthew 5:48)

[2] And he gave some, apostles; and some, prophets; and some, evangelists; and some, pastors and teachers; For the perfecting of the saints, for the work of the ministry, for

Today we walk by faith in God's Word and not by the word of man.

> *So then faith cometh by hearing, and hearing by the word of God.*
>
> *(Romans 10:17)*

Yes, The Bible was written by men, but was divinely inspired and therefore, any reference to it may properly be received as God's Word. The ministries that gave us this vital Word were of Prophets and Apostles, The Old and New Testaments respectively. No human being today has the authority to speak a "word" and then claim it to be equal to that of those from whom our Bible has come. Evangelists, by the nature of their calling, must be endowed with miraculous abilities and Pastors are to illuminate The Bible. God's Word has always been for the growth and development of a people and not a person. Words received from a Prophet or Apostle were immediately supported by an undeniable consequence.

> *And Miriam and Aaron spake against Moses because of the Ethiopian woman whom he had married: for he had married an Ethiopian woman.*
>
> *(Numbers 12:1)*

Since there was no "Word-Bible," it behooved God to make His presence and power known. So, He inflicted Miriam with the dreaded disease, leprosy, and excommunicated her for seven days. Such events proved the authority of those whom God chose to lead His people.

In the developing era of The New Testament, The Apostles were also given visible powers which validated their claims of The Gospel of Jesus Christ.

> *And when Paul had gathered a bundle of sticks, and laid them on the fire, there came a viper out of the heat, and fastened on his hand.*
>
> *(Acts 28:3)*

---

the edifying of the body of Christ: (Ephesians 4:11-12)

God used a miracle to quale the superstitions of the barbarians.

> *Howbeit they looked when he should have swollen, or fallen down dead suddenly: but after they had looked a great while, and saw no harm come to him, they changed their minds, and said that he was a god.*
>
> *(Acts 28:6)*

What did the natives have from Paul that would help them to accept God's Word? Yes, the uneventful outcome of that which they assumed to be deadly. The Island Chief, Publius, received Paul's company and personally lodged them for three days. Surely Paul shared with them the knowledge of The "True and Living God." God suffered Publius' father to *"lay sick of a fever and of a bloody flux."* Paul prayed, *"and laid his hands on him, and healed him."* (Acts 28:8) This event led to a three-month evangelical (healing) mission which powerfully brought Christianity to the people. Such powerful displays attest to the level of spiritual ignorance that overwhelmed the people of that time and era.

Today, God has given the full complement of His magnificent "Word." Therefore, it is the ministry of The Pastor/Teacher who enables the students to follow The Scriptures, word for word, precept upon precept, with perfect accountability.

> *Preach the word; be instant in season, out of season; reprove, rebuke, exhort with all longsuffering and doctrine.*
>
> *(2 Timothy 4:2)*

According to Peter, ignorance leads to personal destruction.[1] The Apostle Paul considered the abolition of ignorance his mission:

> *Now concerning spiritual gifts, brethren, I would not have you ignorant.*
>
> *(1 Corinthians 12:1)*

---

[1] As also in all his epistles, speaking in them of these things; in which are some things hard to be understood, which they that are unlearned and unstable wrest, as they do also the other scriptures, unto their own destruction. (2 Peter 3:16)

Even during his personal tenure, Paul instructed Timothy, his Son in The Ministry, to search The Scriptures.

> *Study to shew thyself approved unto God, a workman that needeth not to be ashamed, rightly dividing the word of truth. But shun profane and vain babblings: for they will increase unto more ungodliness.*
>
> *(2 Timothy 2:15, 16)*

Our Father takes pleasure in the sincere efforts of His people.

> *"These were more noble than those in Thessalonica, in that they received the word with all readiness of mind, and searched the scriptures daily, whether those things were so."*
>
> *(Acts 17:11)*

So, why is it more the norm to major in the minor (listening to and trusting man) and to minor in the major (searching The Scriptures to see if it is so)? It is because The Enemy of Mankind has effectively sewn into the human fabric the desire to focus on the temporal (Carnal) with total disregard for the eternal (Spiritual).[1]

> *For the time will come when they will not endure sound doctrine; but after their own lusts shall they heap to themselves teachers, having itching ears; And they shall turn away their ears from the truth, and shall be turned unto fables.*
>
> *(2 Timothy 4:3, 4)*

Regretfully, that time is now. Those who either refuse the need for or feel that personal Bible Study is not essential, will bear the ill fruit of embedded and reflective theological lies; the circumstances of which shall cause unnecessary and damaging consequences here on Earth and subsequently after departing this life.

---

[1] But seek ye first the kingdom of God, and his righteousness; and all these things shall be added unto you. (Matthew 6:33)

For we must all appear before the judgment seat of Christ; that every one may receive the things done in his body, according to that he hath done, whether it be good or bad.

(2 Corinthians 5:10)

A decision to make Bible Study a priority will greatly enhance one's life. It will expose and remove many of the weeds that choke the precious fruit of God's Word. Such fruit will be the source of God's rewards for a service well done.

Lay not up for yourselves treasures upon earth, where moth and rust doth corrupt, and where thieves break through and steal: But lay up for yourselves treasures in heaven, where neither moth nor rust doth corrupt, and where thieves do not break through nor steal: For where your treasure is, there will your heart be also.

(Matthew 6:19-21)

The most rewarding skills and professions are the ones that challenge us mentally. The mind calls quit long before its potential is exceeded. But because there are few who are willing to press toward the mark of the highest callings, there will always be far more followers than leaders. Knowing how to search Scripture to achieve divine understanding not only enhances your eternal rewards, but it also makes you better at the things you do daily. An old cliché is "the proof is in the pudding." You will be amazed at how easily you will elevate your Bible knowledge, inclusive with the growth that accompanies it, should you take on this and other comparable "Basic Instructions Before Leaving Earth" (B.I.B.L.E).

Brethren, I count not myself to have apprehended: but this one thing I do, forgetting those things which are behind, and reaching forth unto those things which are before, I press toward the mark for the prize of the high calling of God in Christ Jesus.

(Philippians 3:13, 14)

NJM

CHAPTER 1

CHRISTIAN MATHODOLOGY

Roman Numerals & Bible Logic

Logic is the system or principles of reasoning applicable to any branch of knowledge or study. You may be wondering what the learning of Roman Numerals has to do with Bible Study? The answer is nothing. However, one must understand the logic of Roman Numerals before correctly converting Hindu-Arabic (Indo-Arabic) Numerals to Roman Numerals and vice a versa. Learning Roman Numerals in an environment where it may appear unnecessary will require you to push past the inclination to resist such learning.

There is also the tendency to be selective in studying. Don't be surprised if you are tempted to bypass Roman Numerals with the intent to come back later in this study. However, if such is the case, you most likely will rationalize those Roman Numerals truly are not needed. The purpose of this study goes far beyond the accomplishment of Roman Numerals. I have titled this section Christian Mathodology (Quantitative Technique—QT) because math is an exact science and therefore, any disagreements may be proven through strict rules of computation. Truth is also an exact science; however, computing it is not always as simple as 2 + 2 = 4. Remember, Jesus fed more than 5,000 with 2 fish and 5 loaves of bread; and if you would like to hypothesize that the fish were whales and the loaves of bread were the size of trailers, you must also think the child who had them was The Jolly Green Giant.

There is a lad here, which hath five barley loaves, and two small fishes: but what are they among so many?

(John 6:9)

Master the process of translating Roman Numerals and you will have acquired a valuable skill in human reasoning. There is a specific set of rules to which one must adhere before correctly translating Roman Numerals. To apply these rules, one must gain an appreciation for the methodology of converting numerical values to alphabets and vice versa. In his book, Seven Habits of Highly Effective People, Stephen R. Covey's Third Habit is, "Putting First Things First." Putting first things first is the first active trait preceded by, "Begin with the End in Mind," and "Be Proactive." The desire to change (learn) will follow the path of knowledge (study), but it will be challenged by resistance (agony) and shall reap the rewards of success (joy).

A skill is the ability to do something well, usually gained through training or experience. A person who can do with ease that which was once difficult has an accomplished skill. Most adults have reached a pseudo-threshold of learning long before they have surpassed their ability. This is due in part to selective reasoning. Adults do not normally spend time concentrating on things that do not stimulate their interest or need. It is for this very reason that I have chosen Roman Numerals to encourage the ability to surpass the self-imposed threshold of learning. One will have to concentrate on the mathodology of interpreting Roman Numerals to succeed in this venture. Your response to ability becomes the catalyst of response-ability. Now that you can do it, let's get-around-to-it.

Bible Study encounters an additional challenge-Satan! Bible Study must overcome not only the inclination to resist the arduous process, but also the direct attack of The Spirit of Evil to distort the truth. Just having the scholastics of a great student will not defeat the problems lurking in The Halls of Bible Study. Many un-anointed brilliant scholars are clueless in matters revealing spiritual truths.

Few would question the academic accomplishments of Albert Einstein (German-born theoretical physicist). He developed The General Theory of Relativity, one of the two pillars of modern physics (alongside quantum mechanics). (Mar 14, 1879–Apr 18, 1955–age 76). However, his recorded views concerning The Intelligent Creator leaves a lot to be desired. Due to an apparent lack of Spiritual indwelling (Not Born Again-John 3:5), Einstein's views of religion can best be described as "Pantheist/Agnostic." While some have even referred to him as Atheist, he readily dismissed those assumptions. In an interview published in 1930 in G. S. Viereck's book, "Glimpses of the Great Einstein," in response to a question about whether or not he defined himself as a Pantheist, he explained:

Note: *(The indented italicized Scriptures speak to the lack of appropriate Scripture considerations during Einstein's response.)*

"Einstein"

"Your question is the most difficult in the world. It is not a question I can answer simply with yes or no. I am not an Atheist. I do not know if I can define myself as a Pantheist. The problem involved is too vast for our limited minds.

For as the heavens are higher than the earth, so are my ways higher than your ways, and my thoughts than your thoughts.
(Isaiah 55:9)

"Einstein"

May I not reply with a parable? The human mind, no matter how highly trained, cannot grasp the universe. We are in the position of a little child, entering a huge library whose walls are covered to the ceiling with books in many different tongues. The child knows that someone must have written those books. It does not know who or how. It does not understand the languages in which they are written. The child notes a definite plan in the arrangement of the books, a mysterious order, which it does not comprehend, but only dimly suspects.

Therefore speak I to them in parables: because they seeing see not; and hearing they hear not, neither do they understand. And in them is fulfilled the prophecy of Esaias, which saith, By hearing ye shall hear, and shall not understand; and seeing ye shall see, and shall not perceive: For this people's heart is waxed gross, and their ears are dull of hearing, and their eyes they have closed; lest at any time they should see with their eyes, and hear with their ears, and should understand with their heart, and should be converted, and I should heal them.

(Matthew 13:13-15)

"Einstein"

That, it seems to me, is the attitude of the human mind, even the greatest and most cultured, toward God. We see a universe marvelously arranged, obeying certain laws, but we understand the laws only dimly. Our limited minds cannot grasp the mysterious force that sways the constellations.

… For now we see through a glass, darkly; but then face to face: now I know in part; but then shall I know even as also I am known. And now abideth faith, hope, charity, these three; but the greatest of these is charity.

(1 Corinthians 13:11-13)

"Einstein"

I am fascinated by Spinoza's Pantheism. I admire even more his contributions to modern thought. Spinoza is the greatest of modern philosophers because he is the first philosopher who deals with the soul and the body as one, not as two separate things." [1]

For the Word of God is quick, and powerful, and sharper than any twoedged sword, piercing even to the dividing asunder of soul and spirit, and of the joints and marrow, and is a discerner of the thoughts and intents of the heart.

(Hebrews 4:12)

Having no faith in The Bible, but extreme faith in science, led Einstein down a path limited by sight (science).

Beware lest any man spoil you through philosophy and vain deceit, after the tradition of men, after the rudiments of the world, and not after Christ.

(Colossians 2:8)

If only he had applied The Holy Bible as The Table of Contents to the beauty of God's creation, such dispiritedness towards The Creator would have been averted.

As we master the process of calculating Roman Numerals, we will be applying the science of mathematics using grammatical alphabets. The Science of Algebra, the part of mathematics in which letters and other general symbols are used to represent numbers and quantities in formulae and equations, uses similar concepts.

Every student of The Arts, Sciences, and Philosophies will generally excel in the things of the world. Pictures and paintings display explainable images; laboratories are used to document the response of chemicals and agents; literary think tanks are publishing various and sundry projectable persuasions. What they all have in common is matter. How many of the above schools have created anything from nothing? Einstein, like too many others, stumbled at the thought of piercing the veil of the temporal. One must be willing to accept The Creator's account (FAITH) of *why* things are before correctly accounting for *what* things are.

---

[1]   Viereck, George Sylvester. "Glimpses of the Great". Duckworth, 1930. p. 372-373.

For it is written, I will destroy the wisdom of the wise, and will bring to nothing the understanding of the prudent. Where is the wise? where is the scribe? where is the disputer of this world? hath not God made foolish the wisdom of this world? For after that in the wisdom of God the world by wisdom knew not God, it pleased God by the foolishness of preaching to save them that believe.

(1 Corinthians 1:19-21)

Covey's Second Trait is "Begin with the End in Mind." To apply that conditioning to the study of The Bible, one must be prepared to apply faith (absolute confidence in God's Word) to the achievement of spiritual things that are not yet received (HOPE). To know what those things are, one must be able to rightly interpret God's Word. The calculator used in this study of God's Word is the venerable King James Version of The Holy Bible. After four decades of comparing bibles, I have learned to trust the one that doesn't change with time and scholarship, but continues to be the divine principle by which all human creed, conducts and opinions are to be tried. When God's Word is not subject to change, it is easier to hide it in your heart and recall it in your mind.

Thy word have I hid in mine heart, that I might not sin against thee.

(Psalm 119:11)

So, tell your mind that you are about to become an expert in mapping your mental process (As Covey would say "Be Proactive") to accomplish any mindset required to advance your purpose in learning. Prior to the advent of the Arabic symbols that we call numbers, a rendering of numerical values was recorded using alphabets. Such use involved a system that is literally fool proof. There is an age-old adage that says, "numbers do not lie." As true as that statement is, it is handicapped by the fact that mathematicians (humans) do. So, we are going to learn how to convert Arabic numbers to Roman Numerals and to check to ensure correctness. The Bible says that only God is true and that every man is a liar.[1] The youth group, Jesus' Cadets, chose as its motto, "In God we trust, everything else we check."

> *These were more noble than those in Thessalonica, in that they received the word with all readiness of mind, and searched the scriptures daily, whether those things were so.*
>
> *(Acts 17:11)*

And so it is that every person must seek God through His Written Word by prayerfully applying the skills of learning, if an acceptable outcome is to be acquired.

> *Search the scriptures; for in them ye think ye have eternal life: and they are they which testify of me.*
>
> *(John 5:39)*

There is no shortage of brilliant human beings upon The Earth. Consider all the creature comforts, modes of transportation, medical ingenuity, and countless other discoveries and one can only be amazed. However, to have accomplished so much and then to lose it all is a sobering consideration for the truly wise.

> *For what is a man profited, if he shall gain the whole world, and lose his own soul? or what shall a man give in exchange for his soul?*
>
> *(Matthew 16:26)*

> *Ever learning, and never able to come to the knowledge of the truth.*
>
> *(2 Timothy 3:7)*

God gave us an analytical mind. Do not deny those things that are obvious. Such carelessness plays into the deceptive schemes of The Devil. Participating in a structured methodological study minimizes

---

[1] God forbid: yea, let God be true, but every man a liar; as it is written, That thou mightest be justified in thy sayings, and mightest overcome when thou art judged. (Romans 3:4)

one's vulnerability. It is imperative that our fundamental beliefs are well founded before endeavoring mystical interpretations.

Finally, an appreciation for the ability to continue a well-defined process helps to promote innovative and stimulating thought. Expect a struggle. No! Welcome the struggle of learning the methodical process of translating Roman Numerals and you will cultivate a vital conditioning required in Hermeneutics, Exegesis, and Epiphany. The very first step in this process is the memory of the following acronym:

MEDICAL XVID

Forgetting is an essential step in the formulation of memory, therefore, be prepared to forget the above. Being reminded of an x-ray will help the recall. There is no x-ray in our acronym, but there is an x-vid. The medical society's "ray" is our "vid."

There are seven different characters in the repertoire of standard Roman Numerals. MEDICAL XVID has eleven alphabets so we must remove four of them. The first three are the vowels (E-I-A) in the word MEDICAL.

We are left with:

M, D, C, L

Now look closely at the XVID. There are eight characters (M, D, C, L, X, V, I, D) remaining and we only need seven. If you were going to remove one alphabet from XVID, which would it be? Keeping our observation in context, we must consider the first conclusion which gave us M, D, C, L. Now from the X, V, I, D, we must drop an alphabet. Which of the M, D, C, L X, V, I, D is to be removed? Clue: there are only seven characters in standard Roman Numerals and they each are different.

If at the conclusion of this challenge you get it wrong, do not get discouraged. We often learn more from our mistakes than we do from those things that come easily. Simply consider the right answer by examining why it proves to be right. Such consideration is the act of reasoning–"the action of thinking about something in a logical, sensible way."

We know that we are to remove four alphabets from the entire MEDICAL XVID and up to this point, we have removed three. They were the vowels in MEDICAL. We are left with M, D, C, L and XVID. So, where will the last removal come from? Reasoning tells us that the alphabets M, D, C, L are set and therefore, we are to only consider XVID for the alphabet to be removed. Cross referencing the MDCL and XVID will aid in the consideration. Which alphabet did you remove?

If you chose "D," you are correct. "D" is the only alphabet that would be duplicated if not removed from XVID. Logically speaking, there may only be one value for each alphabet.

We are left with:

X, V, I

Together the symbols in descending (value) order are:

M, D, C, L, X, V, I

The seven characters that we have discovered constitute the foundation for Roman Numerals. Ensure yourself that they are to be remembered via several different means:

L–GAP

L–GAP is a mnemonic device that may be used to assist recall of essential data. It stands for Location, General Idea, Association, and Paper.

- Where is the Location of the symbols found in Roman Numerals?
    - o Let's use the hospital as our first clue.
- What is the General Idea of our consideration?
    - o Let's use medical technology.
- Is there anything that we may Associate with Roman Numerals?

- o Let's use the medical x-ray.
- Finally make sure that you write the alphabets (symbols) repeatedly on a piece of paper.
  - o Writing does wonders in solidifying information that is to be remembered.

Be assertive in learning. Use your own system to help in the process of memory. The above acronym MEDICALXVID might be achieved using others that you find more familiar. As an example:

IV–Intravenous
XL–Extra Large
CD–Certificate of Deposit, Compact Disk, etc.
M–Millennium, One Thousand

The above example, as you shall learn, places the numerical values in their appropriate families.

CHRISTIAN THEOLOGICAL STUDIES

Before advancing further into the knowledge of Roman Numerals, take a break and focus on the following Christian Theological Studies. To attempt to read The Bible without an appreciation of the varying viewpoints will certainly lead to misinterpretation.

I. Angelology…the study of angels.
II. Anthropology (Christian)…the study of human nature.
III. Baptiology (Personal Study)
IV. Bibliology…the study of the Volume of Sacred Law (VSL), Bible.
V. Christology…the study of God the Son.
VI. Demonology (Christian) …the study of demons.
VII. Ecclesiology…the study of the nature and mission of The Church.
VIII. Eschatology…the study of end time prophecy and The Apocalypse.
IX. Hamartiology…the study of the nature and effects of sin.

X. Paterology...the study of God the Father.

XI. Pneumatology...the study of God The Holy Ghost.

XII. Soteriology...the study of salvation.

XIII. Theology...the study of The One and Only God, The Creator.

Bible misinterpretation is a result of weak doctrinal foundations built on half-baked ideas concerning Scripture. Example: to not understand the inevitable, unavoidable, and damnable nature of sin has led some to incorrectly believe that sin is conquerable through human diligence. A student of Hamartiology is not likely to fall for such vanity. The web site "GotQuestions.com" defines the study of sin as that which every human being is infected and therefore, incapable of overcoming alone:

> "Hamartiology is the study of sin. Hamartiology deals with how sin originated, how it affects humanity, and what it will result in after death. To sin essentially means to "miss the mark." We all miss God's mark of righteousness (Romans 3:23). Hamartiology, then, explains why we miss the mark, how we miss the mark, and the consequences of missing the mark. These are some important questions in Hamartiology:"

NUMERICAL VALUES/ROMAN NUMERAL FAMILIES (RNF)

The greatest to the least value attributed to Roman Numerals:

- M= 1000
- D= 500
- C= 100
- L= 50
- X= 10
- V= 5
- I= 1

Bible observation is an essential means in the process of reaching a logical spiritual conclusion. There are times when Bible Study may be frustrating. Even the Apostle Peter speaking of Paul's teachings revealed as much:

> *As also in all his epistles, speaking in them of these things; in which are some things hard to be understood, which they that are unlearned and unstable wrest, as they do also the other scriptures, unto their own destruction.*
>
> *(2 Peter 3:16)*

The interpretation of Roman Numerals is based on scientific facts. It is a matter of calculation and not memorization. Therefore, each step in the process becomes a map by which one may venture as far as the Roman road will allow.

What do you notice about the descending values of the previous list? Read each line and sound the alphabet and the number value paying close attention to that which is of the same denomination. The answer is the numbers "1" and "5."

- When we speak of symbols in the "1" family, we are speaking of the "I, X, C and M."
- When speaking of the symbols in the "5" family, we are speaking of "V, L and D."

The numbers "1" and "5" alternate regardless from which end you begin. The first number, whether going from the left or right, is the number "1." The number "1" is followed by the number "5." The only difference is the number of zeros that follow either the "1" or the "5." Our Arabic list of numbers contains the zero; however, it was not given a symbol by the Romans.

The M represents the largest base number in standard Roman Numerals, and it is:

M=1,000

One thousand (1,000) using Arabic symbols has three (3) zeros. Since the Romans did not have a symbol for zero, it is logical that the number "1,000" will only require one symbol when translated to Roman Numerals. We are, therefore, given only one symbol that requires translating. The symbol is the "M", and the value is thousand.

Do you remember the second acronym used to remember the characters used in Roman Numerals? If so, you have the two families increasing value. How many symbols are there in the "1" family? If you answered four, then you were correct. The highest base symbol in Roman Numerals is "M." It represents the Arabic value of "1,000." Each of the three remaining symbols in the "1" family receives one zero less than the higher value symbol.

C=100
X=10
I= 1

"C" gets two zeros (one less than "M"); "X" gets one zero (one less than "C"); and "I" gets no zero.

The "D" represents the largest member of the "5" family.

D=500

"D" is five hundred, the largest number represented in the "5" family. The remaining two symbols, "L" and "V" represent "50" (One zero less than "D") and "5" (No zero).

L= 50
V= 5

On a blank piece of paper, record in an orderly format everything that you have learned thus far about Roman Numerals. Do not look at your notes or the book.

MATHEMATICAL EQUATION:

*Study to shew thyself approved unto God, a workman that
needeth not to be ashamed, rightly dividing the word of truth.*

(2 Timothy 2:15)

Now we shall work on seeing what is beneath the basic knowledge
of Roman Numerals. In other words, we must learn the system's logic.
We shall not add to it nor take away from it. We are simply taking the
system apart paying close attention to how it is constructed. If we do
not correctly apply the steps of interpretation, the result will easily
reveal our mistake. To discover our propensity to error is vital to our
conscientiousness when studying The Bible.

*Whom shall he teach knowledge? and whom shall he make
to understand doctrine? them that are weaned from the milk,
and drawn from the breasts. For precept must be upon precept,
precept upon precept; line upon line, line upon line; here a
little, and there a little:*

(Isaiah 28:9, 10)

The Romans started with the "1" family multiplying each increasing
value by the common denominator of "10."

1 X 1= 1
1 X 10= 10
10 X 10= 100
100 X 10= 1000

The "5" family utilizes "V" as the symbol for "5." The "L" represents
the "V" multiplied ten times. The "D" represents the "L" multiplied
ten times.

5 X 1= 5
5 X 10= 50
50 X 10= 500

INTERPOLATION:

In the mathematical field of numerical analysis, interpolation is a method of constructing new data points within the range of a discrete set of known data points. This is a good place to demonstrate how we shall use math to help our "ology." Now that I know the Roman system, I may take it upon myself to increase the value of Roman Numerals beyond the standard calculations. My first consideration is that of assigning, at a minimum, two additional symbols to the seven that make up the standard foundation.

1,000 X 10= 10,000 "N"

The symbol that I have chosen for 10,000 is "N." Having designated "N" for the highest value in the "1" family, an intermediary position opens between "N & M." I am designating that position to be that of "J." "J" is now, by default, the highest value in the "5" family. Using the logic already learned, what is the correct value for "J?"

Consider the "N" that we have constructed in the "1" family. The value for the "N" following the known calculus is "10,000."

Our known data points are "M" ("1,000") and "N" ("10,000"). For us to correctly determine the "J," which is between the "N" and the "M," we must interpolate. By observing the formula from which each of the Roman symbols derived their value, we may conclude that the "J" in our list represents "5,000."

What is the middle value of "10,000" divided by "2?" You may also reach the same conclusion by the largest member of the "5" family, "500," multiplied by "10" arriving at the same conclusion of "5,000,"

- N= 10,000
- J= 5,000
- M= 1,000
- D= 500
- C= 100
- L= 50

- X = 10
- V = 5
- I = 1

One may continue the numerical method applied in Roman Numerals to infinitum. However, you will have to assign your symbols as you expand your interpolation.

Interpolation is essential to the discovery of certain missing points in bible interpretation. Although The Bible can be a bit challenging, the process of cross-referencing related Scriptures provides for healthy interpolations. Remember those hated fill-in-the-blank tests? Yes, they often required us to look at the words before the blank and the words after the blank to determine what goes in the blank. Interpolating Scriptures, although similar, encounters an additional challenge. The words before the blank and the words after the blank are often in different books. As an example, answer the following question:

FINDING SALOME

WHO WAS THE MOTHER OF JAMES AND JOHN, THE SONS OF ZEBEDEE?

Having an exhaustive concordance and comprehensive bible dictionary are essential tools for Bible Study. In today's culture, one might immediately google the answer and come up with Salome. Truth is not the result of public opinion, nor is it affirmed in the mind of another. I once sought to know the longest sentence in The Bible. My google search revealed, "Ephesians 1:3-14 is probably the longest sentence in The Bible."[1] I'm happy that I didn't restate that statement as fact, since in my Bible, Ephesians 1:3-6 is a complete sentence, thereby omitting verses 7–14 from the equation. Although I have yet to conclude the matter, I am sure that the initial observation cannot be correct, since Ephesians 3:1-7 is clearly a contender.

Be careful with conclusions gained by reason of consensus and no other evidence. One must reach a personal confirmation if the

[1] Harbor Church Honolulu

representation is to be creditable. If you believe that Salome is the name of the wife of Zebedee and the mother of James and John, then write your proof before continuing this study. What proof do you offer for your consideration? Did you make your conclusion based on the opinion(s) of others or can you personally prove your position by Scripture?

THE NAME SALOME IS LISTED IN THE BIBLE ONLY TWO TIMES:

> *There were also women looking on afar off: among whom was Mary Magdalene, and Mary the mother of James the less and of Joses, and Salome;*
>
> *(Mark 15:40)*

> *And when the sabbath was past, Mary Magdalene, and Mary the mother of James, and Salome, had bought sweet spices, that they might come and anoint him.*
>
> *(Mark 16:1)*

Considering the above Scriptures, the inquirer knows with whom Salome participated and where and under what circumstances. But who she is, is unknown at this point. However, these verses are essential to our blank. There are several paths that one might take from this juncture. The one that I will choose is the path of Mary Magdalene. I am going to search for "Magdalene" in The New Testament. It would not be convenient to choose "Mary" since "Mary" is a common name and would reveal more verses (46 total) and different people. I have found that "Magdalene" appears in The Bible, including the two above listings, a total of twelve times. One of the verses separates the words "Mary" and "Magdalene" which might prove to be vital if you needed to discover every reference to her by name. With such consideration, I used only the word "Magdalene" for my search.

> *And certain women, which had been healed of evil spirits and infirmities, Mary called Magdalene, out of whom went seven devils,*
>
> *(Luke 8:2)*

She is mentioned in each of The Four Gospels. After reading each of the verses containing the name "Magdalene," there is a noticeable observation. Of all who dared to follow Jesus, Mary M. (Magdalene) was relentless beyond any other. John dedicated the 20th Chapter of his Gospel to her legacy. She was reportedly the last to remain at the place of His crucifixion and the first to see Him after His resurrection. Mary M. situated herself as the go-between to the disciples. She informed them of His vacant tomb and then of His personal return. Tracing the footsteps of Mary Magdalene reveals valid information in our search of who's who at the scene of the crucifixion.

Included in the following list is *"the mother of Zebedee's Children."*

> *Among which was Mary Magdalene, and Mary the mother of*
> *James and Joses, and the mother of Zebedee's children.*
> *(Matthew 27:56)*

Although it is not concluded exactly who Salome is, it is becoming questionable as to whether she, according to the above, is the mother of Zebedee's children.

> *Now there stood by the cross of Jesus his mother, and his mother's*
> *sister, Mary the wife of Cleophas, and Mary Magdalene.*
> *(John 19:25)*

Cleophas by name appears only in the above verse. Is Mary the wife of Cleophas, the mother of James and Joses? One thing is true. She is not the mother of Zebedee's children. (*see Matthew 27:56 above*) A good bible dictionary or encyclopedia (not to mention google) will provide enough information to conclude that *"Mary the wife of Cleophas"* is unknown and otherwise not mentioned by name elsewhere in The Scriptures.

Did Jesus' mother, Mary, have a sister by the same name? Here is where we shall fill in the blank (<u>who is Salome</u>) by deduction. Studying The Scriptures previously listed provide the following identifications of the women at the burial:

I.   His mother's sister
II. Jesus' mother

III. Mary Magdalene
IV. Mary, the mother of James
V. Mary, the mother of James the less and Joses
VI. Mary, the wife of Cleophas
VII. Salome
VIII. The mother of Zebedee's children

Salome is listed by name as having been one of the women celebrated at the burial of Jesus. The most conclusive of these Scriptures is *John 19:25*. However, one might interpret John as having listed only three women at the burial if ... *and his mother's sister, Mary the wife of Cleophas...* is interpreted as one person. And if so, then who is the fourth person that John failed to record?

There must be a fourth person since Mark (15:40) and Matthew (27:56) each omit Mary, the mother of Jesus, listing three women and cross-referencing Salome as the mother of Zebedee's children. We must have concluded that the mother of Zebedee's children was not the mother of James (the less) or Joses. Now, let's take another look at *Mark: 15:40*.

There were also women looking on afar off: among whom was

1. Mary Magdalene, and
2. Mary, the mother of James the less and of Joses, and
3. Salome
   (Mark 15:40)

The following mentions are excluded by Mark (*listed as they appear in the Scripture*):

I. *"Mary the wife of Cleophas"*
II. *"The mother of Zebedee's children"*
III. *"Jesus his mother"*
IV. *"His mother's sister"*

As previously noted, there were, without a doubt, at least four notable women ministering during the crucifixion of Christ. Looking closely at Mark 15:40, we may conclude that Jesus' mother, Mary, was omitted from Mark's list. Therefore, it is safe to include Mary, the mother of Jesus, with the three women noted by Mark.

May we interpolate the remaining identifications with Mark's list?

"Now there stood by the cross of Jesus his mother, and his mother's sister, Mary the wife of Cleophas, and Mary Magdalene."

(John 19:25)

I.   Jesus' Mother, Mary

II.   His mother's sister <u>is Salome</u>

III.   Mary, the wife of Cleophas, <u>is the mother of James and Joses</u>

IV.   Mary Magdalene

Which of the four women that were known to be present is not listed by name? The answer is Salome. If Salome were present, and we know that she was, which of the women above would have to be her? The answer is Jesus' mother's sister. So, by interpolation (filling in the blank), we may safely conclude that Salome is Jesus' aunt and the mother of Zebedee's children.

Our previous list of each record of the women at the tomb now looks like this:

I.   Mary, the wife of Cleophas
       ✓ Mary, the mother of James the less and Joses
       ✓ Mary, the mother of James

II.   Mary Magdalene

III.   Salome
       ✓ The mother of Zebedee's children
       ✓ His mother's sister

IV.   Jesus' mother
       ✓ Mary, the wife of Joseph

Up to this point we have concluded that Zebedee had sons and their mother is Salome; but what are the names of the sons? Cross referencing Zebedee leads us to the following verse:

And when he had gone a little further thence, he saw James the son of Zebedee, and John his brother, who also were in the ship mending their nets.

(Mark 1:19)

James and John are the names of Zebedee's and Salome's children. This would conclude your research into the woman named Salome. However, if you continue to trace her footsteps in The Scripture, you will find that she, on behalf of her sons, petitioned Jesus, for when He comes into His Kingdom, to allow her sons to sit, one on His Right Hand and the other on His Left Hand.

Then came to him the mother of Zebedee's children with her sons, worshipping him, and desiring a certain thing of him. And he said unto her, What wilt thou? She saith unto him, Grant that these my two sons may sit, the one on thy right hand, and the other on the left, in thy kingdom.

(Matthew 20:20, 21)

Why or what relationship would logically cause the mother of James and John to desire that her sons be allowed to sit in seats of honor in The Lord's Kingdom?

- *Answer: She was the aunt of Jesus and therefore, her children His first cousins.*

Why does The Bible not record such a request from the mother of James the less and Joses?

- *Answer: Because Mary of Cleophas is not the sister of Mary, the mother of Jesus, and therefore, no reasonable expectation of favor.*

Continuing your exegesis into the study of Salome opens other study paths such as that which leads to the disciple of Christ named James, the son of Alphaeus. Who was the mother of this James? Concentrate your study around the name Alphaeus.

And Andrew, and Philip, and Bartholomew, and Matthew, and Thomas, and James the son of Alphaeus, and Thaddaeus, and Simon the Canaanite,

(Mark 3:18)

You may work on that question alone. There are clues in The Scriptures previously used to find Salome. Have fun! After concluding your findings, then you should compare your opinion with those of other bible scholars. If their opinions cause you to change yours's, make sure that it is due to your interpretation of The Bible verses used by them and not them.

THE ROMAN RULES OF ORDER

Now we are going to apply our knowledge to the process of computing Roman Numerals through a logical sequence which allows one to test their results. We must remember these three Roman Rules: (RR)

1. RR1 is the rule of repetition.
2. RR2 is the rule of adding and subtracting.
3. RR3 is the rule of multiplication.

RR1-WHEN TO AND WHEN NOT TO REPEAT A SYMBOL

When to repeat a symbol:

You may repeat a symbol from the "1" family; however, you may only repeat it 3 successive times. There are four symbols from the "1" family. What are they?

The symbols in the "1" family are "M, C, X, I." When they succeed themselves, you should always add. Any combination of the "I" family symbol adds to the value up to three consecutive times. Example,

"MM" is "1,000 + 1,000 equaling "2,000." The limitation is not to use more than three consecutive members of the "1" family.

Example:
o III represents 3
o XXX represents 30
o CCC represents 300 and
o MMM represents 3,000

We are simply adding the numerical value of each symbol three times. What do you think "XX" represents? How about "CC"?[1] In ancient times, some took liberty disregarding the rule of "3." In such cases, one may encounter the "IIII" as the Roman Numeral for the number "4." When coming across this exception, verify the value by the lesser value or the greater value before and after. What value precedes or follows the questionable "IIII?" Only the "IV" may stand unquestionable as "4."

What is wrong with interpreting "MMMM" as "4,000?"

• The Romans derived the number "4" using only two symbols and related them by subtraction. The above incorrect rendering has four symbols that are related through addition.

When not to repeat a symbol:

Never repeat a symbol from the "5" family successively! There are three symbols from the "5" family. What are they?

The symbols from the five family are, from the largest to the smallest, "D, L, V." One member said that she remembers the sequence by repeating "Dorothy Loves Vegetables." Okay, any attempt to place any two of the three listed symbols together will result in indigestion.

Example:

o VV would be 5+5 which equals 10.

---

[1] XX = 20 CC = 200

- o Instead of writing "VV" for ten, the appropriate symbol for "10" is "X."
- o The Arabic number "1" only requires one symbol. Therefore, wherever "1" is, it will only require one symbol regardless to the value.

Different members of the "5" family may be required in a sequence, but never two of the same.

- o "55" is translated "LV," each "5" requiring only one symbol, albeit different.

RR2-Addition versus Subtraction

Now we are going to list the first ten Roman Numerals from the smallest to the largest. We began the sequence following the rules concerning repetition. We repeated the "I" symbols, but was limited to 3 (III). Since we could not use four I's (IIII), we simply went back to one "I" in front of the "V" (IV) which allowed us to take "1" (I) from "5" (V) resulting in "4" ("IV"). We continue to add an additional "1" to the "V" until reaching our maximum allowed "VIII" ("8"). At which point, we must revert to the same logic applied at the rendering of the numeral for "4." The difference is that now the "I" precedes the "X" subtracting "1" from "10" leaving "9" ("IX").

A symbol of smaller value that precedes a symbol of larger value will take away its value from the larger. Whenever there is a 4 or 9, there will be a need to subtract. It does not matter where these two numbers appear, it will always require subtraction.

Fact:

- o Smaller symbol left of a larger subtracts from
    - ✓ "IV" One from five equals four
- o Smaller symbol right of a larger adds to
    - ✓ "VI" Five plus one equals six

Observation review:

When you are trying to remember the correct symbols for any Roman Numeral, start at the beginning. Look at the number in its infancy (first ten symbols) and from there you will know exactly what its family traits are. Let's use as an example the following number:

999,999

9 is IX	One from ten
90 is XC	Ten from one hundred
900 is CM	One hundred from one thousand
9,000 is I̲X̲	One thousand from ten thousand
90,000 is X̲C̲	Ten thousand from one hundred thousand
900,000 is C̲M̲	One hundred thousand from one million

Pay close attention to the Roman Numeral symbols. Notice that at "9,000" the symbols are repeated with the addition of a line underneath. The line indicates that the symbol is being multiplied 1000 times. Don't worry too much about it at this time since you will get the full lay out of multiplication in RR3. Look closely at the calculations to the right of the symbols and try to detect the mathematical process required to go from one level to the next.

As an exercise, choose any number from 1 to 8 and record the family tree just like the one listed above for "9." An interesting observation, if you choose the number "8," is the number of symbols required to record it. Eight requires more symbols than any of the numbers in the Roman Numerical sequence (followed by a close second is the number "7").

Having spent quality time in processing newly learned information is essential. New learnings are likely to slip away much easier than that which is more familiar. What do you need to know at this phase of your study?

I.   The seven symbols of Roman Numerals
II.   The two families of symbols
III.   The rule of repetition
IV.   The first ten basic values
V.   When to add and when to subtract

Observation versus Interpretation

Observation is the ability to recognize the individual values of a Roman Numeral symbol. Interpretation is the ability to correctly interpret any number from "1 to 3,999,999."

Many students of Roman Numerals learn the basic numbers by rote memory. I am sorry to admit, but most bible students also learn their bibles by rote as well. This type of bible knowledge is here referred to as familiarization. It is like being able to almost recite the story about The Five Wise and The Five Foolish Virgins yet, not having a clue what it means prophetically or even personally. The Apostle Paul spoke of such shallow interpretations as, *"For I bear them record that they have a zeal of God, but not according to knowledge." (Romans 10:2)* The goal is not to only be able to play the instrument by ear, but to be able to read and write the symbols that make the sounds.

Review: "666"

Let's convert the Arabic number "666" into Roman Numerals. My first thought is to consider what the number "6" looks like in Roman Numerals. Okay, it looks like "VI."

We must articulate each of the Arabic values in the number "666." The first number is "600."

The basic number "6" is composed of "5" plus "1." Therefore, the "600" must be "500" plus "100." What is the symbol for "500" and "100?"

Next, we must consider "60." Remaining consistent with the system, I must interpret "60" as "50" plus "10." What is the symbol for "50" and "10?"

Finally, we must consider "6." "6" is a forgone conclusion as we have committed it to instant recall.

Having answered each of the above requirements, it is concluded that "666" consist of the following "6" symbols:

"DCLXVI"

Most Bible students will at some point in their study have to deal with the number "666." There is an interesting correlation to the Arabic number 666 and the Roman Numeral "DCLXVI." Take a little time and study the symbols and try to find the mystery. The answer is in the endnotes. But before going there, take some time and meditate.[1]

If you are successful in figuring out the mystery, you might very well have reached an epiphany.

> *Here is wisdom. Let him that hath understanding count the number of the beast: for it is the number of a man; and his number is Six hundred threescore and six.*
>
> *(Revelation 13:18)*

Remember, we use nine numbers and a series of zeros to list an endless number of Arabic values. If you forget any of the first nine numbers or the sequence in which they reside, you will surely fall short in your calculations. The Romans applied the rule of "10" to their calculations, laying the foundation on the first set of ten values.

What do you need to know before going any further?

I.   The first ten Roman Numerals
    a.   The way each is structured
    b.   Does it require adding or subtracting, neither or both
II.   Do not forget that there are two families
    a.   Know them and each of the symbols that constitute them
    b.   What limitations apply to each family

The Bible student must have a base from which he/she will build his/her study. That base is much like the first ten numbers of

---

[1]   For the number 666, the Roman Numerals are from left to right, excluding the "M," a perfect list of the Roman Numerical characters. They are actually one less than a perfect order (7). Umm, as a side note, if the "M" was considered to represent the Millennial, God's earthly Paradise, then it must be separated from 666.

Roman Numerals. Regardless to how many numbers we calculate in Roman Numerals, we will by necessity have to remember to keep our calculations true to the math of the first ten sets.

One may apply the same interpretation to The Bible. Jehovah instituted the "Ten Commandments" (Exodus 20:1–17, Deuteronomy 5:4–21):

THE TEN COMMANDMENTS

I. *Thou shalt have no other gods before me.*

II. *Thou shalt not make unto thee any graven image, or any likeness of anything that is in heaven above, or that is in the earth beneath, or that is in the water under the earth. Thou shalt not bow down thyself to them, nor serve them: for I the LORD thy God am a jealous God, visiting the iniquity of the fathers upon the children unto the third and fourth generation of them that hate me; And showing mercy unto thousands of them that love me, and keep my commandments.*

III. *Thou shalt not take the name of the LORD thy God in vain; for the LORD will not hold him guiltless that taketh his name in vain.*

IV. *Remember the sabbath day, to keep it holy. Six days shalt thou labor, and do all thy work: But the seventh day is the sabbath of the LORD thy God: in it thou shalt not do any work, thou, nor thy son, nor thy daughter, thy manservant, nor thy maidservant, nor thy cattle, nor thy stranger that is within thy gates: For in six days the LORD made heaven and earth, the sea, and all that in them is, and rested the seventh day: wherefore the LORD blessed the sabbath day, and hallowed it.*

V. *Honor thy father and thy mother: that thy days may be long upon the land which the LORD thy God giveth thee.*

VI. *Thou shalt not kill.*

VII. *Thou shalt not commit adultery.*

VIII. *Thou shalt not steal.*

IX. *Thou shalt not bear false witness against thy neighbor.*

X.   *Thou shalt not covet thy neighbor's house, thou shalt not covet thy neighbor's wife, nor his manservant, nor his maidservant, nor his ox, nor his ass, nor any thing that is thy neighbor's.*

These Ten Commandments are the basis of our interpretation of all Scriptures. There are an endless number of possible interpretations and applications. However, they must not conflict with these ten.

As an example, one needs only to research the 613 commandments that the Jews consider to be essential in their application of The Ten:

"The tradition that 613 commandments (Hebrew:, taryag תוצמ ג"ירת mitzvot, "613 mitzvot") is the number of mitzvot in the Torah, began in the 3rd century CE, when Rabbi Simlai mentioned it in a sermon that is recorded in Talmud Makkot 23b."[1]

Interestingly, the Romans instituted two families to represent the computation of all numbers. We have learned them as the "1" family and the "5" family. In The Bible, Jesus categorized The Ten Commandments into two families:

1.   The Divine Family (Relationship)

"Jesus said unto him, Thou shalt love the Lord thy God with all thy heart, and with all thy soul, and with all thy mind. This is the first and great commandment....

2.   The Human Family (Fellowship)

... And the second is like unto it, Thou shalt love thy neighbour as thyself. On these two commandments hang all the law and the prophets."

(Matthew 22:37-40:)

---

[1]   Israel Drazi (2009). Maimonides and the Biblical Prophets. Gefen Publishing House Ltd. p. 209.

Roman Numeral interpretations follow a clear and concise path of interpretation. By simply maintaining the integrity that God established in His Commandments, the same reliability may be applied in the study of The Bible.

The following considerations are examples of Bible truths that every student should use as a foundation. Each question should be answered convincingly before going to the next. Attempting to pick and choose one without having concluded the ones prior is like writing Roman Numerals without knowing all the symbols or their values.

TWELVE AFFIRMATIONS

I.   Do you believe that The Bible is divinely inspired?

II.   Do you believe that Jesus is God?

III. Do you believe that every human is a sinner?

IV.   Do you believe in a literal Heaven and Hell?

V.   Do you believe that Jesus died for you?

VI.   Do you believe that salvation is eternal?

VII. Do you believe that to be absent from the body (For the Saved) is to be present with The Lord?

VIII. Do you believe that everyone must give account for their works?

IX.   Do you believe in The Feast of The Lamb, The Marriage Feast?

X.   Do you believe in The Second Advent of Jesus?

XI.   Do you believe that Jesus will rule in Earth as He does in Heaven?

XII. Do you believe in The New Heaven, and The New Earth, New Jerusalem?

The above are samplings of facts that must be confirmed before going deeply into the spiritual truths of The Scripture. Much of what you think you will see in your search of Scripture is affected by your knowledge or lack of the same concerning questions such as those above. Do not confuse this to mean that The Bible responds to the way you answer these questions, because it does not! The truth, however, is often distorted by incorrect assumptions. Why do I need to be sure about

Bible interpretation? Because if I misinterpret it, I have everything to lose; if I interpret it correctly, I have everything to gain.

RR3–WHEN TO MULTIPLY IN ROMAN NUMERALS

There is a symbol that we briefly mentioned, but shall now interpret. It is the symbol for one thousand times (1000 X). It is the horizontal line (vinculum) above or below a symbol. For the sake of convenience, we will use the underline feature to represent the 1000 X symbol. Look at the following:

I   1,000 (not to be confused by the "M")

V   5,000

X   10,000

L   50,000

C   100,000

D   500,000

M   1,000,000

The line over the top (underneath in this study) adds three zeros to the value of the symbol that it crowns (underscore in this study). Simply stated, the line over a symbol multiplies the value of that symbol times 1,000.

Before we really take on some big numbers, let's do a quick review of that which we have learned up to this point. Oh, and by the way, how much paper have you used for your notes and problem solving? If the answer is none and you are correct in converting those numbers that we have covered, you have an exceptional aptitude for math comprehension and a near photographic memory. But for the rest of us, having paper and pencil is a must. Writing reinforces our learning skills and gives us a method to review our progress.

If you have done all the above and are still being challenged, welcome to the club. In more than one way, The Lord instructs us to stand when we have become convinced that we cannot stand any longer. Why does He do it like that? He wants us to know that it is He who strengthens us and not we ourselves.

Wherefore take unto you the whole armour of God, that ye
may be able to withstand in the evil day, and having done all,
to stand. Stand ...

(Ephesians 6:13, 14)

One way to check your Roman Numeral is to apply the number of symbols required as a rule. It does not matter where in the numerical sequence a number appears, it will always require the same family and value as that of the initial number in the first 10 symbols.

For example, the number "2,222,222" will only require 14 symbols (2 for each "2" because "2" requires "2" [II]. "MMCCXXMMCCXXII" is the Roman Numeral for "2,222,222." The number "1,111,111" requires how many symbols?

The "I" with a line under or over it is only used when you are subtracting "1,000" from a larger value that is multiplied by one thousand. The "I" cannot be applied when the value of "1,000" is to be added.

Example:

"56,000" is "50,000 plus 6,000." To correctly write the value in Roman Numerals will require "3" symbols. "1" to record the "50,000" and "2" to record "6,000." One may be tempted to write it as "LVI."

"LVI"-The "I" in this sample would logically represent "1,000" being added to the preceding "55,000." However, when adding "1,000" to the equation, the symbol "M" is required. The correct Roman Numeral for "56,000" is "LVM."

"1,000" represented by the line over the "I" must only be to the left of the "V" or the "X." Knowing this establishes a rule. What is the rule? The answer is in the footnotes. But before going there, write your rule.[1]

---

[1] The "I" may only be used when subtracting 1,000 from V 5,000 or X 10,000. Otherwise, M is the correct symbol for 1,000.

There are only seven symbols in one million, one hundred and eleven thousand, one hundred and eleven. There is only one symbol required for 1. So, it is for each of the numbers in the sequence. Imagine having to write the Roman Numeral for "888,888." How many symbols would be required?[1]

Let's look at 9,000 and 4,000. Since the Romans did not have a symbol for zero, there is no need to try to find one when converting large numbers. Since it takes only two symbols to write the "9" or the "4," there are only two symbols required to write "9000 or 4000," albeit they are different. Here is where you will apply logic before seeking the symbol. If it takes "1" from "5" to compute "4," then it will take "1000 from "5000" to compute "4,000."

"IV" = "4,000." When the multiplication line is used, any symbol to its left will also have to use it. If the "M" 1,000 symbol was used to the left of the "V", we would have had to use the "M" symbol which is "1,000 X 1,000" or one million. In which case, we would have written one million and five thousand (1,005,000). Therefore, the exception to the "M," which is the correct symbol for 1,000, must be "I" when subtracting "1000 from "V" 5,000 or "X" 10,000."

Answer these questions:

- How many symbols are required to write the Roman Numeral for 9?
- What is the relationship of the symbols to each other?
- What family of symbols is used to write the Roman Numeral for 9?
- How are the numbers calculated when computing the number 9?

Using this logic, try your hand on writing the Roman Numeral for 999,999.

- How many symbols are required for the above number? _____
- What is the relationship of the symbols to each other? _____

---

[1] DCCCLXXXVMMMDCCCLXXXVIII

- What family of symbols is used for the above? _____
- How are the numbers calculated when computing the above? _____

Quick Glance/At Face Value

One of the quickest ways to check a Roman Numeral is by observing the last number in the sequence (the number furthest to the right). Let's say that you are looking for the correct Roman Numeral for the following Arabic number. One of the three numbers listed in Roman Numerals is correct. Look at the Arabic number and quickly assess which is correct.

"3,562,955"

- <u>MMMDLX</u>CMLVI
- <u>MMMDLX</u>MMCMLV
- <u>MMMDLX</u>CMLIV

The first clue is to look for the symbol for the last number (5). There is only one of the choices that ends in "5" (V). You could get confused if you look only at the "V" which ends two of our choices. However, a close look reveals that one of them is an "IV" or "4." If there is one that is right, it must be the second one. However, it does not have to be right.

Our next observation is to count the number of symbols required for each of the Arabic numbers when converted to Roman Numerals. It will require the same number of symbols to write the Roman Numeral for each of the Arabic numbers being considered.

"3,562,955"

- 3 requires III=3
- 5 requires V=1
- 6 requires VI=2
- 2 requires II=2,
- 9 requires IX=2

- 5 requires V=1
- <u>5 requires V=1</u>
  Total 12

The middle symbol has the right number of symbols. Therefore, it is close to being proven correct. Now let's take the number apart using each of the Arabic numbers as if it were the only number on the page.

"3,000,000"

We begin with (3,000,000) three million. It requires "3" identical symbols and they will come from the "1" family adding value. How do I know that? Because the base number "3" is "III." Three identical symbols I + I + I total "III" ("3"). Next is the fact that the largest symbol in the "1" family is "M" representing "1000." Okay, if I add a crown to <u>"M"</u> (underscore), it multiplies "1000" "1000" times totaling "1,000,000" (one million). For "3" million, I will simply use the one million three identical times: <u>MMM</u> = 3 million.

Observation:

• 3	III
• 30	XXX
• 300	CCC
• 3,000	MMM
• 30,000	<u>XXX</u>
• 300,000	<u>CCC</u>
• 3,000,000	<u>MMM</u>

"500,000"

The next number in the sequence is "500,000" (five hundred thousand). It requires "1" symbol from the, you guessed it, "5" family. How did you know that? Because the base number "5" is only one symbol, "V." Since five requires only one symbol, then five hundred thousand will require only one symbol. The largest symbol in the 5 family is "D" representing "500." Why do you think that we should start our consideration with the "D?" Answer: It wouldn't be logical to use either of the other two (V or L) when we have sounded the word "five hundred."

The same logic applies if you were looking for "50,000."
The sound of fifty is a clue to start at the symbol for fifty (L).

Okay, if I add a crown to the "D", it multiplies "500" x "1000" totaling "500,000" (five hundred thousand).

Observation:

- 5   V
- 50   L
- 500   D
- 5000   V̲
- 50,000   L̲
- 500,000   D̲

Using the same logic, work out the remaining values of the Roman Numeral for "3,562,955." Break down each one in long hand just as the three million and five hundred thousand were computed above.

That places you at figuring out how to write:

➢ sixty thousand (60,000),
➢ two thousand (2,000),
➢ nine hundred (900),
➢ Fifty (50),
➢ five (5).
   o Good luck.

After finishing the above exercise, you are to write the Arabic value for:

- <u>MMMDLXCMLVI</u>
- <u>MMMDLXCMLIV</u>

The correct answers for the above are in the end notes of this line.[1]

A common mistake is thinking that logic is applied based on perception alone. Such is the problem when bible interpretation is based on feelings rather than faith. Faith requires an object which, in either Roman Numerals or bible interpretation, is based on written laws.

> *(For we walk by faith, not by sight:)*
>
> *(2 Corinthians 5:7)*

Remember, there is a system to these equations that cannot be disregarded without messing up the conclusion. Often the number "49" is recorded in Roman Numerals as "IL." If you did not know the dos and don'ts of Roman Numerals, "I" (1) placed before the "L" (50) looks good for "49." Doesn't one from fifty equal forty-nine? Yes, and if you are at liberty to write your own code of logic, then so be it. However, if you are to interpret the number based on a given set of commands, then you must exhaust all points of consideration. None of the cardinal concerns may be violated. The above rendering, "IL," is recorded with only two symbols and therefore, cannot be correct!

However, if the answer followed the correct observation:

- "40" requires how many symbols?
- "9" requires how many symbols?
- "49" requires how many symbols?
    - "2" to make "40" ("XL")
    - "2" to make "9" ("IX")
    - "4" to make "49."
        - ✓ "XLIX"

You must first convert the "40" which requires "2" symbols just as does the "4." And they must calculate via subtraction (the relationship

---

[1] MMMDLXCMLVI 3,560,956
MMMDLXCMLIV 3,560,954

of the symbols). The same logic is required for the "9." The result for "49" is "XLIX"–"10 from 50 (=40) and 1 from 10 (=9)." Together they are forty plus nine, "49" / "XLIX."

> But the anointing which ye have received of him abideth in you, and ye need not that any man teach you: but as the same anointing teacheth you of all things, and is truth, and is no lie, and even as it hath taught you, ye shall abide in him.
>
> (1 John 2:27)

Many have interpreted the above Scripture as confirmation that a saved person does not need to attend church, i.e., receive additional teachings. They conclude that The Holy Ghost within is the only teacher required. What should one think of the following Scriptures?

> Teaching them to observe all things whatsoever I have commanded you: and, lo, I am with you alway, even unto the end of the world. Amen.
>
> (Matthew 28:20)

> And the things that thou hast heard of me among many witnesses, the same commit thou to faithful men, who shall be able to teach others also.
>
> (2 Timothy 2:2)

> Therefore, brethren, stand fast, and hold the traditions which ye have been taught, whether by word, or our epistle.
>
> (2 Thessalonians 2:15)

To interpret "1 John 2:27" as meaning that you have no need for God's organization of Spiritual development through The Church is like writing the Roman Numeral "IL" for "49." You may convince yourself that it is correct by some means of logical interpretation. However, it is wrong.

1 John 2:27 speaks of the efficacy of salvation. It says that the anointed person has the indwelling (Inspiration) of The Holy Ghost and shall receive unending teachings through The Holy Commands of

The Lord. These truths are The Scriptures found in The Holy Word of God, The Bible. The understanding of which requires the interaction of an inspired teacher and an inspired student.

> *For when for the time ye ought to be teachers, ye have need that one teach you again which be the first principles of the oracles of God; and are become such as have need of milk, and not of strong meat.*
>
> *(Hebrews 5:12)*

> *And Philip ran thither to him, and heard him read the prophet Esaias, and said, Understandest thou what thou readest? And he said, How can I, except some man should guide me? And he desired Philip that he would come up and sit with him.*
>
> *(Acts 8:30, 31)*

To ensure the appropriate interpretation of His Holy Word, God places us in The Church for Spiritual growth and development.

> *...And the Lord added to the church daily such as should be saved.*
>
> *(Acts 2:47)*

He commits us to those whom He has anointed with the pastoral calling. (Ephesians 4:11)

> *Remember them which have the rule over you, who have spoken unto you the word of God: whose faith follow, considering the end of their conversation.*
>
> *(Hebrews 13:7)*

That there are consequences determined by our response to God's decree are just as certain.

> *Obey them that have the rule over you, and submit yourselves: for they watch for your souls, as they that must give account,*

that they may do it with joy, and not with grief: for that is unprofitable for you.

(Hebrews 13:17)

BIBLE INTERPRETATION / SIMPLE DEDUCTION / LOGIC

Read the two verses below and interpret from them the correct answers to the questions that follow.

Know therefore this day, and consider it in thine heart, that the Lord he is God in heaven above, and upon the earth beneath: there is none else.

(Deuteronomy 4:39)

And without controversy great is the mystery of godliness: God was manifest in the flesh, justified in the Spirit, seen of angels, preached unto the Gentiles, believed on in the world, received up into glory.

(1 Timothy 3:16)

1. How many Gods are there?
2. Was God ever manifested (to reveal its presence or make an appearance) in the flesh?

The above questions are answered simply through applied logic.

- Question one is answered "One" by the first Scripture.
- Question two is answered "Yes" by the second Scripture.

To interpret either question differently does what to The Scriptures above?

If there is more than one God, then Deuteronomy 4:39, among a great number of other Scriptures, is lying.

If God never appeared in the flesh, then 1 Timothy 3:16, among a great number of other Scriptures, is lying.

We simply do not believe that The Bible lies. Therefore, applied logic is trust/faith. Such becomes the basic approach to Bible Study.

The three Scriptures below speak of the act of creation. Read them and then, using simple logic, answer the questions that follow.

> *Thus saith the Lord, thy redeemer, and he that formed thee from the womb, I am the Lord that maketh all things; that stretcheth forth the heavens alone; that spreadeth abroad the earth by myself;*
>
> *(Isaiah 44:24)*

> *He was in the world, and the world was made by him, and the world knew him not.*
>
> *(John 1:10)*

> *For by him were all things created, that are in heaven, and that are in earth, visible and invisible, whether they be thrones, or dominions, or principalities, or powers: all things were created by him, and for him:*
>
> *(Colossians 1:16)*

1. What assistance did God receive during The Creation?
2. Did Jesus receive credit for the act of Creation?

The above questions are answered simply through applied logic.

- Question one is answered "None" by the first Scripture.
- The second question is answered "Yes" by the second and third Scriptures.

To interpret either question differently does what to The Scriptures above?

- If God got assistance, then He did not act alone and therefore, Isaiah 44:24 is lying.
- If Isaiah 44:24 is true, then the only way John 1:10 &Colossians 1:16 may be true is by Jesus being God.

Keeping Scripture in Context and proving it by Cross References are simple approaches to logical deductions. Scripture truths learned are like the truths learned about Roman Numerals. It is upon them that all other conclusions must be built. If your consideration does not fit the foundation, do not force it!

Before venturing further in this study, please answer the following questions correctly: (*Footnote has the answers*)

1. What is the Roman Numeral and its' Arabic conversion that has the most symbols of any Roman Numeral?[1]

2. What is the largest Arabic number that may be translated into Roman Numerals using the seven standard symbols?[2]

3. Using two additional symbols (9), what is the largest Arabic number that may be translated into Roman Numerals?[3]

4. Utilizing the additional "N & J" to the standard "7" symbols, write the Roman Numeral equivalent of the largest Arabic number.[4]

5. Since the "M" and the "Ī" both represent the number "1,000," what simple rule determines which to be correct?[5]

You may check your numerical translations (7 standard symbols) @ WWW.Calculateme.com

---

[1] MMMDCCCLXXXVMMMDCCCLXXXVIII 3,888,888

[2] 3,999,999 Three million nine hundred ninety-nine thousand nine hundred ninety-nine

[3] 39,999,999 Thirty-nine million nine hundred ninety-nine thousand nine hundred ninety-nine

[4] NNNMNCMXCIXCMXCIX

[5] The "M" is never used to subtract "1,000" and the "Ī" is never used to add "1,000 (but the M is used to subtract I million)."

CHAPTER 2

THE BIBLE

KING JAMES (AUTHORIZED-AV) VERSION (KJV)

The Bible is the book written by divinely inspired men. God is its author and salvation is its means. Truth without any mixture of error is its matter. And it alone is the divine principles by which all human creeds, conduct and opinions are tried.

Verbal Plenary Inspiration (VPI) complies with God's position of being responsible for the words that fill His Book. There are however, at least two other theories that bid for acceptance alongside VPI. The three are:

INSPIRATIONAL THEORIES

- *Dictation theory: God dictated the books of The Bible word for word as if the biblical authors were being mechanized.*
- *Dynamic Inspiration: The thoughts contained in The Bible are inspired. But the words used were left to the individual writers.*
- *Verbal Plenary Inspiration: In the simplest terms, VPI concludes that God used human skills to produce a divine book. God authored The Bible through the intellect, skills, and personal traits of His human host.*

  "All scripture is given by inspiration of God, and is profitable for doctrine, for reproof, for correction, for instruction in righteousness:"

  (2 Timothy 3:16)

Revelation… is the revealing or disclosing of some form of truth or knowledge through communication with God. "God speaks directly to man – Bat kol."

Inspiration…is the breathing (*theopneustos*, literally, "God-breathed") of matter into existence through supernatural power. "Biblical inspiration is the doctrine in Christian theology that the authors and editors of the Bible were led or influenced by God with the result that their writings may be designated in some sense the word of God."[1] "Man records God's Words-Ruach Hakodesh."

> *And the Lord appeared again in Shiloh: for the Lord revealed himself to Samuel in Shiloh by the word of the Lord.*
> *(1 Samuel 3:21)*

Illumination… is the spiritual enhancement of the mind of humanity by the anointing of The Holy Spirit (Paraclete). The Spirit of God moves the human mind to receive enlightenment from The Written Word (Unction). "Man receives understanding of God's Word-Spirit Filled."

The book that we call The Bible is the Christian's written message from God. It explains creation, existence and prophecy covering human existence from the beginning to the very end. It explains the conditions that plague humanity and offers consolation to all who will hear.

> The Bible was written over a span of 1500 years by 40 writers. Unlike other religious writings, The Bible reads as a factual news account of real events, places, people, and dialogue. Historians and archaeologists have repeatedly confirmed its authenticity.

> Using the writers' own writing styles and personalities, God shows us who He is and what it's like to know Him.

---

[1] Wikipedia® is a registered trademark of the Wikimedia Foundation, Inc., a non-profit organization.

There is one central message consistently carried by all 40 writers of The Bible: God, who created us all, desires a relationship with us. He calls us to know Him and trust Him.

The Bible not only inspires us, but it also explains life and God to us. It does not answer all the questions we might have, but enough of them. It shows us how to live with purpose and compassion; how to relate to others. It encourages us to rely on God for strength, direction, and enjoy His love for us. The Bible also tells us how we can have eternal life.

© EveryStudent.com

Today The Bible is a composition of two covenants: The Old Testament (OT) and The New Testament (NT). There are ten separate genres in the complete Protestant Bible: Five in The Old and Five in The New.

The Five Genres in The Old Testament are listed in the order of their appearance:

1. 5 Books of Law
2. 12 Books of History
3. 5 Books of Poetry
4. 5 Books of Major Prophets
5. 12 Books of Minor Prophets
   39 Total Books

The Five Genres in The New Testament are in the order in which they are listed:

1. 4 Books of Gospel
2. 1 Book of History
3. 14 Books of Pauline Epistles

4. 7 Books of General (Catholic) Epistles
5. 1 Book of Prophecy
    27 Total Books

Anytime you are reading from The Old Testament, you are reading God's message to His chosen people, The House of Israel. You must discipline yourself to understand the context of those writings or else you may misperceive New Testament truths.

> *And certain men which came down from Judæa taught the brethren, and said, Except ye be circumcised after the manner of Moses, ye cannot be saved. When therefore Paul and Barnabas had no small dissension and disputation with them, they determined that Paul and Barnabas, and certain other of them, should go up to Jerusalem unto the apostles and elders about this question.*
>
> *(Acts 15:1, 2)*

As you can see in the above Scriptures, conflict resolution began between The Jews and The Church at the conception of The Church. Judaism and Christianity are two different religions. Although there is but one God, His persona is different to each Testament. Jehovah is The God of The Old Testament and Jesus is The God of The New Testament. Keep in mind that there is a bright line between the two Testaments. Although The Jews are yet holding on to their Old Testament rituals, God's presence was exclusively with Jesus during His walk on Earth and now with The Holy Ghost in His absence. That means that God does not confuse us with His presence. As a matter of fact, His different personas are for our benefit rather than for our misunderstanding. God's identity continues to be illusive to those who fail to distinguish the two Testaments. Although The Old Testament is essential to the understanding of The New Testament, they are as different as night and day.

> *God, who at sundry times and in divers manners spake in time past unto the fathers by the prophets, Hath in these last days*

spoken unto us by his Son, whom he hath appointed heir of
all things, by whom also he made the worlds;

(Hebrews 1:1, 2)

The terms "Father" and "Son" have left many with a dilemma. How can He be both? Such also was the concern of the disciples:

Philip saith unto him, Lord, shew us the Father, and it sufficeth
us. Jesus saith unto him, Have I been so long time with you,
and yet hast thou not known me, Philip? he that hath seen
me hath seen the Father; and how sayest thou then, Shew us
the Father?

(John 14:8, 9)

Such would not be the case if the reader would transpose the word "Son" to "Manifestation of God."

And without controversy great is the mystery of godliness: God
was manifest in the flesh, justified in the Spirit, seen of angels,
preached unto the Gentiles, believed on in the world, received
up into glory.

(1 Timothy 3:16)

The same concern caused The Jewish Religious Leaders to violently resist Jesus' personal claims to be God.

The Jews answered him, saying, For a good work we stone thee
not; but for blasphemy; and because that thou, being a man,
makest thyself God.

(John 10:33)

There is a phrase not too often repeated, but everyone still knows the meaning: "begotten or begetting." People "beget" people; dogs "beget" dogs; fowls "beget" fowls. No one expects any species of creation to beget a species unlike itself. The problem with many, when it comes to Jesus, is their misinterpretation of the phrase-"Only begotten Son."

*For God so loved the world, that he gave his **only begotten Son**, that whosoever believeth in him should not perish, but have everlasting life.*

(John 3:16)

Although Jesus is certainly the human child of Mary, His divinity precedes all forms of creation. He "alone" created everything, *"And he is before all things, and by him all things consist." (Colossians 1:17)* Such logic has already been considered. However, the understanding of Him being *The Begotten Son* must be explained.

The "begotten" of God must be God just as the begotten of humanity must be human. Any reference to Jesus as the "only begotten Son of God" precedes His earthly walk and should, therefore, prompt the reader's mind to the fact that Jesus is God. The Jews, like too many today, could not think beyond the flesh birth; and because of it, did not reason Jesus' divinity.

And they said, Is not this Jesus, the son of Joseph, whose father and mother we know? how is it then that he saith, I came down from heaven?

(John 6:42)

To them, He was not The "Begotten Son of God." He was the son of Joseph. God creates all but Himself. If God could create God, there would be innumerable opinions to justify polytheism. Yet, it is often repeated and of truth, there is but one God. Therefore, when The Scriptures proclaim Jesus as The "Only Begotten," it is not referencing Him as one who came later. It is, by the very nature of God, proclaiming Him to be the only Human Incarnation of The Creator.

For those who understand that The Creator came to His world, through The Testaments of time, to free His human creatures from the damnation of sin, the understanding of The Trinity is easy. The Old Testament is the book of the first revelations of God and the promises (covenants) that He made. The New Testament is the book of the fulfillments of those promises. New Testament prophecy guides the human mind to the ultimate fulfillment. Therefore, much of what The

New Testament reveals is supported by God's promises as recorded in The Old Testament. The present dispensation holds to The Dispensation of Grace experienced through the power of The Holy Spirit. Although not recorded in The Bible as such, the reader who is saved is a member of The "You Testament."

> *Let us therefore, as many as be perfect, be thus minded: and if in any thing ye be otherwise minded, God shall reveal even this unto you.*
>
> *(Philippians 3:15)*

Not being able to apply The Old and New Testaments in context has led to entire denominations erroneously basing their existence on Old Testament Scripture that has reached fulfillment in The New Testament. The Seventh Day Adventist Church and The Jehovah Witnesses are two examples. The latter considers themselves to be the replacement of Israel; and the former considers themselves to be responsible for rituals rather than truth.

The Jews and The Church are unique bodies; each having an appointed destiny in God's plan. Although for the time being, they are traveling different roads; but shall meet at the crossroad in the end.[1] It was of such a time (the end) that the disciples begged of Jesus to know. They asked Him pointedly:

> *And as he sat upon the mount of Olives, the disciples came unto him privately, saying, Tell us, when shall these things be? and what shall be the sign of thy coming, and of the end of the world?*
>
> *(Matthew 24:3)*

The disciples were Jewish and certainly questioning the consequences of those who were rejecting Jesus as God. The Bible covers Jesus'

---

[1]   And had a wall great and high, and had twelve gates, and at the gates twelve angels, and names written thereon, which are the names of the twelve tribes of the children of Israel: (Revelation 21:12) And the wall of the city had twelve foundations, and in them the names of the twelve apostles of the Lamb. (Revelation 21:14)

answers with eschatological views that include The Jews as well as The Church.

> *Then shall the kingdom of heaven be likened unto ten virgins,*
> *which took their lamps, and went forth to meet the bridegroom.*
>
> *(Matthew 25:1)*

The Wise Virgins are The Church; and The Foolish Virgins are The Jews. The Jews were not accepting Jesus and therefore, could not receive The Holy Ghost referred to as The "Oil" in their lamps.

> *The fool hath said in his heart, There is no God. They are*
> *corrupt, they have done abominable works, there is none that*
> *doeth good.*
>
> *(Psalm 14:1)*

A minor observation to the above Scripture may begin with *"The Jew hast said in his heart, Jesus is no God"*. Such are the expectations of the present dispensation with overwhelming proof that time will change the outlook of The Jews.

> *(According as it is written, God hath given them the spirit*
> *of slumber, eyes that they should not see, and ears that they*
> *should not hear;) unto this day.*
>
> *(Romans 11:8)*

The intertestamental period between The Old and New Testaments is generally known as The 400 Years of Darkness. It is during this time that God ceased from speaking to His people via bat kol, prophet, or angel messenger. However, God's Will, supported by His Written Word, remained as a guide to light the path of the faithful.

Such studies require both testaments if the reader is going to reach an unadulterated conclusion. The New Testament is filled with Old Testament prophecy that is fulfilled. The New Testament prophecy opens our understanding to those that are yet to be fulfilled with perfect assurance of it. Another way of putting it is, "The Old Testament is The

New Testament Concealed. The New Testament is The Old Testament Revealed.

The Bible student does well to take the time to learn the sixty-six books of The Bible. It is also advisable to prepare an easy to remember statement about each of them. The ability to group the books in their respective genres is also essential in maintaining Bible context when studying.

As students of The Bible, we must conclude what is and what is not, Bible. The world has accepted hundreds of so-called versions of The Bible. Such acceptance speaks loudly of human vanity and the lack of reverence extended to God's Word. The word "version" is defined as-a particular form of something, differing in certain respects from an earlier form or other forms of the same type of thing.

Of the three excerpts taken from official documents shown below, only one has been subjected to versions. Which would you consider subjecting to such liberty by the public?

ROMEO AND JULIET (EXCERPT)
William Shakespeare

Act III, Scene ii

> Come, night, come, Romeo, come, thou day in night,
> For thou wilt lie upon the wings of night
> Whiter than new snow on a raven's back.
> Come, gentle night, come, loving, black-browed night,
> Give me my Romeo, and, when he shall die,
> Take him and cut him out in little stars,
> And he will make the face of heaven so fine
> That all the world will be in love with night,
> And pay no worship to the garish sun.
> Oh, I have bought the mansion of love,
> But not possessed it, and though I am sold,
> Not yet enjoyed.

IN CONGRESS, July 4, 1776. (EXCERPT)

The unanimous Declaration of the Thirteen United States of America,

> We hold these truths to be self-evident, that all men are created equal, that they are endowed by their Creator with certain unalienable Rights, that among these are Life, Liberty and the pursuit of Happiness.—That to secure these rights, Governments are instituted among Men, deriving their just powers from the consent of the governed, —That whenever any Form of Government becomes destructive of these ends, it is the Right of the People to alter or to abolish it, and to institute new Government, laying its foundation on such principles and organizing its powers in such form, as to them shall seem most likely to affect their Safety and Happiness.

THE HOLY BIBLE, ENGLISH (EXCERPT)
Acts 8:37

> *And Philip said, If thou believest with all thine heart, thou mayest. And he answered and said, I believe that Jesus Christ is the Son of God.*

If you chose neither, you chose wisely and respectfully.

Autograph-a word meaning: any manuscript handwritten by its author, either in alphabetical or musical notation. An autograph may be an early or corrected draft of a manuscript and provide valuable evidence of the stages of composition or of the "correct" final version of a work. Although The Bible was originally written in Hebrew (Old Testament) and Greek (New Testament), the original authenticity translates to the language of those honorable translators into their native tongues.

The people of Corinth were often hearing The Words of God from Saints of other tongues; and in such cases, were admonished to have the services of a translator. *"If any man speak in an unknown tongue, let it be by two, or at the most by three, and that by course; and let one interpret. But if there be no interpreter, let him keep silence in the church; and let him speak to himself,* and to God." *(1 Corinthians 14:27, 28)* The sound, as does the spelling of words, changes from one language to the next. But the meaning may not change if the message is to be considered authentic, unadulterated.

For English speaking people, the venerable Authorized Version by King James is God's Inspired Word. It bears the painstaking scholarship of the best Bible scholars (1604 – 1611) at the service of The King of England, King James I.

Of the fifty-four translators, four were college presidents, six were bishops, five were deans, thirty held PhD's, thirty-nine held Masters degrees; there were forty-one university professors, thirteen were masters of the Hebrew language, and ten had mastered Greek. Every man involved in the King James Bible translation believed in the verbal inspiration of the Scriptures, all believed in the deity of our Lord Jesus Christ, and all were men of prayer. Many were not only Biblical scholars and master linguists, but also God-called, Spirit-filled preachers. Yet the translators considered themselves "poor instruments to make God's holy truth to be yet more and more known unto the people."

A look at some of the statements of the translators themselves reveals the depth of their convictions concerning the eternal Word of God. They spoke of the Scriptures as "that inestimable treasure which excelleth all the riches of the earth." They acknowledged the Bible as being "so full and so perfect," "a fountain of most pure water, springing up into everlasting life." They believed "the original (Scriptures) were from heaven, not earth; the author being God, not men; the penmen, such as were sanctified from the womb and endued with a principal portion of God's Spirit." They referred to the Bible as "God's Word," "God s Truth," "God's testimony," "the Word of salvation." Study of the Scriptures brought "light of understanding, stableness of persuasion, repentance from dead works, newness of life, holiness, peace, joy in the Holy Ghost, fellowship with the saints, participation of the heavenly nature, fruition of an inheritance immortal, undefiled, and that shall never fade away." From the translators Epistle Dedicatory, the dedication letter of their Bible translation to King James I:

"Among all our joys, there was not one that more filled our hearts, than the blessed continuance of the preaching of God's sacred Word among us."

Some closing comments from The Translators to the Reader: Gentle Reader, we commend thee to God, and to the Spirit of His grace. He removeth the scales from our eyes, the veil from our hearts, opening our wits that we may understand His Word, enlarging our hearts, yea correcting our affections, that we may love it above gold and silver, yea that we may love it to the end. Ye are brought unto fountains of living water which ye digged not. Others have labored, and you may enter into their labors; O receive not so great things in vain, O despise not so great salvation! It is a fearful thing to fall into the hands of the living God; but a blessed thing it is, and will bring us to everlasting blessedness in the end, when God speaketh unto us, to hearken; when He setteth His Word before us, to read it; when He stretcheth out His hand and calleth, to answer, Here am I, here we are to do thy will O God."

In the final analysis, the translators of the King James Bible believed that what they had spent nearly seven years of their lives producing was an "exact translation of the holy Scriptures into the English tongue."

By Bill Bradley, Professor of Bible and History,
Landmark Baptist College,
The Landmark Anchor, May 2003

Note that which God spoke concerning His Word: *"The words of the Lord are pure words: as silver tried in a furnace of earth, purified seven times. Thou shalt keep them, O Lord, thou shalt preserve them from this generation for ever." (Psalm 12:6, 7) "All scripture is given by inspiration of God, and is profitable for doctrine, for reproof, for correction, for instruction in righteousness:"* *(2 Timothy 3:16)* No, they may not be contaminated; but, too sadly, they are counterfeited!

Excerpt From: David W. Daniels, "Look What's Missing." Chick Publication 2009

> *"When you have a Bible changed by men, all you have are men's words. But when you have the words of God preserved in your language, you have a book like no other book. You have The Book. You no longer encounter a book —you encounter a Person. When you see what is missing —and what is at stake— I hope you will stop trusting in the false Bible versions and trust the true and consistent Bible that has been passed down through history, which in English is known as the King James Bible."*

It was stated of a well renowned Bible Scholar and Pastor who publicly teaches and preaches from The "New International Version" (NIV) of The Bible that he personally studies from The King James Bible. Maybe his consideration of those who listen to him is like those of Paul's time in Corinth: *"And I, brethren, could not speak unto you as unto spiritual, but as unto carnal, even as unto babes in Christ. I have fed you with milk, and not with meat: for hitherto ye were not able to bear it, neither yet now are ye able." (1 Corinthians 3:1, 2)* But then, Paul was not feeding his students a contaminated Scripture, for he said: *"But though we, or an angel from heaven, preach any other gospel unto you than that which we have preached unto you, let him be accursed." (Galatians 1:8)*

Paul's knowledge of spiritual warfare equipped him for the inevitable assaults of Satan against the truth of God's message. So, that world-renowned pastor and preacher must not have read Paul's declaration of the singular authenticity of The Scripture or else he surely wouldn't be feeding his congregates that which he reportedly doesn't eat himself. If one of his students were to take it upon him/herself to venture down the road of Acts Chapter 8, he or she is certain to arrive at a roadblock:

ACTS 8:37 NEW INTERNATIONAL VERSION (NIV).

"Acts 8:37 is removed from the Holy Scriptures in the NIV" (Technically no Acts 8:37)

> *36 As they traveled along the road, they came to some water and the eunuch said, "Look, here is water. What can stand in the way of my being baptized?"* [37] [c]1 *(Acts 8:36, 37 NIV)*

Given the option to choose to remove a verse from the existing Bible, would you choose this one?

> *And Philip said, If thou believest with all thine heart, thou mayest. And he answered and said, I believe that Jesus Christ is the Son of God.*
>
> *(Acts 8:37) KJV*

Another example of human counterfeiting may be observed in the now infamous Johannian comma: 1 John 5:7.

> *For there are three that bear record in heaven, the Father, the Word, and the Holy Ghost: and these three are one.*
>
> *And there are three that bear witness in earth, the Spirit, and the water, and the blood: and these three agree in one.*
>
> *(1 John 5:7, 8) KJV*

Regardless to one's scholarship, there is little to no disagreement in Christendom of the fact that God, Who is a Spirit, presents Himself to humanity in the persons of Father, Word (Son) and Holy Spirit. Yet, Bible counterfeiters seemingly have no problem abusing this well documented fact:

---

1   Acts 8:37 Some manuscripts include here Philip said, "If you believe with all your heart, you may." The eunuch answered, "I believe that Jesus Christ is the Son of God."

⁷ For there are three that testify: ⁸ the[1a] Spirit, the water and the blood; and the three are in agreement.

(1 John 5:7, 8) NIV

If you were to examine the 7th verse of 1 John 5 (NIV), who would you understand to be the three that testify? And, of the three that are listed in verse 8, "Spirit, the water and the blood;" where might they be found? Since The Word of God (KJV) answers those questions and the above Scriptures do not, it stands to reason that the answers were intentionally removed!

DR. FRANK LOGSDON, BIBLE TRANSLATION LEADER SAYS, "I'M IN TROUBLE WITH THE LORD."

Dr. Frank Logsdon, project member of the translation committee for The New American Standard Version (NASB), has denounced his work on that bible and urged all Christians to return to The Authorized Version, commonly known as The King James Bible.

Although the most popular modern translation at the present time is The New International Version, both modern bibles are based upon the same Catholic text and Logsdon's concerns apply to both.

Being involved with the project from the very beginning, Logsdon helped publisher F. Dewey Lockman with the feasibility study that led to the translation. He interviewed some of the translators, sat with them, and even wrote the preface. But soon the questions began coming in.

His old friend, Dr. David Otis Fuller, began to put his finger on the many shortcomings of the Catholic text used in all modern bibles, which include the NASB and today's NIV.

Logsdon finally said, "I'm in trouble; I can't refute these arguments; it's wrong; it's terribly wrong; it's frightfully wrong; and what am I going to do about it?"

Logsdon shocked publisher Dewey Lockman by writing, "I must under God renounce every attachment to the New American Standard."

---

[1] 1 John 5:8 Late manuscripts of the Vulgate testify in heaven: the Father, the Word and the Holy Spirit, and these three are one. 8 And there are three that testify on earth: the (not found in any Greek manuscript before the fourteenth century)

Logsdon then began to travel extensively, trying to make up for his error by explaining to people the very simple reasons why The Authorized Version is the one Bible which is absolutely 100% correct.[1]

Frank Logsdon Repudiates the NASB

> *Frank Logsdon was asked two questions about the Bible version issue and used the occasion to explain why he finally rejected the Critical Text and **repented of his involvement** in the creation of the New American Standard Version in 1960.*

Transcript of lecture given by Frank Logsdon, 1973, follows:

> *Two questions were handed me tonight which if I could answer them would take care of almost all the other questions: "Please tell us why we should use the Authorized Version and why the New American Standard is not a good version, and the background from which it came." "What is your opinion of the 1881, 1901 and other variations of the Bible in relation to the Authorized Version?" May I point out to you very specifically, not that you do not know but to stir up your pure minds by way of remembrance, we are in the end time. And this end time is characterized by a falling away, and of course that is apostasy. That is the meaning of the word: Falling away from truth. And when there is a falling away from truth, concurrently there is always confusion because they are sort of Siamese twins.*

> *With confusion there is mental and heart disturbance, and people naturally come short of the high standard of the Lord. Everything we have or ever will have will be found here [in the Bible], as we have said so many times. All that God does for us, in us, with us, through us, to us must come by the way of this Word. It's the only material the Spirit of God uses to produce life and to promote it. Name it, and it has to be here. So you can understand why the archenemy of God and man would want to do something to destroy this book. I ought to*

---

[1]

whisper to you, and this is no compliment to the devil, but he knows it can't be destroyed. He tried to destroy the Living Word. You don't see this depicted on Christmas cards, but the night Jesus Christ was born a devil was there in that stable with one third of the fallen angels whom he had dragged down, to devour the man-child as soon as He was born (Rev. 12:6). Now he couldn't do it. Just think. Satan was there when Jesus was born, with all of those cohorts, those fallen angels, for one purpose: to devour the man-child. He couldn't do it.

So failing to abort the Saviorhood of Jesus Christ both at the manger and at the cross-when he said come down from the cross, that is, before your work is finished come down-he is going to do what he knows is the next most effective thing, that is try to destroy the Written Word.

You understand, I am sure, there are places in this book where you can't differentiate between the Living Word and the Written Word. You know that. John 14:6- "I am the life." John 6:63—My words are life." Different life? The same life. You can't differentiate because after all the Written Word is the breath, if you please, of God, and Jesus Christ is God made flesh or the Word that came to earth.

THE DEVIL'S ATTACK ON THE BIBLE

Nevertheless, getting back to this, the devil is too wise to try to destroy the Bible. He knows he can't. He can't destroy the Word of God. But he can do a lot of things to try to supplant it, or to corrupt it in the minds and hearts of God's people.

Now he can only do it in one of two ways: either by adding to the Scriptures or by subtracting from the Scriptures. And you mark it down in your little red book: He's too wise to add to because those who have been in the Word for a long time would say, "Wait a minute; this is not in the Bible." So he subtracts from it. The deletions are absolutely frightening.

For instance, there are in the revisions (1881 and 1901), so we are told 5337 deletions, subtractions if you please. And here is the way it is done. It is done so subtly that very few would discover it. For instance, in the New American Standard we are told that 16 times the word "Christ" is gone. When you are reading through you perhaps wouldn't miss many of them. Some you might. And 10 or 12 times the word "Lord" is gone. For instance, if you were in a church when the pastor is speaking on the words of the Lord Jesus in His temptation, "Get thee behind me, Satan," if you have a New American Standard you wouldn't even find it. It's not even in there. And there are so many such deletions.

So this is done in order to get around it and further blind the minds and hearts of people, even though it may be done conscientiously. There isn't any worse kind of error than to have conscientious error. If you are conscientiously wrong it's a terrible situation to be in.

Nevertheless, when there is an omission that might be observed, they put in the margin, "Not in the oldest manuscripts." But they don't tell you what those oldest manuscripts are. What oldest manuscripts? Or they may say, "Not in the best manuscripts." What are the best manuscripts? They don't tell you. You see how subtle that is? The average man sees a little note in the margin which says "not in the better manuscripts" and he takes for granted they are scholars and they must know, and then he goes on. That's how easily one can be deceived.

The New American Standard Version is not the King James Version. It never was, isn't, and never will be. Not many perhaps have caught this, but when King James gave his seal to the order to have the Bible translated it was just the permission or authority to go ahead with it. It wasn't his Bible. And for some 200 years his name was not connected to it; he didn't want his name connected with it. And long, long after he had gone from this scene in some sly, clever way "King James" was attached to it. You see, that is attaching God's Word to a man, or man's name to God's Word, and it shouldn't be. It is the Authorized Version.[1]

Thoughtful and sincere English-Speaking Bible Students should not compromise their studies with counterfeits. *The King James Version* (AV) is as the translators stated, *"that inestimable treasure which excelleth all the riches of the earth."*

OLD TESTAMENT

THE HEBREW (JEWISH) OLD TESTAMENT

The Christian Bible contains an Old and New Testament. The Old Testament consists of the books received from The Hebrew Writings before The Advent of Jesus Christ. The Tanakh (/tɑːˈnɑːx/;[1] תָּנָ״ךְ, pronounced [taˈnax] or [təˈnax]; also Tenakh, Tenak, Tanach) or sometimes the Miqra (מִקְרָא) is the canonical collection of Hebrew Scriptures, including the Torah.

These texts are almost exclusively in Biblical Hebrew, with a few passages in Biblical Aramaic instead (in the books of Daniel and Ezra, the verse Jeremiah 10:11, and some single words). The Hebrew Bible is also the textual source for The Christian Old Testament. The form of this text that is authoritative for Rabbinic Judaism is known as The Masoretic Text (MT). It consists of 24 books, while the translations divide essentially the same material into 39 books for The Protestant Bible.

The Title of The Hebrew Bible, TaNaKh, is an acronym of its contents. There are three sections: Torah-Five Books, Nevi'im-Eight Books, and Ketuvim-Eleven Books. The Torah consist of The Law or Pentateuch. The Nevi'im is The Prophetical section, and The Ketuvim contains The Poetry, Praise and History.

Modern scholars seeking to understand the history of The Hebrew Bible use a range of sources, in addition to The Masoretic Text.[1] These sources include early Greek (Septuagint) and Syriac (Peshitta) translations, The Samaritan Pentateuch, The Dead Sea Scrolls and quotations from rabbinic manuscripts. Many of these sources may be older than The Masoretic Text and often differ from it.[2] These differences have given rise to the theory that yet another text, an Urtext of The Hebrew Bible, once existed and is the source of the versions extant today.[3] However, such an Urtext has never been found. The answer to the question of which of the three commonly known versions (Septuagint, Masoretic Text, Samaritan Pentateuch) is closest to the Urtext is not fully determined.[4]

THE PROTESTANT OLD TESTAMENT

A Protestant Bible is a Christian Bible whose translation or revision was produced by Protestants. Such Bibles comprise 39 books of The Old Testament (according to The Jewish Hebrew Bible Canon, known especially to Non-Protestants as The Protocanonical Books) and 27 books of The New Testament for a total of 66 books.

Some Protestants use bibles which also include 14 additional books in a section known as the Apocrypha (though these are not

---

[1] "Scholars seek Hebrew Bible's original text – but was there one?". Jewish Telegraphic Agency. 2014-05-13. Retrieved 25 September 2015.

[2] "Controversy lurks as scholars try to work out Bible's original text". The Times of Israel. Retrieved 25 September2015.

[3] Isaac Leo Seeligmann, Robert Hanhart, Hermann Spieckermann: The Septuagint Version of Isaiah and Cognate Studies, Tübingen 2004, pages 33-34

[4] Shanks, Herschel (August 4, 1992). Understanding the Dead Sea Scrolls (1st ed.). Random House. p. 336. ISBN 978-0679414483.

considered canonical) bringing the total to 80 books.[1] [2] This is often contrasted with the 73 books of The Catholic Bible, which includes seven Deuterocanonical Books as a part of The Old Testament.[3] The division between Protocanonical and Deuterocanonical Books is not accepted by all Protestants who simply view books as being canonical or not; and therefore, classify books found in The Deuterocanon, along with other books, as part of The Apocrypha.[4]

THE LAW BOOKS OF THE OLD TESTAMENT–5 BOOKS

The Five Books of Moses were collectively called The Pentateuch, a word of Greek origin meaning "the five-fold book." The Jews called them The Torah, i.e., "the law." It is probable that the division of The Torah into five books proceeded from The Greek Translators of The

---

[1]   King James Version Apocrypha, Reader's Edition. Hendrickson Publishers. 2009. p. viii. ISBN 9781598564648. The version of 1611, following its mandate to revise and standardize the English Bible tradition, included the fourteen (or fifteen) books of the Apocrypha in a section between the Old and New Testaments (see the chart on page vi). Because of the Thirty-Nine Articles, there was no reason for King James' translators to include any comments as to the status of these books, as had the earlier English translators and editors.

[2]   Tedford, Marie; Goudey, Pat (2008). The Official Price Guide to Collecting Books. House of Collectibles. p. 81. ISBN 9780375722936. Up until the 1880s every Protestant Bible (not just Catholic Bibles) had 80 books, not 66. The inter-testamental books written hundreds of years before Christ, called the "Aprocrypha," were part of virtually every printing of the Tyndale-Matthews Bible, the Great Bible, the Bishops Bible, the Protestant Geneva Bible, and the King James Bible until their removal in the 1880s. The original 1611 King James contained the Apocrypha, and King James threatened anyone who dared to print the Bible without the Apocrypha with heavy fines and a year in jail.

[3]   Roman Catholic Code of Canon Law, 825

[4]   Henze, Matthias; Boccaccini, Gabriele (20 November 2013). Fourth Ezra and Second Baruch: Reconstruction after the Fall. Brill. p. 383. ISBN 9789004258815. Why 3 and 4 Esdras (called 1 and 2 Esdras in the NRSV Apocrypha) are pushed to the front of the list is not clear, but the motive may have been to distinguish the Anglican Apocrypha from the Roman Catholic canon affirmed at the fourth session of the Council of trent in 1546, which included all of the books in the Anglican Apocrypha list except 3 and 4 Esdras and the Prayer of Manasseh. These three texts were designated at Trent as Apocrypha and later included in an appendix to the Clementine Vulgate, first published in 1592 (and the standard Vulgate text until Vatican II).

Old Testament. The names by which these several books are generally known are Greek.

1. **Genesis**
2. **Exodus**
3. **Leviticus**
4. **Numbers**
5. **Deuteronomy**

THE HISTORY BOOKS OF THE OLD TESTAMENT–12 BOOKS

After The Five Books of Moses (The Law), The Bible contains The 12 Books of History. These books track the significant events encountered by The People of Israel and those that contended with them. The time covered expands to approximately 800 years. Israel will take possession of Canaan, be empowered with the gifts of Judges and the coronation of Kings. Israel will be divided into two nations, The Northern and Southern Kingdoms. The Northern Kingdom will fall to Assyria and The Southern Kingdom will be exiled into Babylon. God will, at the leadership of men such as Nehemiah and Ezra, lead The Jews back to Jerusalem.

1. **Joshua**
2. **Judges**
3. **Ruth**
4. **1st Samuel**
5. **2nd Samuel**
6. **1st King**
7. **2nd King**
8. **1st Chronicles**
9. **2nd Chronicles**
10. **Ezra**
11. **Nehemiah**
12. **Esther**

THE POETRY BOOKS OF THE OLD TESTAMENT-5 BOOKS

The preceding 17 books are often referenced as The Books of The History of Mankind, specifically God's Chosen People, up to the inaugural Books of Poetry. The following five books introduces the reader to The Books of Wisdom and stories that enlighten one to God's Providence, Provisions, and Protection.

1. **Job**
2. **Psalms**
3. **Proverbs**
4. **Ecclesiastes**
5. **Song of Solomon**

THE MAJOR PROPHET BOOKS OF THE OLD TESTAMENT-5 BOOKS

The Christian Bible includes Five Books of Major Prophets. The Hebrew Bible includes in The Nevi'im (Prophets) the initial three books and places Lamentations and Daniel among The Ketuvim (Writings). The term "Major," regarding The Prophets, is not to be understood in the sense of importance when comparing them to The Minor Prophets. "Major" speaks of the length and scope of the work and not its importance. The Major Prophets' work had a more global impact than that of The Minor Prophets.

Although Christians tend to avoid these books more than any of the others in The Bible, they offer priceless guidance and direction fulfilling the hope that directs the path of every sincere Saint. The language of The Prophets also reached deeply into the veil of mysticism, often revealing matters that even The Prophets themselves were not completely cognizant of. *"And these all, having obtained a good report through faith, received not the promise:" (Hebrews 11:39)*

1. **Isaiah**
2. **Jeremiah**
3. **Lamentations**

4. **Ezekiel**
5. **Daniel**

THE MINOR PROPHET BOOKS OF THE
OLD TESTAMENT-12 BOOKS

The last twelve books of The Christian Old Testament are The Books of The Minor Prophets. The reference to the word "Minor" is not to be misunderstood in comparison to the validity or importance of the books or their writers. Generally speaking, "Minor" verses "Major" speaks only of the time required of The Prophet, the volume of the work of The Prophet, and the total outreach of the contents. Each book addresses a unique event that dealt more with those to whom The Prophet spoke rather than a world impact. Exceptions to that fact are noticed in interpretations that expand themselves beyond the pages of prophesy and bid for fulfillment observed in the writings of The New Testament. Tithing, as an example, is expressly instructed in Malachi, Chapter 3. But some New Testament Students find such reference to be dated and not applicable. However, a closer study of the word "tithe(s)" reveals thirty-two appearances in The Bible; seven of which are in The New Testament. The very first rendering was prior to the giving of The Law and was received by Melchizedek (Christ pre-incarnate) from Abram. (Genesis 14:20)

There are also other inferences of the tithe, such as God's reservation of one-tree in The Garden of Eden. Although it was accessible, it was not to be touched (Genesis 3.3). It is recorded in The Book of Leviticus, Chapter 27, that there are three things that belong to God alone, yet they are in the dominion (control) of humanity. They are The First of everything that a person possesses (verse 26), Anything Dedicated to The Lord (verse 28), and The Tithe (verse 30). There are no biblical changes to these facts. Therefore, all of humanity have been tasked, from Adam to the future coming of Jesus' Kingdom on Earth, to maintain compliance for that which God uses to help humanity properly prioritize their purposes. The Minor Prophets, although taught, preached, or discussed less than any of the other books of The

Bible (apart from The Book of Revelation), are great messages for growth, obedience, and fellowship.

1. **Hosea**
2. **Joel**
3. **Amos**
4. **Obadiah**
5. **Jonah**
6. **Micah**
7. **Nahum**
8. **Habakkuk**
9. **Zephaniah**
10. **Haggai**
11. **Zechariah**
12. **Malachi**

NEW TESTAMENT

The New Testament is the second half of The Christian Bible. The first half is The Old Testament. Each testament references a condition by which God allowed humanity to achieve fellowship with Him. The word "Testament" means something or someone that serves as a sign or evidence of a specific fact, event, or quality. Blood, in which is the life of a being, was evidenced in Eden as that which The Lord determined to be the substance of human redemption (*"Unto Adam also and to his wife did the Lord God make coats of skins, and clothed them." (Genesis 3:21).*

In The Old Testament, sacrifices were made systematically symbolizing that ultimate plan of salvation. In The New Testament, there was to be only one sacrifice which would cover the sins of the whole world. There are 27 books that make up 5 sections in The New Testament. It opens with The Gospels. The 4 Books of The Gospel cover the Lord Jesus' life, death, and resurrection. Jesus, at the displeasure of the prevailing religion of The Jews, taught of Himself as the following personas: King in The Book of Matthew-Lion; Sacrifice in The Book of Mark-Ox; Human in The Book of Luke-Man; and God in The Book of John-Eagle.

After the resurrection and ascension of Christ, The Holy Spirit gave birth to The New Testament Church. The Book of The Acts of The Apostles chronicles the challenges and teachings of The First Century Church. The Pauline Epistles (Including Hebrews by this author) are the 14 books that follow The Acts. After The Pauline Epistles, there are 7 General Epistles written by James (Brother of our Lord Jesus), Peter, John, and Jude (Brother of our Lord Jesus). Revelation, the final book of The Bible was written by John The Apostle (Author of The Gospel of John, and The 3 General Epistles with his name).

GOSPELS – 4 BOOKS

The Gospel, by definition, means something good. The Greek word from which our word "Gospel" comes is "Euangelion." Eu is the prefix of several familiar terms; euphonic (pleasing to the ear) and eulogy (good message). Therefore, our "Gospel" or "Euangelion" consists of eu-good and angelion-message or good message. Most notably, The Gospels are referred to, by definition, as Good-News. However, too many preachers treat it like anything but. Closely associated with The Gospel are the words "angels" and "angelos." The former is a messenger, and the latter is one who delivers a message.

The first three books, Matthew, Mark, and Luke are generally referred to as The Synoptic Gospels. So designated by their similarity, each references the human family of Jesus and their distinction from The Gospel of John. John is the only Gospel that omits Christ's human pedigree and presents Him as God from the beginning.

The reader should expect to receive a powerful redeeming message of God's love and personal sacrifice for all who truly desire to live with Him forevermore.

1. **Matthew**
2. **Mark**
3. **Luke**
4. **John**

HISTORY 1-BOOK

ACTS

The Acts of The Apostles is the biblical account of the events leading up to and after the birth of The Church. It is the account of The "You Testament" i.e., the indwelling of The Holy Spirit. It is evidenced here that the foundation of The Church, that being The Twelve, were filled with The Power of God and subsequently empowered those who were willing to heed their call. Although the title rightly acknowledges The Acts of all The Apostles, the book more specifically outlines the ministries of Peter and Paul. Ironically, each of them is also represented in The Gospels by their associates Mark-Peter and Luke-Paul. The book was written by Luke with the intent to show the continuation of all that Jesus began to do and teach (1:1). As in each of The Gospels, there is a recording of The Great Commission (Matthew 28:19, Mark 16:15, Luke 24:49, John 20:21). There is also a recording of the same in Acts 1:8.

PAULINE EPISTLES-14 BOOKS

The Pauline Epistles consist of 13 books claiming authorship by Paul The Apostle (Saul was his Jewish name-Paul his Roman name). For many years, Church Fathers also assigned the writing of The Book of Hebrews to Paul. However, recent scholars tend to question the authenticity of such due to an apparent difference in writing style. Such concern tends to deny The Power of The Holy Spirit (Verbal Plenary Inspiration-VPI) as the actual author of all canonical writings. As for me, assigning The Book of Hebrews to Paul is rather logical. First and foremost, who would be better than he who was a Pharisee and noted to have come from the linage of Israel through the family of Benjamin (Philippians 3:5)? Add to those facts, Paul was considered the *"Hebrew of the Hebrews"; "Circumcised the eighth day, of the stock of Israel, of the tribe of Benjamin, an Hebrew of the Hebrews; as touching the law, a Pharisee;" (Philippians 3:5)* When assigning the first 14 epistles to Paul, it is rather easy to remember that half as many more books, 7, conclude the 21 books of epistles in The New Testament. Another memorable fact is

Paul wrote to 7 churches, as did John in The Book of Revelation. Paul's writings are the earliest extant writings of The New Testament.

1. **ROMANS**
2. **I CORINTHIANS**
3. **2 CORINTHIANS**
4. **GALATIANS**
5. **EPHESIANS**
6. **PHILIPPIANS**
7. **COLOSSIANS**
8. **I THESSALONIANS**
9. **2 THESSALONIANS**
10. **I TIMOTHY**
11. **2 TIMOTHY**
12. **TITUS**
13. **PHILEMON**
14. **HEBREWS**

GENERAL EPISTLES – 7 BOOKS

The General or Catholic Epistles were written to The Universal Church. Unlike the Pauline Epistles which were written initially to a particular place or person, The General Epistles were apparently meant to address common concerns that were needful for all Christians. Having survived the attacks of certain scholars, such as Martin Luther and others, these epistles overcame attempts to list them as the lesser epistles. Such designation would assign to The Pauline Epistles more authority. The authors are The Apostles James, Peter, John, and Jude. The first and the last of these men are believed to be the earthly brothers of Jesus.

1. **JAMES**
2. **1ST PETER**
3. **2ND PETER**
4. **1ST JOHN**
5. **2ND JOHN**

6. 3RD **JOHN**
7. **JUDE**

PROPHECY – 1 BOOK

REVELATION

The Book of Revelation is my favorite book. It has endured controversial criticisms much like that of The Lord that it represents. The Early Church Fathers thought it unworthy to be listed in the canon. However, due to empirical proof of authenticity, they chose to include it as poetry with little to no use otherwise. Today, it is recognized by many to be the essential truth and divine key to the understanding of current, as well as future, worldly affairs.[1] It is now, for the most part, appropriately classified as A Book of Prophecy. It opens the understanding of its reader with God's personal assurance of blessings.

> *Blessed is he that readeth, and they that hear the words of this prophecy, and keep those things which are written therein: for the time is at hand.*
>
> *(Revelation 1:3)*

The author is The Apostle John. There are several dates published for the writing of this book. The differences are relative to The Schools from which it is interpreted. The date of AD 95-96 is confirmed through several undeniable facts. The least of which places the period to be during the time of Domitian Caesar. This date is determined by the following statement by Irenaeus (AD 130 to AD 202), as quoted by Eusebius, The Church Historian, in AD 325: *"We will not, however, incur the risk of pronouncing positively as to the name of Antichrist; for if it were necessary that his name should be distinctly revealed in this present time, it would have been announced by him who beheld the apocalyptic vision. For that was seen no very long time since, but almost in our day, towards the end of Domitian's reign."*

---

[1] "Write the things which thou hast seen, and the things which are, and the things which shall be hereafter;" (Revelation 1:19)

"The Revelation of Jesus Christ, which God gave unto him, to shew unto his servants things which must shortly come to pass; and he sent and signified it by his angel unto his servant John:"

(Revelation 1:1)

John was chosen to succeed the other Apostles long before the matter became a known fact. He and his brother James asked Jesus to allow them to sit one on His Right Hand (Heart-Love) and the other on His Left (Mind-Justice) in The Kingdom. The same request was reported by Matthew to have been made by Zebedee's wife Salome. Salome (Hebrew: שלומית, Shelomit) was a follower of Jesus who appears briefly in The Canonical Gospels and in more detail in Apocryphal Writings. She is sometimes identified as the wife of Zebedee, the mother of James and John, and sometimes also as the sister of Mary, mother of Jesus. Possibly motivated by family ties, she and her sons made their request known to The Lord. John lived to be an old man, yet he never ceased from The Commission to spread The Gospel. He was resolved to experience the baptism of suffering and persecution. And now, such relentless determination has gotten him his home among other exiles in Patmos. John was well into his 90's or more as he pinned The Revelation.

I John, who also am your brother, and companion in tribulation, and in the kingdom and patience of Jesus Christ, was in the isle that is called Patmos, for the word of God, and for the testimony of Jesus Christ.

(Revelation 1:9)

Rome housed many of those who disagreed with her at Patmos, where political and religious slaves literally served out their lives working in the mines. Although John was reportedly a survivor of human boiling by Emperor Domitian, his exploits were believed to be hidden from the world due to the absence of social media. However, such was apparently not the plan of God. God used John's imprisonment to author one, if not the most, dynamic book in The Bible.

The Revelation has stifled the world and was denied by many as a book of literal interpretation. Not too many years past, The Book of Revelation was given the genre of Poetry. Some believe that the rise of unbiblical and dangerous Allegorical Hermeneutics by such men as Clement, Alexandria, Origen and finally Augustine was the culprit. Chiliasm, or Premillennialism, has undergone many interpretations over the years as to whether it shall include an earthly kingdom for The Jew or a heavenly one. Such considerations are well defined in the study of The Book of Revelation. Its message is timely. Age and experience have opened the windows of Revelation allowing today's scholar to see clearly that which was yet obscured to The Early Church Fathers.

The Book of Revelation is, without a doubt, the most controversial of them all. Because of its Spiritual depths and literal observations, scholars confuse its interpretations as either being one or the other when it is clearly both. Yes, when it speaks of locusts the size of horses (Revelation 9:7), it means exactly that. Yet, these locusts are carnivorous and their prey humans. (Revelation 9:4, 5) Such are the events of God's wrath poured out on evil during The Tribulation. While some shy away from The Book because of such depictions, the opposite should be the case, seeing as how these things are the destiny of those who love to hurt humanity.

John's message covers The Past, Present and The Future. *"Write the things which thou hast seen, and the things which are, and the things which shall be hereafter;" (Revelation 1:19)* Chapter One covers The Past, Chapters Two and Three cover the Present, and except for the closing of Chapter 22, from Chapters Four to the end cover The Future.

Seven Churches are highlighted from Asia Minor. These were not the only Churches. Therefore, the number becomes important. (Genesis 2:2) The Number Seven is repeated mysteriously throughout The Scriptures (Jude 1:14). It is the representation of divine completeness. (Psalm12:6) It is the composition of Four (Earthly-Genesis 13:14) and Three (Heavenly-I John 5:7). Although this Book is studied from The Schools of Preterism, Historicism, and Idealism/Spiritism, it personally ascribes itself to Futurism/Prophesy. As such, it is the eschaton of human existence. Each of The Seven Churches (Message to All Churches) is examined based on Seven Conditions. The following breakdown is The Church of Ephesus:

1. ***Instruction:*** *Unto the angel of the church of Ephesus write;*
2. ***Introduction:*** *These things saith he that holdeth the seven stars in his right hand, who walketh in the midst of the seven golden candlesticks;*
3. ***Commendation:*** *I know thy works, and thy labour, and thy patience, and how thou canst not bear them which are evil: and thou hast tried them which say they are apostles, and are not, and hast found them liars: And hast borne, and hast patience, and for my name's sake hast laboured, and hast not fainted.*
4. ***Condemnation:*** *Nevertheless, I have somewhat against thee, because thou hast left thy first love.*
5. ***Correction:*** *Remember therefore from whence thou art fallen, and repent, and do the first works; or else I will come unto thee quickly, and will remove thy candlestick out of his place, except thou repent.*
6. ***Admonition:*** *But this thou hast, that thou hatest the deeds of the Nicolaitans, which I also hate. He that hath an ear, let him hear what the Spirit saith unto the churches;*
7. ***Assurance:*** *To him that overcometh will I give to eat of the tree of life, which is in the midst of the paradise of God.*

Like Ephesus, Pergamos and Thyatira also received both Commendations and Condemnations. Smyrna and Philadelphia received no Condemnations while Sardis and Laodicea received no Commendation. For the scholar, The Revelation not only reveals The Personage of Christ as the only means of salvation (Revelation 5:9), but also the conditions of the world from introspective (Revelation 16:9-11) to the poligious (politics–religion) controls that dominate it. (Revelation 17 & 18) Revelation pulls the cover off the evil pretenders and exposes their deeds. (Revelation 21:8) John was told to "write," not speak to The Churches. God, through John, was authoring His Last Book. All The Prophets and Apostles had finished their course.

The law and the prophets were until John: since that time the kingdom of God is preached, and every man presseth into it.

(Luke 16:16)

I have fought a good fight, I have finished my course, I have kept the faith:

(2 Timothy 4:7)

Yet today, many are parading across the stage of life with a personal message from God exclusive of The Written Word. Such acclaims should immediately send up red flags:

For such are false apostles, deceitful workers, transforming themselves into the apostles of Christ. And no marvel; for Satan himself is transformed into an angel of light. Therefore it is no great thing if his ministers also be transformed as the ministers of righteousness; whose end shall be according to their works.

(2 Corinthians 11:13-15)

The Church at Ephesus tried The Messengers at a time when Apostles were prevalent and proved many to be liars. (Revelation 2:2) Today, such proof is revealed in the fact that The Apostle John was the last of The Apostles as his book is the last of The Books of the Bible.

And he saith unto me, Seal not the sayings of the prophecy of this book: for the time is at hand. He that is unjust, let him be unjust still: and he which is filthy, let him be filthy still: and he that is righteous, let him be righteous still: and he that is holy, let him be holy still. And, behold, I come quickly; and my reward is with me, to give every man according as his work shall be. I am Alpha and Omega, the beginning and the end, the first and the last. Blessed are they that do his commandments, that they may have right to the tree of life, and may enter in through the gates into the city.

(Revelation 22:10-14)

In the final analysis, The Book of Revelation serves to encourage and warn with one swipe of the sword. It warns those who position themselves as serving in The Office of The Divinely Inspired (VPI); while encouraging those who position themselves as Students of Divine Illumination:

> *For I testify unto every man that heareth the words of the prophecy of this book, If any man shall add unto these things, God shall add unto him the plagues that are written in this book: And if any man shall take away from the words of the book of this prophecy, God shall take away his part out of the book of life, and out of the holy city, and from the things which are written in this book.*
>
> *(Revelation 22:18, 19)*

Historical annotations are well documented by most reputable publishers of Bibles. Relevant information, such as this provided for Revelation, may be studied normally at the beginning of every book in most study bibles. Additional information may be gleaned from cross references and annotations that usually accompany each page throughout The Bible.

CHAPTER 3

BIBLE PHILOSOPHY

Philosophy is the study of general and fundamental problems concerning matters such as existence, knowledge, values, reason, mind, and language. The Ancient Greek word φιλοσοφία (philosophia) was probably coined by Pythagoras and literally means "love of wisdom" or "friend of wisdom." Philosophy has been divided into many sub-fields. Loving wisdom is a worthy challenge for all of God's people.

> *And the spirit of the Lord shall rest upon him, the spirit of wisdom and understanding, the spirit of counsel and might, the spirit of knowledge and of the fear of the Lord;*
>
> *(Isaiah 11:2)*

> *For the Lord giveth wisdom: out of his mouth cometh knowledge and understanding.*
>
> *(Proverbs 2:6)*

The problem with human philosophy is that such studies are subjective. Human philosophy is a mere expansion of human logic. Human logic is dependent on created matter without which perception is impossible. Words are mere descriptions of something tangible providing a recognizable image to the mind. Such words must have been learned by training, association, or an unexplainable cognizant intuitive response. The first act performed by Adam, prior to the creation of Eve, was that of naming all the creatures in The Garden of Eden.

And Adam gave names to all cattle, and to the fowl of the air, and to every beast of the field; but for Adam there was not found an help meet for him.

(Genesis 2:20)

For one to accept The Bible's report on Creation, faith must be applied. Why? Because there is no material proof known to man to support a human being literally standing from the dirt as is reported of Adam. Adam's intelligence (mind development), like his physical structure, was fully mature at Creation.

Charles Robert Darwin, the English Naturalist and Geologist remains to this very day the renowned professor and founder of The Theory of Evolution. You would think, that after over 100 years of academic growth, The Theory of Evolution would have diminished like that of The Theory of Geocentrism. Today, no one questions whether The Earth is the center of the universe. Astrologers unanimously agree that that position belongs to the sun. So why, in such an intellectively astute society, are we yet holding on to Evolution as a worthy study? Because to reject the teachings of Darwin concerning Evolution would give rise to the teaching of Creationism, and certainly the fruit of "The Tree of The Knowledge of Good and Evil" will not stand idly by and allow that to happen.

In John's Gospel (John 3:3), Christ made it perfectly clear, that except a man be born again (becomes A New Creature), he could not see The Kingdom of God. God's Kingdom is A Spiritual Kingdom and therefore, is invisible to the carnal eye. Attempting to learn the things that are of God through conventional schools of intelligentsia is futile. The ability to interpolate Scripture is a product of Spiritual Illumination.

For the invisible things of him from the creation of the world are clearly seen, being understood by the things that are made, even his eternal power and Godhead; so that they are without excuse:

(Romans 1:20)

Worldly philosophers tend to hypothesize which often leads to extrapolations; the process of going from a known to an unknown without any proof other than scholarship and speculation. Such was the problem of Albert Einstein's theory of the spirit world.

> *Beware lest any man spoil you through philosophy and vain deceit, after the tradition of men, after the rudiments of the world, and not after Christ.*
>
> *(Colossians 2:8)*

> *Because that, when they knew God, they glorified him not as God, neither were thankful; but became vain in their imaginations, and their foolish heart was darkened. Professing themselves to be wise, they became fools,*
>
> *(Romans 1:21, 22)*

To the contrary, God, through the presence of the Holy Spirit (Ruach Hakodesh), gives each convert spiritual discernment. A far too often neglected condition when it comes to truth is that without Spiritual discernment it is virtually impossible to find it. However, one who has been born again and desiring truth will find an endless reservoir of knowledge, wisdom and understanding.

> *But ye have an unction from the Holy One, and ye know all things. I have not written unto you because ye know not the truth, but because ye know it, and that no lie is of the truth.*
>
> *(1 John 2:20, 21)*

> *But strong meat belongeth to them that are of full age, even those who by reason of use have their senses exercised to discern both good and evil.*
>
> *(Hebrews 5:14)*

Understanding the Bible as the volume of truth without any mixture of error is contingent. If humanity accepted the Bible as God's personally authored book its contents would survive as the principles by which all human creeds, conducts and opinion are to be tried. Without such acceptance, one is left to philoso-lie his / her existence as though they have the mind of the Creator. There is no logical evidence that any human has ever given personal proof of their birth. Amazingly, even with such admitted limitations some still attempt to explain existence without the words of the Creator. How might one expect to know spiritual existence when, unassisted, no one has ever written a true book about their personal gestation?

> But the natural man receiveth not the things of the Spirit of God: for they are foolishness unto him: neither can he know them, because they are spiritually discerned.
>
> (1 Corinthians 2:14)

Note that the natural man considers spiritual things to be foolish. For that to occur the natural man must consider himself wise in his own right. Paul mentioned this fact when he proclaimed the Jews to be in denial of God's righteousness by the establishment of their own righteousness.

> For they being ignorant of God's righteousness, and going about to establish their own righteousness, have not submitted themselves unto the righteousness of God.
>
> (Romans 10:3)

Humanity's ignorance to God's righteousness does not mean that humanity is oblivious and unintelligent. As a matter of fact, God personally spoke to the powerful abilities that the human host possesses. It is stated in the Old Testament:

> And the Lord said, Behold, the people is one, and they have all one language; and this they begin to do: and now nothing will be restrained from them, which they have imagined to do.
>
> (Genesis 11:6)

Paul explained God's wisdom and strength by comparing the same to the wisdom and strength of humanity. In other words, Paul used the best example of the virtues of knowledge and power to reveal the supremacy of God's virtues.

> *Because the foolishness of God is wiser than men; and the weakness of God is stronger than men.*
>
> *(1 Corinthians 1:25)*

"A, P, D, T" is a quick to remember acronym of the religions of the world. There are two "A^s," two "P^s," two "D^s," and only one "T."

- o *The two "A^s"*
  - *Atheist and Agnostic*
- o *The two "P^s"*
  - *Polytheist and Pantheist*
- o *The two "D^s"*
  - *Deist and Dualist*
- o *The one and only true religion*
  - *The Theist*

The one constant in each of the philosophies is God. Even the atheist is defined by his/her obsession with what is believed to be the absence of God. The following definitions are simple explanations of the spirits that contend within the human mind.

SEVEN MAJOR RELIGIONS

I.   Atheist–*A person who disbelieves or lacks belief in the existence of God or gods: "he is a committed atheist"*

II.   Agnostic–*A person who believes that, at our present level of knowledge, we cannot know whether a God exists. Some Agnostics believe that we can never know whether a deity exists.*

III. Polytheist – *One who accepts as true, the worship of or belief in multiple deities, which are usually assembled into a pantheon of gods and goddesses, along with their own religions and rituals.*

IV.   Pantheist–*The pantheist holds to the doctrine that God is the transcendent reality of which the material universe and human beings are only manifestations: it involves a denial of God's personality and expresses a tendency to identify God and nature.*

V.   Deist – *The Deist is one who believes in the existence of a God on the evidence of reason and nature only, with rejection of supernatural revelation.*

VI.   Dualist – *One who holds to the doctrine that there are two independent divine beings or eternal principles, one good and the other evil. The belief that a human being embodies two parts, as body and soul.*

VII.   Theist-*One who holds to the belief in one God as the creator and ruler of the universe, without rejection of revelation.*

Surely as time progresses other schools of philosophy are added, for such is the endless quandry of hypothesis. Imagine the great number of Bible students who readily accept the above position of theism, yet we find in their commentary posits of many, if not all, of the others. Such spiritual volleying is referred to as antithetical. A person or thing that is the direct opposite of someone or something else: "love is the antithesis of selfishness."

Bible students must maintain those core values we refer to as doctrines. A great example of such is the acceptance of the Bible as the Word of God. The Bible does not offer any proof of its validity. It simply states truths that go back beyond the existence of humanity as well as the unforeseeable future. Having accepted the Bible as God's truths chronicled for the development of His intelligent creatures is the beginning of faith.

There are a few congregations in Christidome that disagree on critical doctrinal facts. Sadly, there are too many Christians who rely totally on the perceivable knowledge of their pastors without any personal desire to benefit from the same. It brings to mind those members who spend years in a particular church denomination and then upon relocating find themselves in a church of conflicting doctrine. Such actions only confirm the lack of conviction emphasized by the ease with which the change was made.

A report by studiopress (http://www.studiopress.com/) an online information source, stated that according to Gordon-Conwell

Theological Seminary, in 2012 there existed roughly 43,000 Christian denominations worldwide. Today it is stated that a new denomination is formed every 10.5 hours, or 2.3 denominations a day. If nothing else convinces one of the validity of the Gospel, these facts alone should be proof.

> *For I know this, that after my departing shall grievous wolves enter in among you, not sparing the flock. Also of your own selves shall men arise, speaking perverse things, to draw away disciples after them.*
>
> *(Acts 20:29, 30)*

> *I marvel that ye are so soon removed from him that called you into the grace of Christ unto another gospel:*
>
> *(Galatians 1:6)*

Paul's astonishment of the Galatians was in part because of the apparent conviction and commitment that he thought they possessed. The other gospel of which he spoke was not a gospel at all. It was a mere philosophy with which those who sought to appease the minds of the Galatians tendered. Christian scholars and students alike must be vigilant in prayer and due diligence to rightly divide the Words of God.[1] It is imperative that the Bible student understands that it is God's way or no way. These many different philosophies that tickle the intuition of humanity are idle pursuits.

> *Which is not another; but there be some that trouble you, and would pervert the gospel of Christ. But though we, or an angel from heaven, preach any other gospel unto you than that which we have preached unto you, let him be accursed.*
>
> *(Galatians 1:7, 8)*

Being aware of the seven religious beliefs greatly enhances one's ability to recognize those occasions when the path of wisdom leads

---

[1] Study to shew thyself approved unto God, a workman that needeth not to be ashamed, rightly dividing the word of truth. (2 Timothy 2:15)

away from the "strait and narrow" venturing into the wide and broad (Matthew 7:13, 14). Even the theist must be alert to the threads of apostasy sewn into the garment of Christianity. While many believers evaluate a church based entirely on sound, sight, and sensationalism the presence of seeds contrary to comprehensive Bible interpretation may go unnoticed.

> But while men slept, his enemy came and sowed tares among the wheat, and went his way.
>
> (Matthew 13:25)

ECLECTICISM / SYNCRETISM

Eclecticism and Syncretism are the two most common occurrences of self-designed religion contrary to Bible truths.

Eclecticism is a conceptual approach that does not hold rigidly to a single paradigm or set of assumptions, but instead draws upon multiple theories, styles, or ideas to gain complementary insights into a subject, or applies different theories in particular cases. However, this is often without conventions or rules dictating how or which theories were combined."[1]

Syncretism (/'sɪŋkrətɪzəm/) is the combining of different beliefs, while blending practices of various schools of thought. Syncretism involves the merger and analogizing of several originally discrete traditions, especially in the theology and mythology of religion, thus asserting an underlying unity and allowing for an inclusive approach to other faiths." [2]

Humanity has a predisposition of "can't we all just get along," and therefore some find it hard to stand firm on biblical truths that may offend others. However, in the final analysis we must each stand before the Lord and give account for the things done in the flesh. And contrary to an ever-increasing opinion some will enter everlasting life and too sadly, some everlasting damnation.

---

[1]   From Wikipedia, the free encyclopedia
[2]   https://en.wikipedia.org/wiki/Syncretism

But whosoever shall deny me before men, him will I also deny before my Father which is in heaven. Think not that I am come to send peace on earth: I came not to send peace, but a sword. For I am come to set a man at variance against his father, and the daughter against her mother, and the daughter in law against her mother in law. And a man's foes shall be they of his own household. He that loveth father or mother more than me is not worthy of me: and he that loveth son or daughter more than me is not worthy of me. And he that taketh not his cross, and followeth after me, is not worthy of me.

(Matthew 10:33-38)

Marvel not at this: for the hour is coming, in the which all that are in the graves shall hear his voice, And shall come forth; they that have done good, unto the resurrection of life; and they that have done evil, unto the resurrection of damnation.

(John 5:28, 29)

GLOSSARY

- **A.D.—** Stands for Anno Domini, which is Latin for "year of our Lord," and it means the number of years since the birth of Jesus Christ.

- **AMILLENARISM OR AMILLENNIALISM—** (from Latin mille, one thousand; "a" being a negation prefix) is a type of chillegorism which teaches that there will be no millennial reign of the righteous on earth. Amillennarists interpret the thousand years symbolically to refer either to a temporary bliss of souls in Heaven before the general resurrection, or to the infinite bliss of the righteous after the general resurrection.

- **AGES—**Biblically defined periods revealing the creation of matter, such as the universe and the earth. There are three distinct periods, each containing dispensations, relating to the fulfillment of God's plan for all of creation.

- **ALLEGORY**— The representation of abstract ideas or principles by characters, figures, or events in narrative, dramatic, or pictorial form.

- **ANADIPLOSIS**— Repetition of the last word or phrase of one line as the first word of the next. ("rely on his honor—honor such as his?")

- **ANAPHORA**—Repetition of a word or phrase at the beginning of several subsequent clauses or phrases. (Lincoln's "we cannot dedicate—we cannot consecrate—we cannot hallow—this ground")

- **APOCRYPHAL**—(of a story or statement) of doubtful authenticity, although widely circulated as being true.

- **APOCALYPSES**—In the Greek New Testament, apocalypses appear in two senses. When used figuratively, it has the sense of "bringing someone to knowledge," as in the English phrase "remove the veil of ignorance." For example, when we say that a mystery is unveiled, we mean that the veil of ignorance is lifted so that the matter can be plainly understood. In terms of the book of Revelation, this is the sense that most interpreters and readers recognize in it. They see it as the unveiling of prophetic events to understanding.

- **APOCALYPTIC**—Relating to or predicting the end of the world, especially as described in the Bible or another religious text.

- **ARMAGEDDON**—(Bible) New Testament, the battle at the end of the Tribulation between the forces of evil and the Lord. (Revelation 16:16, Revelation 19:19)

- **AUTOGRAPH**—An original writing of a biblical document. The original manuscript written.

- **B.C.**—The terms anno Domini (AD) and before Christ (BC) are used to label or number years in the Julian and Gregorian calendars. ... However, BC is placed after the year number (for example: AD 2018, but 68 BC), which also preserves syntactic order.

- **BIBLIOLOGY**—(from Greek biblos meaning "book") refers to the study of the nature of the Bible as revelation. It often includes such topics as revelation, inspiration, inerrancy, canonicity, illumination, and interpretation.

- **CANON**—The collection of books that are considered inspired from God and authoritative in all areas addressed.

- **CHILIASM**—Is the ancient name for what today is known as premillennialism, the belief that when Jesus Christ returns, He will not execute the last judgment at once but will first set up on earth a temporary kingdom, where resurrected saints will rule with Him over non-resurrected subjects for a thousand years of peace and righteousness.

- **CODEX**—An early book form made from papyri leaves cut, folded, and sewn together in the middle to make a book. First used in the 2nd century.

- **CONTEXT**—Study the Bible with an eye on its ancient setting and develop an understanding of its key people, places, and civilizations with Historical and Chronological Context of the Bible. Take in the full history of the Bible with a detailed account that focuses on its major empires, events, and personalities.

- **COPTIC**—The Afro-Asiatic language of the Copts, which survives only as a liturgical language of the Coptic Church.

- **COVENANT THEOLOGY**—(also known as Covenantalism, Federal theology, or Federalism) is a conceptual overview and interpretive framework for understanding the overall flow of the Bible. It uses the theological concept of a covenant as an organizing principle for Christian theology.

- **CREATIONISM**—The term creationism most often refers to belief in special creation; the claim that the universe and lifeforms were created as they exist today by divine action, and that the only true explanations are those which are compatible with a Christian fundamentalist literal interpretation of the creation myths found in the Bible's Genesis creation narrative.

- **DEUTEROCANONICAL BOOKS**— (from the Greek meaning "belonging to the second canon") are books and passages considered by the Catholic Church, the Eastern Orthodox Church, the Oriental Orthodox Churches and the Assyrian Church of the East to be canonical books of the Testament but which are considered non-canonical by Protestant denominations.

- **DISPENSATIONAL THEOLOGY**— Refers to the unified teachings of Dispensationalism that address what other views teach as divergent theologies in the Old Testament and New Testament. Its name reflects a view that biblical history is best understood as a series of dispensations, or separated time-periods, in the Bible.

- **DIVINE APPOINTMENT**— Is a meeting with another person that has been specifically and unmistakably ordered by God.

- **ECLECTICISM**— is a conceptual approach that does not hold rigidly to a single paradigm or set of assumptions, but instead draws upon multiple theories, styles, or ideas to gain complementary insights into a subject, or applies different theories in particular cases.

- **EISEGESIS**— The interpretation of a text, esp. a biblical text, using one's own ideas. which is to 'read into' a particular text.

- **ELLIPSIS**—An ellipsis is a series of dots (typically three, such as "…") that usually indicates an intentional omission of a word, sentence, or whole section from a text without altering its original meaning.

- **EMPIRICISM**—the theory that all knowledge is derived from sense-experience. Stimulated by the rise of experimental science, it developed in the 17th and 18th centuries, expounded by John Locke, George Berkeley, and David Hume. Compare with phenomenalism.

- **EPIPHANY**— refers to a realization that Christ is the Son of God. Western churches generally celebrate the Visit of the Magi as the revelation of the Incarnation of the infant Christ and commemorate the Feast of "The Epiphany" on January 6. In our study of the Bible, it is a usually sudden manifestation or perception of the essential 'nature or meaning' of something pertaining to the spirit world.

- **EPISTLE**— (Bible) New Testament, any of the apostolic letters of Saints Paul, Peter, James, Jude, or John. The genre also appears in the second and third chapters of The Book of Revelation.

- **EPISTROPHE**—: Repetition of the same word at the end of every line or phrase. (Abraham Lincoln's Gettysburg Address: "...and that government of the people, by the people, for the people, shall not perish from the earth.")

- **ESCHATOLOGY**—From the Greek "eschatos," which means "last," and "logos," which means "word." It is the study of last things: the tribulation, the rapture, the return of Jesus, the final judgment, etc.

- **ESCHATON**—The return of Jesus. From the Greek "eschatos," which means "last."

- **ETYMOLOGY**— The study of the origin of words and the way in which their meanings have changed throughout history.

- **EVOLUTIONISM**— was a common 19th century belief that organisms inherently improve themselves through progressive inherited change over time (orthogenesis) and increase in complexity through evolution. The belief went on to include cultural evolution and social evolution.

- **EXEGESIS**— is when a person interprets a text based solely on what it says. That is, he extracts out of the text what is there as opposed to reading into it what is not there (Compare with Eisegesis). There are rules to proper exegesis: read the immediate context, related themes, word definitions, etc., that all play a part in properly understanding what something says and does not say.

- **EXTANT**—That which exists.

- **FULFILLMENT THEOLOGY**— also called replacement theology is a Christian doctrine which has parallels in Islam. In Christianity, supersessionism is a theological view on the status of the church in relation to the Jewish people and Judaism.

- **FUTURISM—** is a Christian eschatological view that interprets portions of the Book of Revelation and the Book of Daniel as future events in a literal, physical, apocalyptic, and global context. By comparison, other Christian eschatological views interpret these passages as past events in a symbolic, historic context (Preterism and Historicism), or as present-day events in a non-literal and spiritual context (Idealism). Futurist beliefs usually have a close association with Premillennialism and Dispensationalism.

- **GENRE—** A Biblical genre is a classification of Bible literature according to literary genre. The genre of a particular Bible passage is ordinarily identified by analysis of its general writing style, tone, form, structure, literary technique, content, design, and related linguistic factors; texts that exhibit a common set of literary features (very often in keeping with the writing styles of the times in which they were written) are together considered as belonging to a genre.

- **GOG AND MAGOG—** are names that appear in the Hebrew Bible (Old Testament), notably Ezekiel, and the Book of Revelation, sometimes indicating individuals and sometimes lands and peoples. Sometimes, but not always, they relate to the end times. Passages from the Book of Ezekiel and Revelation have attracted attention for this reason.

- **HAMARTIOLOGY—**is the study of sin. Hamartiology deals with how sin originated, how it affects humanity, and what it will result in after death. To sin essentially means to "miss the mark." We all miss God's mark of righteousness (Romans 3:23). Hamartiology, then, explains why we miss the mark, how we miss the mark, and the consequences of missing the mark. These are some important questions in Hamartiology:

- **HERMENEUTICS—**The branch of knowledge that deals with interpretation, especially of the Bible or literary texts.

- **HISTORICISM**— is a mode of thinking that assigns major significance to a specific context, such as historical period, geographical place, and local culture. As such it stands in contrast to individualist theories of knowledge such as empiricism and rationalism, which neglect the role of traditions.

- **HISTORICITY**— holds that the book of Revelation predicts the future, but it has been progressively fulfilled through church history—not some future tribulation. This view began with Joachim of Fiore in the twelfth century AD. This was the view of Martin Luther and the Reformers, who believed that the Antichrist was the Roman papacy and Babylon was the Roman church. This view generally has a minimal following today because it is difficult to align Revelation with any significant portion of church history. It has also led to wild speculation.

- **HOMILETICS**— (Gr. homiletikos, from homilos, to assemble together), in theology, is the application of the general principles of rhetoric to the specific department of public preaching. One who practices, or studies homiletics may be called a homilist or more colloquially a preacher.

- **IDEALISM**— (also called the spiritual approach, the allegorical approach, the nonliteral approach, and many other names) in Christian eschatology is an interpretation of the Book of Revelation that sees all of the imagery of the book as symbols.

- **ILLUMINATION**—From paper (Bible) to the heart of humanity (See Revelation and Inspiration).

- **INERRANCY**—Without error. The Bible is without error.

- **INSPIRATION**—The teaching that the Bible is "God-breathed." It is, therefore, accurate in all it addresses. The authors of the Bible were inspired of God; that is, they wrote under the divine guidance of God. From Man to paper (Bible). See Revelation and Illumination.

- **ISOGESIS**— (Common misspelling of eisegesis) It basically means reading preconceived ideas into the Bible rather than exegesis which means observing and taking out the obvious literal meaning of the Bible.

- **KRATER**— in ancient Greece, a large two-handled bowl, used to mix wine with water.

- **LXX**—The Roman numerals for 70. It is used to describe the Septuagint which is a Greek translation of the Hebrew Scriptures done (traditionally) by 70 scholars around 250-150 B.C.

- **MANUSCRIPT**—A document or a copy of an original writing.

- **MATHODOLOGY**—A study (Quantitative Technique—QT) founded by the Christian author Nathaniel J. McClain of converting Arabic numbers to Roman numerals with the intention of learning the methodology of math conversions and applying the science to Bible Hermeneutics.

- **METHODOLOGY**— is the systematic, theoretical analysis of the methods applied to a field of study. It comprises the theoretical analysis of the body of methods and principles associated with a branch of knowledge. Typically, it encompasses concepts such as philosophical or theoretical frameworks, theoretical model, phases and quantitative or qualitative techniques.

- **MILLENNIUM**—a thousand years; the name given to the era mentioned in Revelation 20:1-7. Some maintain that Christ will personally appear on earth for the purpose of establishing His kingdom at the beginning of this millennium. Those holding this view are usually called "millenarians."

- **MINUSCULE**—The Greek characters of lower case: abgde, etc. Different copies of Greek manuscripts appear in minuscule form. See Uncial.

- **MONERGISM**— is the view within Christian theology which holds that God works through the Holy Spirit to bring about the salvation of an individual through spiritual regeneration, regardless of the individual's cooperation.

- **OPISTHOGRAPH**—a scroll with writings on both sides.

- **PALIMPSEST**—Vellum that was previously used for a writing surface that has been scraped clean and dressed, and then another writing is made on the surface. Codex Ephraemi rescriptus is one of these. It is possible to use certain chemicals and ultraviolet light to uncover the writings underneath the second writing.

- **PAPYRUS**—A plant growing along the Nile in Egypt during biblical times. It was used as writing material. Papyrus scrolls were made by cutting and pressing sections of the papyri plant together at right angles. The typical maximum length of a scroll was about 35 feet. The scribe, when using papyrus, would often use the natural horizontal fibers of the papyrus plant as guidelines. He would take a blunt instrument and score horizontal lines and then score two or more vertical lines as margins for the edge of the sheet or to define columns on it. We get the word "paper" from this word. Many of the biblical manuscripts were on papyrus.

- **PARABLE**—A short fictional story told to illustrate one or more moral / mystical points.

- **PARACLETE**— The word parakletos is a verbal adjective, often used of one called to help in a lawcourt. In the Jewish tradition the word was transcribed with Hebrew letters and used for angels, prophets, and the just as advocates before God's court. The word also acquired the meaning of 'one who consoles' (cf. Job 16:2, Theodotion's and Aquila's translations; the LXX has the correct word parakletores). It is probably wrong to explain the Johannine parakletos on the basis of only one religious background. The word is filled with a complex meaning: the Spirit replaces Jesus, is an advocate and a witness, but also consoles the disciples.

- **PARALLELISM**— The use of components in a sentence that are grammatically the same; or similar in their construction, sound, meaning, or meter. Multiple words, phrases, terms, or verses bringing clarity to valid interpretations or meanings.

- **PENTATEUCH**—The first five (penta) books of the Bible: Genesis, Exodus, Leviticus, Numbers, and Deuteronomy. These are attributed to Mosaic authorship.

- **PERICOPE**—per-ik-o-pee—A selection from a book. A small set of Bible verses, read.

- **PHARISEE**— a member of an ancient Jewish sect, distinguished by strict observance of the traditional and written law, and commonly held to have pretensions to superior sanctity.

- **PHENOMENALISM**— the doctrine that human knowledge is confined to or founded on the realities or appearances presented to the senses.

- **PHONOLOGY**— the branch of linguistics that deals with systems of sounds (including or excluding phonetics), especially in a particular language.

- **PILCROW**— The pilcrow (¶), also called the paragraph mark, paragraph sign, paraph, alinea (Latin: a lineā, "off the line"), or blind P,[1] is a typographical character for individual paragraphs.

- **PNEUMATOLOGY**—The study of the Holy Spirit.

- **POLYPTOTON**— Repetition of the words with the same root but different endings. (as in Tennyson's "my own heart's heart, and ownest own, farewell")

- **POSTMILLENNIALISM**— Holds that Jesus Christ establishes His kingdom on earth through His preaching and redemptive work in the first century and that He equips His church with the gospel, empowers her by the Spirit, and charges her with the Great Commission (Matt 28:19) to disciple all nations.

- **PRAGMATICS**— the branch of linguistics dealing with language in use and the contexts in which it is used, including such matters as deixis, taking turns in conversation, text organization, presupposition, and implicature.

- **PREMILLENNIALISM**—-In Christian eschatology, is the belief that Jesus will physically return to the earth to gather His saints before the Millennium, a literal thousand-year golden age of peace. This return is referred to as the Second Coming. The doctrine is called "premillennialism" because it holds that Jesus' physical return to earth will occur prior to the inauguration of the Millennium. It is distinct from the other forms of Christian eschatology such as postmillennialism or amillennialism which view the millennial rule as occurring either before the second coming, or as being figurative and non-temporal.

- **PRETERISM**—-Is a Christian eschatological view that interprets some (Partial Preterism) or all (Full Preterism) prophecies of the Bible as events which have already happened. Daniel is interpreted as events that happened in the second century BC, while Revelation is interpreted as events that happened in the first century AD.

- **PROTESTANT**— a member or follower of any of the Western Christian churches that are separate from the Roman Catholic Church and follow the principles of the Reformation, including the Baptist, Presbyterian, and Lutheran churches.

- **PROTOCANONICAL BOOKS**— Are those books of the Old Testament that are also included in the Hebrew Bible (the Tanakh) and that came to be considered canonical during the formational period of Christianity.

- **PROPITIATION**— For the Christian the propitiation was the shed blood of Jesus on the cross. It turned away the wrath of God so that He could pass "over the sins previously committed," (Rom. 3:25). It was the Father who sent the Son to be the propitiation (1 John 4:10) for all (1 John 2:2).

- **PSEUDEPIGRAPHA**— Spurious or pseudonymous writings, especially Jewish writings ascribed to various biblical patriarchs and prophets but composed within approximately 200 years of the birth of Jesus Christ.

- **PUBLICAN**—-(Tax Collector) one who farmed the taxes (e.g., Zacchaeus, Luke 19:2) to be levied from a town or district, and thus undertook to pay to the supreme government a certain amount. To collect the taxes, the publicans employed subordinates (5:27; 15:1; 18:10), who, for their own ends, were often guilty of extortion and peculation. In New Testament times these taxes were paid to the Romans, and hence were regarded by the Jews as a very heavy burden, and hence also the collectors of taxes, who were frequently Jews, were hated, and were usually spoken of in very opprobrious terms. Jesus was accused of being a "friend of publicans and sinners" (Luke 7:34).

- **QUALITATIVE TECHNIQUES**— Examine the why and how of decision making, not just what, where, when, or "who", and have a strong basis in the field of sociology to understand government and social programs. Qualitative research is popular among political science, social work, and special education and education searchers.

- **QUANTITATIVE TECHNIQUES**—QT-Research is the systematic empirical investigation of observable phenomena via statistical, mathematical, or computational techniques. The objective of quantitative research is to develop and employ mathematical models, theories and/or hypotheses pertaining to phenomena.

- **QUIRE**—A collection of leaves of parchment or paper folded one within the other, in a manuscript or book.

- **RAPTURE**—The teaching that those Christians who are alive at the beginning, middle, or end of the tribulation period will be transformed (resurrected) and caught up to meet the Lord Jesus in the clouds. (1 Thess. 4:16-5:2; 2 Thess. 2)

- **RATIONALISM**—a belief or theory that opinions and actions should be based on reason and knowledge rather than on religious belief or emotional response.

- **REGENERATION**—Spiritual or physical change. biblically, it is the saving of a person from his or her sins. It is being born again (John 3). It is a spiritual change in a person, whereby he/she becomes indwelt by the Holy Spirit.

- **REPLACEMENT THEOLOGY**—See Supersessionism.

- **REVELATION**—From God to Man (See Inspiration and Illumination)

- **RUACH HAKODESH**— In Judaism, Holy Spirit (Hebrew: חור שדוקה, ruach ha-kodesh) refers to the divine force, quality, and influence of God over the universe or over God's creatures, in given contexts. The term "holy spirit" appears three times in the Hebrew Bible: Psalm 51 refers to "Your holy spirit" (ruach kodshecha) and Isaiah refers twice to "His holy spirit" (ruach kodsho) (63: 10, 11).

- **SANHEDRIN**— (Hebrew and Aramaic: סַנְהֶדְרִין; Greek: Συνέδριον, synedrion, 'sitting together,' hence 'assembly' or 'council') were assemblies of either twenty-three or seventy-one elders (known as "rabbis" after the destruction of the Second Temple), who were appointed to sit as a tribunal in every city in the ancient Land of Israel. (There were also Lesser Sanhedrin's of 23 Judges for local communities.)

- **SCRIBE**—(Judaism) Old Testament a recognized scholar and teacher of the Jewish Law. (Judaism) A man qualified to write certain documents in accordance with religious requirements.

- **SEMANTICS**— Is the study of meaning. It focuses on the relationship between signifiers—like words, phrases, signs, and symbols—and what they stand for, their denotation.

- **SOTERIOLOGY**—The study of the doctrine of salvation.

- **SUPERSESSIONISM**—Also called **replacement theology** or fulfillment theology, is a Christian doctrine which has parallels in Islam. In Christianity, supersessionism is a theological view on the current status of the church in relation to the Jewish people and Judaism.

- **SYMPLOCE**— Combination of anaphora and epistrophe. Repetition is both at the end and at the beginning. ("When there is talk of hatred, let us stand up and talk against it. When there is talk of violence, let us stand up and talk against it." — Bill Clinton)

- **SYNECDOCHE**— a figure of speech in which a part is made to represent the whole or vice versa, as in Cleveland won by six runs (meaning "Cleveland's baseball team"). (Also, Metonymy— The use of a link term to stand in for an object or a concept. "Ex. The pen is mightier than the sword")

- **SYNOPTIC GOSPELS**—The first three gospels: Matthew, Mark, and Luke. They are referred to as the synoptic because of their great similarity.

- **SYNCRETISM**— involves the merging or assimilation of several originally discrete traditions, especially in the theology and mythology of religion, thus asserting an underlying unity and allowing for an inclusive approach to other faiths.
- **SYNERGISM**— In Christian theology, synergism is the position of those who hold that salvation involves some form of cooperation between divine grace and human freedom.
- **SYNTAX**— The arrangement of words and phrases to create well-formed sentences in a language: "the syntax of English"
- **TANAKH**— תַּנַ"ךְ, pronounced [taˈnaχ] or [təˈnax];also Tenakh, Tenak, Tanach), or sometimes the Miqra(מִקְרָא), is the canonical collection of Hebrew Scriptures, including the Torah (24 books – 3 sections).
- **TESTAMENT**—Latin for Covenant. Old Testament and New Testament Are Old and New Covenants.
- **TEXTUAL CRITICISM**—The study of the biblical documents, their copying, transmission, writing style, instruments, etc. It deals with the reconstruction of the original writings through these elements.
- **THEOLOGY**—The study of the things of God.
- **TORAH**—In its narrowest sense, Torah the first five books of the Bible: Genesis, Exodus, Leviticus, Numbers and Deuteronomy, sometimes called the Pentateuch or the Five 5 Books of Moses. It is the first of three sections of the Jewish Bible known as the TANAKH. In its broadest sense, Torah is the entire body of Jewish teachings.
- **TRINITY**—The Doctrine that there is one God in three persons: not three gods, but one God.
- **UNCIAL**—The Greek characters of upper case: ABGDE, etc. Different copies of Greek manuscripts appear in Uncial form. See Minuscule.
- **UNCTION**—Kings, prophets, and priests were anointed, in token of receiving divine grace. All believers are, in a secondary sense, what Christ was in a primary sense, "the Lord's anointed." (I John 2:20, 27)

- **URTEXT**—In biblical studies refers to the assumption that there once was a uniform text of the Hebrew Bible(Tanakh) to precede both the Septuagint (LXX) and the Masoretic Text (MT).

- **VELLUM**—A material used for writing, like paper. It was made from animal skins, usually from cattle, sheep, goats, and antelope. The hair was scraped off of the skins, then they were washed, smoothed, and dressed with chalk. Vellum was used until the late Middle Ages until paper was introduced into Europe from China via Arab traders. Vellum lasted longer than papyrus and was tougher, but the edges sometimes became torn and tattered. The two oldest parchment manuscripts are the Codex Vaticanus (from Egypt) and the Codex Sinaiticus.

- **YHVH**—The tetragrammaton (/ˌtɛtrəˈɡræmətɒn/; from Greek Τετραγράμματον, meaning "[consisting of] four letters"), יהוה☐ in Hebrew and YHWH in Latin script, is the four-letter biblical name of the God of Israel

CHAPTER 4

PLANET WORSHIP

3-AGES
6-PHASES
8-DISPENSATIONS

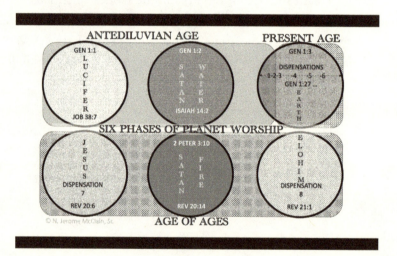

ANTEDILUVIAN AGE — PRESENT AGE

GEN 1:1 / L U C I F E R / JOB 38:7

GEN 1:2 / S A T A N / W A T E R / ISAIAH 14:2

GEN 1:3 / DISPENSATIONS 1-2-3 -4 -5 -6 / GEN 1:27 ... / E A R T H

SIX PHASES OF PLANET WORSHIP

J E S U S / DISPENSATION 7 / REV 20:6

2 PETER 3:10 / S A T A N / F I R E / REV 20:14

E L O H I M / DISPENSATION 8 / REV 21:1

© N. Jerome McClain, Sr.

AGE OF AGES

Taking The Bible Scriptures out of context is probably the greatest culprit to Bible misinterpretation. The Bible chronicles The Creation, inclusive of "matter" and "humanity." The Scriptures uncover the events leading to The Fall, the consequences, and the ultimate destiny of His intelligent beings. Understanding Ages, Phases and Dispensations opens a wide window of distinctions that prevent many of the pitfalls that are responsible for incorrect interpretations.

Bible Dispensational understanding is essential for the unadulterated study of God's Word. Like the life of a child from infancy (New Birth) to death (Fullness of Time), all of humanity is likened to the first two sons of Eve (Cain & Abel). Having entered life through the birth canal of humanity, they each chose their individual destiny (Abel-Heaven, Cain-Hell).

The Bible contains many maps, some written centuries ago prior to the coming of Jesus. Therefore, we must be sure that the map that is being followed is relevant to our location and time. Otherwise, we may find ourselves lost on a dead-end street or wandering in an endless circle going nowhere.[1]

AGES

The term "Ages" denotes the very instant that God created "matter." Therefore, Ages began an immeasurable period prior to the creation of heavenly or earthly beings. Vegetation and beast were created inestimable years after the creation of Planet Worship. Planet Worship (Earth) shall endure a total of Three Ages:

1. *Antediluvian Age*
2. *Present Age*
3. *Age of Ages*

1. THE ANTEDILUVIAN AGE

The Age prior to The Flood, the Antediluvian, consisted of the creation of The Universe of Angels, The Fall of Lucifer, The Creation, and subsequent Fall of Humanity. It continued with the struggle between The People who are of God, The Clan of Abel/Seth, and Those who are of The Devil (The Clan of Cain). It is the home of Three of The Six Phases of Planet Worship and Two of The Eight Dispensations of Humanity.

Long before the creation of man, angels resided in Eden singing praises and worshipping God.[2] Imagine a pristine world where God's Creatures praised Him without ceasing. Yet, the leader of The Worship

---

[1]   Ever learning, and never able to come to the knowledge of the truth. (2 Timothy 3:7)
[2]   When the morning stars sang together, and all the sons of God shouted for joy? (Job 38:7)

Team (Lucifer The Anointed Cherub) attempted to rise above all The Creatures of God. Lucifer desired the praise and worship that was due God.[1] Then imagine God's response to such treason—He cast Satan (Lucifer) headlong into Earth, which resulted in a state of chaos and that which became void.[2]

God caused the previously pristine environment (mountains of fire, gleaming reflections of light flickering off substances such as *"the sardius, topaz, and the diamond, the beryl, the onyx, and the jasper, the sapphire, the emerald, and the carbuncle, and gold"*) to implode, resulting in chaos and that which became void.[3] Such were the conditions of The Antediluvian Age, prior to The Advent of Dispensations (Humanity).

After the fallen world was birthed from the waters of destruction, God brought forth a planet habitable for humankind. Adam and Eve failed by the execution of their Will (Synergism), were forced out of Eden, and were destined to a life of sin that resulted in the inheritance of death. Their two sons became mutual victims of The Fall: Cain, the murderer, and his brother, Abel, the murdered.

Cain's descendants were successful craftsmen and admirably intelligent. But they fell to the wiles of The Evil Angelic Host who indiscriminately took wives of their people and begot The Nephilim.[4]

The Antediluvian ended with God's judgement against a world contaminated by The Spirit of The Devil and that of man. The angels that sexually assaulted humankind were condemned to Tartarus to await

---

[1] I will ascend above the heights of the clouds; I will be like the most High. (Isaiah 14:14)

[2] And he said unto them, I beheld Satan as lightning fall from heaven. (Luke 10:18)

[3] "They that see thee shall narrowly look upon thee, and consider thee, saying, Is this the man that made the earth to tremble, that did shake kingdoms; That made the world as a wilderness, and destroyed the cities thereof; that opened not the house of his prisoners? Isaiah 14:16-17 By the multitude of thy merchandise they have filled the midst of thee with violence, and thou hast sinned: therefore I will cast thee as profane out of the mountain of God: and I will destroy thee, O covering cherub, from the midst of the stones of fire." (Ezekiel 28:16)

[4] There were giants in the earth in those days; and also after that, when the sons of God came in unto the daughters of men, and they bare children to them, the same became mighty men which were of old, men of renown (Genesis 6:4)

the final judgment of The Great White Throne.[1],[2] Noah's family of eight, seven of every clean kind, and two of every unclean kind rode the waves of The Flood in God's Ark of Safety. They embarked in The Antediluvian and disembarked in The Postdiluvian.

2. THE PRESENT AGE

The Postdiluvian is The First Dispensation of The Present Age. After The Flood, Noah and his family repopulated Planet Worship. This is the beginning of the 2nd of the 3 Ages. The Present Age continues Phase 3 of the 6 Phases of Planet Worship and is the home of 4 of the 8 Dispensations. She bares The Divinity of Grace and Outreach, The Priesthood of The Family, The Laws of Godliness and The Embodiment of The Holy Spirit. She is home to the lion's share of the toils of salvation. History shall report of all that was necessary to complete the journey back to a semblance of peace and prosperity. She shall end with The Second Advent of Jesus Christ, preceded by The Judgement of The Church (Bema) and The Judgement of The Jews (Tribulation). The Judgment of The Nations shall immediately follow.

3. THE AGE OF AGES

Operation "Armageddon" will remove The Unholy Trio-Satan, Antichrist, and False Prophet-which leads to a Millennium of Righteousness on Earth. A Millennium of Righteousness on Earth is the inaugural existence of the final of The Three Ages. Jesus' triumph over His enemies and His bodily presence (2nd Advent) brings an existence of time likened only by The Garden of Eden. The exception being there is no enemy amid the people. Jesus fulfills each of the awaiting prophecies and establishes His Kingdom on Earth just as it is in Heaven.

At Jesus' Second Coming, the world will reside in constant fellowship with Christ in The Final Age, The Age of Ages.

---

[1] For if God spared not the angels that sinned, but cast them down to hell, and delivered them into chains of darkness, to be reserved unto judgment; (2 Peter 2:4)

[2] And the devil that deceived them was cast into the lake of fire and brimstone, where the beast and the false prophet are, and shall be tormented day and night for ever and ever. (Revelation 20:10)

PHASES

Earth Phases are periods defined by unique occurrences brought about by cataclysmic events. The Six Days of Creation, as explained in Genesis, are six days of re-creation of Planet Worship for the habitation of humankind. Each day represents an essential need for humanity to survive. By comparison, The Six Phases are essential to the survival of Planet Worship.

1. *WORSHIP BY THE SON OF THE MORNING*
2. *WATER THAT COVERED THE PLANET*
3. *LAND THAT ROSE FROM THE WATERS*
4. *LIGHT OF THE SON OF GOD (MILLENNIUM)*
5. *FIRE THAT DESTROYS THE EARTH AND THE HEAVENS*
6. *THE NEW HEAVEN AND THE NEW EARTH*

PHASE 1

WORSHIP BY THE SON OF THE MORNING

The original Planet Worship (Planet Earth) was layered with the precious ores that are presently buried beneath the crust of the earth.

> *How art thou fallen from heaven, O Lucifer, son of the morning! how art thou cut down to the ground, which didst weaken the nations!*
>
> *(Isaiah 14:12)*

> *Thou hast been in Eden the garden of God; every precious stone was thy covering, the sardius, topaz, and the diamond, the beryl, the onyx, and the jasper, the sapphire, the emerald, and the carbuncle, and gold: the workmanship of thy tabrets and of thy pipes was prepared in thee in the day that thou wast created. Thou art the anointed cherub that covereth; and I have set thee so: thou wast upon the holy mountain of God; thou hast walked up and down in the midst of the stones of fire.*
>
> *(Ezekiel 28:13, 14)*

The original Planet Worship (Earth) was created to house the angels that sang praises and glory to God. Of all the planets in the universe, Planet Earth is unique as headquarters for Worship.

PHASE 2

WATER THAT COVERED THE PLANET

The original Planet Worship (Earth) became dark and chaotic because of The Fall of Lucifer (Satan) and his angelic host.

> *They that see thee shall narrowly look upon thee, and consider thee, saying, Is this the man that made the earth to tremble, that did shake kingdoms; That made the world as a wilderness, and destroyed the cities thereof; that opened not the house of his prisoners?*
>
> *(Isaiah 14:16, 17)*

Imagine the brilliant glowing ores of the original planet imploding beneath the now exposed crust of dirt that covers Planet Worship. Such is the result of Lucifer being cast down from Heaven:

> *And he said unto them, I beheld Satan as lightning fall from heaven.*
>
> *(Luke 10:18)*

The result is noted in the second verse of Genesis Chapter 1: *"And the earth was without form, and void; and darkness was upon the face of the deep…" (Genesis 1:2)* Of such a time spoke God's Word when The Earth was delivered from the waters.[1]

---

[1] And God made the firmament, and divided the waters which were under the firmament from the waters which were above the firmament: and it was so. (Genesis 1:7)

PHASE 3

LAND THAT ROSE FROM THE WATERS

The angels of God that failed in their duty to worship God by yielding to Lucifer's desire to rise above all intelligent beings and his desire to receive the praises and glory are the reasons for the conditions of Phase Two of Planet Worship (Earth).[1] Satan would receive an earthly kingdom that, through subsequent Ages, Phases and Dispensations, would eventually be re-formed to its original glory.[2]

It was not just a metaphor that Christ said: *"I tell you that, if these should hold their peace, the stones would immediately cry out." (Luke 19:40)* After-all, God created man from the dust of the earth: *"And the Lord God formed man of the dust of the ground, and breathed into his nostrils the breath of life; and man became a living soul." (Genesis 2:7)* Before the creation of man, God created and renovated every possible need for humanity. This Phase (3rd Phase) would exist until after The Rapture of The Church and The Tribulation.

PHASE 4

LIGHT OF THE SON OF GOD (MILLENNIUM)

The Millennial Kingdom (1000 years) is the earthly home of Christ's Kingdom and the fulfillment of The Covenants made to The House of Israel. Because of the absence of The Unholy Trio-Satan (Abyss), Antichrist and False Prophet (Lake of Fire)-the unique characteristics of Phase 4 are void of "the Presence, Penalty, and Power of Sin." The infant is 100 years old. This is The Second Eden (Paradise) where death is suspended, and all Creatures will reside harmoniously together. Of those that are born during The Millennial, there will ultimately be a

---

[1] For thou hast said in thine heart, I will ascend into heaven, I will exalt my throne above the stars of God… (Isaiah 14:13)

[2] And I saw a new heaven and a new earth: for the first heaven and the first earth were passed away; and there was no more sea. (Revelation 21:1)

need to choose whether they repent and accept Christ, or default to the lead of Satan when he is loosed from The Abyss.

PHASE 5

FIRE THAT DESTROYS THE EARTH AND THE HEAVENS

Phase 5 is the aftermath of the events following the release of Satan after 1,000 years of incarceration.

> *And they went up on the breadth of the earth, and compassed the camp of the saints about, and the beloved city: and fire came down from God out of heaven, and devoured them.*
> *(Revelation 20:9)*

Reminiscent of the catastrophic impact of Phase 2, where Planet Worship was transformed from a glowing place of worship to a dark chaotic heap of clay, She must now be destroyed by an inferno unlike any before. It is of this matter that The Apostle Peter wrote:

> *But the day of the Lord will come as a thief in the night; in the which the heavens shall pass away with a great noise, and the elements shall melt with fervent heat, the earth also and the works that are therein shall be burned up.*
> *(2 Peter 3:10)*

Phase 2 reclassified the angels that followed Satan as "fallen." Phase 5 includes those humans who rejected the salvation once freely offered by Jesus The Christ. They must all now stand before that same Jesus. Albeit this time He is The Judge!

Phase 5 is the deportation of all that have risen against The Divine Will of God. It is the substance of the reason for The Lake of Fire. The Lake of Fire was made for The Devil, his angels, and all humans that follow them. *"Then shall he say also unto them on the left hand, Depart from me, ye cursed, into everlasting fire, prepared for the devil and his angels:"* (Matthew 25:41)

Hell, at best, is the reception center; and physical death is the passport that renders The Unsaved before The Lord at The Final Judgement-"The White Throne" (Revelation 20:11). The White Throne is The Sentencing Judgement that occurs at the end of Phase 5, which cleanses The Universe of all contaminates that corrupt an otherwise perfect existence.

> *"And the sea gave up the dead which were in it; and death and hell delivered up the dead which were in them: and they were judged every man according to their works. And death and hell were cast into the lake of fire. This is the second death."*
> *(Revelation 20:13, 14)*

The Second Death is the final death of those who die (separation of soul from the body) and will be reembodied to stand before Jesus for their eternal sentencing. The one constant is that there shall never be an opportunity for betterment, probation, or parole, but instead an everlasting period of damnation:

> *"And shall come forth; they that have done good, unto the resurrection of life; and they that have done evil, unto the resurrection of damnation."*
> *(John 5:29)*

Zachariah The Prophet had this to say of the depiction of such death:

> *"And this shall be the plague wherewith the Lord will smite all the people that have fought against Jerusalem; Their flesh shall consume away while they stand upon their feet, and their eyes shall consume away in their holes, and their tongue shall consume away in their mouth.*
> *(Zechariah 14:12)*

The removal of all that offends the perfection of God opens the way for The New Heaven and The New Earth.

PHASE 6

THE NEW HEAVEN AND THE NEW EARTH

Phase 6 is reminiscent of the original phase–Phase 1–with the exception being the presence of An Adorned Bride, The Body of The Lord. She is The Consummated House of Israel (The Bride of Jehovah) and The Church (The Bride of Jesus). They together constitute The New Heaven (Church) and The New Earth (Israel).[1] She is called by name, New Jerusalem.

> *"And I saw a new heaven and a new earth: for the first heaven and the first earth were passed away; and there was no more sea. And I John saw the holy city, new Jerusalem, coming down from God out of heaven, prepared as a bride adorned for her husband."*
>
> *(Revelation 21:1, 2)*

God, Who is a Spirit, must be worshipped In Spirit and In Truth! (John 4:24) Phase 6 is the fulfillment of Planet Worship. She has endured through time, Ages and Dispensations. She has been the home of angels and humans alike. All have been given adequate time to choose their Eternal Destiny. Each Persona of God has completed His Mission and The Abdication is ready. [2]

Each Persona of God has completed His mission and The Abdication is ready.

---

[1] And he carried me away in the spirit to a great and high mountain, and shewed me that great city, the holy Jerusalem, descending out of heaven from God, Having the glory of God: and her light was like unto a stone most precious, even like a jasper stone, clear as crystal; And had a wall great and high, and had twelve gates, and at the gates twelve angels, and names written thereon, which are the names of the twelve tribes of the children of Israel: On the east three gates; on the north three gates; on the south three gates; and on the west three gates. And the wall of the city had twelve foundations, and in them the names of the twelve apostles of the Lamb. Revelation 21:10-14

[2] (1 Corinthians 15:24-28) "See Dispensation 8"

DISPENSATIONS

Dispensations are to "the progress of humanity" that which Ages & Phases are to "the endurances of matter." To dispense means to give; therefore, Dispensationalism is the study of how God instructs humanity to (give) "worship, walk, and work" worthily. Each dispensation is characterized by an additional virtue marking an essential phase of Human Spiritual Development. The perfection of Adam and Eve at the moment of their creation was highlighted by their innocence. The Edenic Dispensation is, therefore, The Dispensation of The Innocence that synthesizes the efforts of humanity with the purpose of God.

Dispensationalism, as a theology, has its roots in the teachings of John Nelson Darby (1800-1882). Over the years, Dispensationalism, as a study, has become different depending on interpretation. As a result, there are several different schools.

1. Classical
2. Traditional (Revised)
3. Progressive
4. Hyper (Ultimate)
5. And others

It is sometimes taught to be an Evangelical, Futurist teaching. Most dispensationalists hold to The Doctrine of Premillennialism and The Pre-Tribulation Rapture. The Nation of Israel and The Church are seen as separate and distinct human factions, each having unique requirements, although sharing the same ultimate Spiritual quest. For the dispensationalist, The Book of Revelation is a Book of Prophecy and not Poetry. The Millennium is understood to be a literal time consisting of one thousand years where Jesus will personally establish His Kingdom on Earth, thereby fulfilling His covenant promise to The House of Israel.

The abiding contradiction to the theological Doctrine of Dispensationalism is Covenantalism. The central focus of each is the ultimate outcome of The House of Israel. The promises that God made with Abraham (Genesis 12:1-3) and David (2 Samuel 7:12-16) were without condition and forever. Dispensationalists take these promises to be literal (Dual-Covenant Theology). Covenantalist believe that Israel, through lack of faith in Jesus, forfeited their rights (Replacement Theology).

The Jehovah's Witnesses are a good example of professed Christians who hold to the teaching that they are "the replacement" of The House of Israel. This Replacement Theology is called Supersessionism. It is their belief that they, under The New Testament, have replaced The Jews; therefore, they are the recipients of the ultimate fulfillment of the promises made by God.

The Islamic Faith, although of a different religion-yet theistic-believes itself to be the final and most authentic expression of Abraham's belief in "The One God." They clearly acknowledge both Judaism and Christianity. However, they are, to themselves, paths to the ultimate and final Faith of Islam.

Dispensationalists examine each Scripture to determine its reference in the mystery of human growth and development. On the journey, their faithfulness is challenged by growth potentials afforded during the various developmental periods. Each dispensation is an economy benefiting from the maturity of the previous one(s). One must also be mindful of the fact that those of the prior dispensations were not subjected to the unique challenges of those of the latter.

The intro to The Initial Five of The Eight Dispensations correlates with One of Each of The Five Crowns discovered in The New Testament (each related to a person). Whereas The Final Three Dispensations are dedicated to The Three Personages of God. Consider them as types of mission objectives during the growing phases of humanity. As an example, Adam is here, represented as having received The Incorruptible Crown, which speaks to his sinless nature at Creation. After The Fall (Sin), Adam and Eve were expelled from The Garden of Eden. They entered another quest (Dispensation) for that which was lost (Fellowship with God). On the road back to enviable Eden, they would need to exercise "consciousness" (The Knowledge of Good and Evil) with the potential loss of life (Martyrdom) for doing the right thing. So, in Eden, the requirement was "obedience." After Eden, there is an additional requirement, "consciousness."

Note, in Eden, doing the right thing (being obedient) prevented death, whereas outside of Eden, death is the consequence of having disobeyed God. Therefore, death outside of Eden is the destiny for all mankind and can also come because of being obedient to God i.e., martyrdom (Cain killed his brother Abel). The one constant in dispensational studies is the fact that each succeeding dispensation will feel the pains of omissions by those of the past while growing from the commissions uniquely placed upon them.

Each dispensation will advance toward the final dispensation which is a literal return to the created purpose of humanity, albeit Spiritual. That is the ultimate fulfillment of being the sacred souls which we are as demonstrated by God when He initially breathed into a vessel created to combat the very evil displayed by the different dispensations.

THE FIVE-FIVES

(BIBLICAL NUMEROLOGY 5)

The number "5" is a symbol of God's grace. Grace is God's special provision for the rescue of mankind from the snare of Satan. The "Five-Fives" combine to represent grace for grace, *"And of his fulness have all we received, and grace for grace." (John 1:16).* The Ten Commandments are divided by 5 upper (Relationship) and 5 lower (Fellowship) commands. The "upper" are relative to God's Holiness and His Relationship with mankind. The "lower" are relative to man's fellowship with mankind. God's "two-edged sword" is His Word, The Bible. The Old Testament begins with 5 Books of Law defining the critical reality of life and the perpetual failure of mankind. The New Testament begins with 5 books displaying The Gospel and The Acts of those who accept His grace.

God's abundance may be seen in His miraculous multiplication of 5 loaves that fed five thousand, not counting the women and the children (Matthew 14:17). John (The Apostle) introduced the world to the manifestation of God in his Gospel and concluded 5 books later with his penning of The Revelation. If one was inclined to research it, they would find that there are 5 ingredients in The Holy Oil used to sanctify The Tabernacle. The Tabernacle was made to contain 5 curtains, 5 pillars, 5 bars etc. There are countless other references to God's use of the number "5" to illustrate His love and grace for His Human Creation. The following is but an example of how the study of 5 may lead to an epiphany in the understanding of God's plan for people.

The "Five-Fives" (5x5) is a list of unique associations that pertain to a specific *person, anointing, condition, atonement, and period*, respectively. Through the study of each and the synthesis of their efforts, we are better able to interpret God's Will in an ever-changing culture. A synopsis of this study may be remembered as the following:

A Memorable Acronym:

1. P   Personage
2. C   Crown
3. C   Condition
4. S   Sola
5. D   Dispensation

1. PERSONAGE

The first Five Dispensations are headed by a human progenitor, hereafter referred to as "Personage." God, through His Word, introduced us to Adam-specifically Adam and Eve-His personal Creation of Humanity. The Seed of God's Creation will grow through the toils and labors, both good and evil, in time.

The Personages are:

1. Adam & Eve
2. Adam & Abel
3. Noah
4. Abram
5. Moses

2. CROWN

There are Five Crowns listed in The Bible that represent the judgement of The Saints of God. As the dispensations were fulfilled, the means and criteria associated with each were clearly defined by God's Word. Man is, therefore, held responsible for the obedience required.

The Crowns are:

1. The Incorruptible Crown (1Corinthians 9:25)
2. The Crown of Life/The Martyrs Crown (James 1:12 – Revelation 2:10)
3. The Crown of Rejoicing/The Soul Winners Crown (1 Thessalonians 2:19)
4. The Crown of Righteousness/The Crown of Faith (2 Timothy 4:7, 8)
5. The Crown of Glory/The Pastor-Teachers Crown (1 Peter 5:8)

A mnemonic that will help you to remember The Crowns:

My Crown is [1]**Incorruptible** in [2]**Life** or **Death**. My [3]**Rejoicing** is [4]**Righteousness** in [5]**Glory**.

3. CONDITION

The culture of each dispensation is represented by challenges presented to each progenitor and those people present at the time. Adam and Eve inherited a "Condition of Innocence" and were thereby challenged only by their individual Wills. Of course, their Wills were challenged by Satan, who afforded them the opportunity to choose. Although they were beguiled by The Serpent and followed His direction, they did so by their own Will. After inheriting The Sin Nature, they were removed from fellowship with God and dispatched through Ages and Dispensations of challenges in the hope of returning to enviable Eden.

The Conditions are:

1. Innocence

2. Consciousness
3. Government
4. Priesthood
5. Legal

4. SOLA

The Solas speak to a condition that God alone has assigned to Himself over periods of growth in the development of mankind. Although they are represented individually in one of The Fives, they are-like The Crowns-combined in the life potential of every person. As students of The Bible, we can apply them in context when interpreting a particular passage of Scripture.

The Solas are:

1. Sola Scriptura (According to Scripture Alone.)
2. Solus Christus (In Christ Alone.)
3. Sola Gratia (By Grace Alone.)
4. Sola Fide (Through Faith Alone)
5. Soli Deo Gloria (To the Glory of God Alone)

5. DISPENSATION

The initial revelation of the development of mankind in the affairs of The Creator are scripted in a segment of The Bible classified as a Dispensation. The "Five," as previously stated, are introduced by a man chosen by God to bring to the mind of humanity a unique accomplishment that builds on those from the previously chosen. These "Five" Dispensations lead up to The Final Three which are headed by The Tri-Personage of God.

The Dispensations are:

1. The Edenic Dispensation (Adam-Eve)
2. The Antediluvian Dispensation (Adam-Abel)
3. The Postdiluvian Dispensation (Noah)
4. The Patriarchal Dispensation (Abraham)
5. The Legal Dispensation (Moses)

6. The Ecumenical/Ecclesiastical Dispensation (The Holy Spirit)
7. The Righteous Dispensation (Jesus The Christ)
8. The Holy Dispensation (God Elohim)

The ability to associate each of these dispensations with a unique reference specific to that dispensation opens ones' interpretive skills into the depths of a specific time and place with less chance of misinterpreting The Scripture being studied.

DISPENSATION 1

(The Antediluvian Age-Phase 3)

1. Adam & Eve
2. Incorruptible Crown
3. Innocence
4. Sola Scriptura
5. Edenic Dispensation

The first requirement placed on humanity was the need to be obedient to God. Their faithfulness was tested by the presence of Satan (The Serpent) and The Fruit of The Tree of The knowledge of Good and Evil.[1] Simply put, they would either rest in the knowledge of God or seek to prove Him wrong. They chose the latter, and subsequent thereto, the world is now in the maze of dispensationalism, trying to get back to enviable Eden.

The things that God required in one dispensation would carry on to each succeeding dispensation. Adam and Eve learned that there are consequences to disobedience. They lost the fellowship that they had enjoyed in Eden and would learn to apply "consciousness" (Knowledge of Right and Wrong) in their pursuit of salvation.

---

[1] Genesis 3:2-4 And the woman said unto the serpent, We may eat of the fruit of the trees of the garden: But of the fruit of the tree which is in the midst of the garden, God hath said, Ye shall not eat of it, neither shall ye touch it, lest ye die. And the serpent said unto the woman, Ye shall not surely die:

DISPENSATION 2

(The Antediluvian Age-Phase 3)

1. Adam & Abel
2. The Crown of Life/The Martyrs Crown
3. Consciousness
4. Solus Christus
5. Antediluvian Dispensation

Adam and Eve's disobedience caused them to be expelled from The Garden of Eden. While in The Garden, they were fully aware of right, as seen in the directions of God. After disobedience, they became fully aware of wrong, as perpetrated by Satan. The result is "consciousness," The Knowledge of Good and Evil, right and wrong.

The Second Dispensation is named The Antediluvian because it is the dispensation prior to The Flood. It was there that God challenged humanity to incorporate the virtues of "obedience" with the knowledge of "consciousness."

With every dispensation, humanity gains a wealth of experience that enables succeeding families to get closer to the ultimate Will of God. It is God's Will to have perfect fellowship with His Creation. Sin renders animosity between God and humanity, and therefore "fellowship" would have to be facilitated by "justification." Justification required full payment for The Penalty of Sin, which is death.

Adam and Eve became intimately aware of death through the loss of their son, Abel, at the hands of his brother, Cain. Although death is The Power of Sin, it must not be confused with Damnation, which is the final disposition (Penalty) of The Lost. For The Saved, death is a transition to life; but for The Unsaved, it is a transition to eternal damnation.[1] The first two dispensations conclude the Antediluvian Age. Jehovah reserved eight human beings to survive The Flood and to replenish Earth at the beginning of The Present Age. Noah, his

---

[1] And these shall go away into everlasting punishment: but the righteous into life eternal. (Matthew 25:46)

wife, and their three sons with their wives represent The Eight (8) Dispensations destined for the journey back to Eden.

The Antediluvian and The Present Age (The Age that follows) are the bookends of the plight of humanity, Jew–Gentile–Church.[1] The Final Age, The Age of Ages, will constitute the fulfilling of God's Kingdom on Earth as it is in Heaven.

The following Age (The Present Age) and its Dispensations fulfill the accountability of humanity at large.

DISPENSATION 3

(The Present Age-Phase 3)

1. Noah
2. The Crown of Rejoicing (Soul Winners)
3. Government
4. Solar Gratia
5. Postdiluvian Dispensation

The Present Age began with The Dispensation of Government as God reinstructed humanity to be fruitful in replenishing the earth.[2] Noah's family and their descendants were supposed to combine the experiences of "obedience" and "consciousness" with the strength of "unity" (Government), thereby reclaiming authority over the earth. But rather than learning from Cain's ineptness, *"Am I my brother's keeper?" (Genesis 4:9),* humanity continued the role of selfishness. The city that they set out to build was completely void of the true worship that God sought. There were evident traces of failures found in each of the previous dispensations. They were disobedient, following their own minds and not the mind of God. Their selfishness displayed the attributes of Cain and his desire to build a monumental city unto

---

[1] For I would not, brethren, that ye should be ignorant of this mystery, lest ye should be wise in your own conceits; that blindness in part is happened to Israel, until the fulness of the Gentiles be come in. (Romans 11:25)

[2] And God blessed Noah and his sons, and said unto them, Be fruitful, and multiply, and replenish the earth. (Genesis 9:1)

himself[1/2] Religion, albeit contrary to God, had its beginning during the inaugural of The Dispensation of Government. Rather than helping his brother, those at the top found ways to subjugate their brothers and sisters. Such actions logically lead to Jehovah calling out of The Nations a family that he would deliver for the good of His relationship with humanity.

DISPENSATION 4

(The Present Age-Phase 3)

1. Abram
2. The Crown of Righteousness
3. Priesthood
4. Solar Fide
5. Patriarchal Dispensation

Following The Dispensation of Government is The "Patriarchal Dispensation." God called from the ranks of The Gentiles a family led by a man named Abram. God used the family of Abram to showcase His divine love. God instructed Abram to leave his home, yet he was not told exactly where he was to go. Thus, Abram had to walk by faith. The family experienced many unbelievable successes, demonstrating to the world the power of absolute trust in God. Like Adam and Noah, Abram was the product of one dispensation and the beginning of another. His travels would demonstrate to the world God's love and care for His own. Even in the bowels of neglect and failure, God's chosen would experience the success of having The Creator as their Father.

---

[1] And Cain knew his wife; and she conceived, and bare Enoch: and he builded a city, and called the name of the city, after the name of his son, Enoch. (Genesis 4:17)

[2] And they said, Go to, let us build us a city and a tower, whose top may reach unto heaven; and let us make us a name, lest we be scattered abroad upon the face of the whole earth. (Genesis 11:4)

DISPENSATION 5

(The Present Age-Phase 3)

1. Moses
2. The Crown of Glory (Pastor-Teacher)
3. Law
4. Soli Deo Gloria
5. Legal Dispensation

Moses, born in The Patriarchal Dispensation, would go on to be used of God to begin the dispensation revealing The Written Laws of God. Written laws prevented the human spin that too often was impressed upon God's people by pagan cultures. God's people found themselves going back to the customs that God had delivered them from, each act carrying them further away from Eden and closer to Hades. Consequently, God called Moses to the task of delivering His people from bondage, and again, the people rebelled. They had soon forgotten the record of Abram's faith and subsequent victories; consequently, they failed to trust God by preferring the things of their past. Their enculturation was obvious.

> *And the children of Israel said unto them, Would to God we had died by the hand of the LORD in the land of Egypt, when we sat by the flesh pots, and when we did eat bread to the full; for ye have brought us forth into this wilderness, to kill this whole assembly with hunger.*
>
> *(Exodus 16:3)*

Although the people saw God's power and love, they still failed to trust Him exclusively. It was at the hand of Moses that God delivered His Commandments.

> *And Moses turned, and went down from the mount, and the two tables of the testimony were in his hand: the tables were written on both their sides; on the one side and on the other*

were they written. And the tables were the work of God, and the writing was the writing of God, graven upon the tables.

(Exodus 32:15, 16)

Moses is the human author of The First Five Books of The Bible (Jewish Pentateuch), known as The Torah (The Law) and The Book of Job. The period governed by the service of Moses constitutes The Legal Dispensation.

A remarkable fact concerning humanity is that each dispensation proves man's inability to defeat his adversary. Since sin and death are synonymous, only life can defeat sin. God's Justice requires death, and therefore all born under sin must die. This is the point of consideration that separates Christianity from all other religions. Christianity answers the question that asks, "How can a dead man recover life?" If restitution is to be made, the answer is in the fact that a sinless member of the human family is required. Only God can relieve The Penalty (The Separation) of Sin; and by necessity, God would have to become man to do so.

And without controversy great is the mystery of godliness: God was manifest in the flesh, justified in the Spirit, seen of angels, preached unto the Gentiles, believed on in the world, received up into glory.

(1 Timothy 3:16)

The Writings of Moses paved the way for all Sacred Writings that God would preserve for His posterity. It would be through The Writings of God that humanity would be required to study His "Word" and to submit to His directions. Although The Enemy (Satan) does miraculous deeds attempting to contaminate The Truth, it is impossible for Him to succeed, if only we believe.[1]

---

[1] As newborn babes, desire the sincere milk of the word, that ye may grow thereby: (1 Peter 2:2)

The words of the Lord are pure words: as silver tried in a furnace of earth, purified seven times. Thou shalt keep them, O Lord, thou shalt preserve them from this generation for ever.

(Psalm 12:6, 7)

DISPENSATION 6

(The Present Age-Phase 3)

1. The HOLY SPIRIT
2. 5-Crowns
3. Grace (The New Birth)
4. Solar 5
5. Ecclesiastical Dispensation

It was on The Sixth Day of Creation that God completed His work of renovating The Universe for the habitation of Humanity. It was on the day that God breathed into the nostrils of Adam, A Living Soul. It is in The Sixth Dispensation that Humanity is enabled by the indwelling of The Holy Spirit/Born Again.

> *But ye shall receive power, after that the Holy Ghost is come upon you: and ye shall be witnesses unto me both in Jerusalem, and in all Judaea, and in Samaria, and unto the uttermost part of the earth.*
>
> *(Acts 1:8)*

Jesus (God-Himself) was born in The Legal Dispensation and personally established The Dispensation of Grace by The Advent of The Holy Spirit, which followed His death and resurrection. Jesus' Blood, being free of sin, was the acceptable sacrifice which relieves all that receive Him (Grace) from The Penalty of Damnation.

For since by man came death, by man came also the resurrection of the dead. For as in Adam all die, even so in Christ shall all be made alive.

(1 Corinthians 15:21, 22)

For he hath made him to be sin for us, who knew no sin; that we might be made the righteousness of God in him.

(2 Corinthians 5:21)

Today, the world has unprecedented privileges purchased by The Blood of Almighty God. Mercy keeps The Enemy at bay in hopes that The Prey will yield to Grace by Faith and become Justified. The mission of saving The Lost Souls of the world is Gospel (Good News) to all who will receive it.

Seven years before the end of The Dispensation of Grace, The Church and The World (Nations) will simultaneously enter their defining destiny. The Church will be Raptured to meet The Lord in The Heavens and The World will enter Tribulation. The massive egress of The Church, which will include all children under the age of personal accountability, will cause worldwide awareness due to its cataclysmic nature. The resurrected bodies of The Departed Saints will precede The Translation of The Saints. After The Souls of The Departed are clothed in their Glorious Bodies, then The Living Saints will be translated. Paul references the swiftness of The Translation as *"in the twinkling of an eye."*

In a moment, in the twinkling of an eye, at the last trump: for the trumpet shall sound, and the dead shall be raised incorruptible, and we shall be changed.

(1Corinthians 15:52)

For the Lord himself shall descend from heaven with a shout, with the voice of the archangel, and with the trump of God: and the dead in Christ shall rise first: Then we which are alive and remain shall be caught up together with them in the clouds, to

meet the Lord in the air: and so shall we ever be with the Lord.
Wherefore comfort one another with these words.

(1 Thessalonians 4:16-18)

While The Church is engaged in The Bema Judgment (Judgement of The Saints in Heaven) and being suited for The Marriage Feast of The Lamb (Jesus), The World will continue its course toward an unavoidable day of reckoning. During the first three and one-half years, Moses, Elijah, countless angels, and many new converts will actively evangelize The Nations while awaiting The Lord's return, "The Second Advent."

And I will give power unto my two witnesses, and they
shall prophesy a thousand two hundred and threescore days,
clothed in sackcloth. These are the two olive trees, and the two
candlesticks standing before the God of the earth.

(Revelation 11:3, 4)

The Tribulation is the term used to define the conditions that will plague The Nations at the departure of The Church. Israel will suffer The Desecration of The Temple by the satanic-led religious system that will dominate The One-World Order. At the middle of The Tribulation, Satan and his angelic host will be cast out of Heaven into Earth. This event occurs three and a half years into The Tribulation. Satan's fury will at that time be unmatched; therefore, the last three and a half years are properly referred to as The Great Tribulation. The Twelve Elected Tribes of Israel will be protected during The Great Tribulation.

Therefore rejoice, ye heavens, and ye that dwell in them. Woe
to the inhabiters of the earth and of the sea! for the devil is come
down unto you, having great wrath, because he knoweth that
he hath but a short time. And when the dragon saw that he
was cast unto the earth, he persecuted the woman which brought
forth the man child. And to the woman were given two wings
of a great eagle, that she might fly into the wilderness, into her

place, where she is nourished for a time, and times, and half a
time, from the face of the serpent.

(Revelation 12:12-14)

DISPENSATION 7

(The Age of Ages-Phase 4)

1. JESUS CHRIST
2. 5-Crowns
3. Millennium
4. Solar 5
5. Dispensation of Righteousness

The Millennium (Dispensation of Righteousness) is the first dispensation of the Age of Ages. The Present Age and its final dispensation (Grace) will end with the Second Coming of Jesus The Christ. This coming is The Second Advent where those who will be martyred during The Tribulation will receive their resurrected bodies. It will occur seven years after The Rapture of The Church at the conclusion of The Great Tribulation. The Age of Ages and its dispensations, unlike all the previous ones, is led by the physical presence of God Himself.

In route to Earth, Christ will engage The Battle known as Armageddon. At the conclusion of this epic event, The Antichrist and The False Prophet are cast into The Lake of Fire. Those remaining armies that followed the commands of The Unholy Trio will be utterly slain and imprisoned until the dreadful day of The White Throne Judgment.

> *And the beast was taken, and with him the false prophet that*
> *wrought miracles before him, with which he deceived them that*
> *had received the mark of the beast, and them that worshipped*
> *his image. These both were cast alive into a lake of fire burning*
> *with brimstone. And the remnant were slain with the sword of*

him that sat upon the horse, which sword proceeded out of his mouth: and all the fowls were filled with their flesh.

(Revelation 19:20, 21)

Satan will be locked in The Abyss (The Bottomless Pit) until the end of The Millennium (One-Thousand-Year Period). For one thousand years He will expend energy trying to either hover or struggle at The Gate. Otherwise, He will be in a perpetual fall.

And I saw an angel come down from heaven, having the key of the bottomless pit and a great chain in his hand. And he laid hold on the dragon, that old serpent, which is the Devil, and Satan, and bound him a thousand years, And cast him into the bottomless pit, and shut him up, and set a seal upon him, that he should deceive the nations no more, till the thousand years should be fulfilled: and after that he must be loosed a little season.

(Revelation 20:1-3)

The Judgment of The Nations will commence immediately following Armageddon. Those who are saved will accompany Christ and His Church (Bride) to The Millennium Kingdom (Dispensation Number Seven). Those who are lost will be killed and sent to Hell to await The Resurrection of The Condemned.

When the Son of man shall come in his glory, and all the holy angels with him, then shall he sit upon the throne of his glory: And before him shall be gathered all nations: and he shall separate them one from another, as a shepherd divideth his sheep from the goats: And he shall set the sheep on his right hand, but the goats on the left.

(Matthew 25:31-33)

And these shall go away into everlasting punishment: but the righteous into life eternal.

(Matthew 25:46)

To strive for greatness in total disregard for The Creator places one on the same path taken by Satan with the assurance of arriving at the same final destination.

> *But the rest of the dead lived not again until the thousand years were finished. This is the first resurrection. Blessed and holy is he that hath part in the first resurrection: on such the second death hath no power, but they shall be priests of God and of Christ, and shall reign with him a thousand years.*
>
> *(Revelation 20:5, 6)*

THE FIRST RESURRECTION:

The use of the words "First Resurrection" has given rise to the words "Second Resurrection" and can be confusing. There is no literal term in The Bible that says Second Resurrection. However, The Bible chronicles several events that qualify for a type of resurrection. Take for instance the resurrection of the widow of Zarephath's son by Elijah (1 Kings 17:17-24) or the Shunamite's son by Elisha. (2 Kings 4:22-37) These are resurrections.

Then there was an event when a dead man was about to be buried and the people saw a band of raiders approaching. In haste, they threw the dead man's body into Elisha's tomb. According to God's Word, when the body of the dead man touched the bones of Elisha, the man revived. (2 Kings 13:21)

Add to those Old Testament examples The New Testament's records of the widow of Nain's son (Luke 7:11-16), the Synagogue ruler Jairus' twelve-year old daughter (Matthew 9:18, 19, 23-26, Mark 5:21-24, 35-43, Luke 8:40-42, 49-56, Lazarus (John 11:1-44), the monumental resurrection of The Saints following Jesus' resurrection (Matthew 27:51-53), Tabitha/Dorcas by Peter (Acts 9:36-41), and Eutychus by Paul (Acts 20:7-12), and even Paul was stoned and believed by many to be dead, yet miraculously revived. (Acts 14:19)

To all of these add the countless out-of-body admissions by many who are living today, and one might truly become confused by the term First Resurrection.

The number designation "first" determines **the condition of the soul** and **not the sequence of the resurrection.** Any soul that leaves the flesh and receives its Glorified Body may be classified as First Resurrection. Those souls that are destined to damnation are held in The Prison of The Earth until after the final mortal combat (Gog and Magog), which follows The One-Thousand-Year Reign of Christ on Earth. At that time, all that are not of God will be resurrected into physical bodies of flesh and ushered before The Sentencing Throne, "The Great White Throne," of God. After receiving their just penalty for denying The Creator, they will be killed, thereby leaving the flesh a second time (This is The Second Death) and sent to The Eternal Lake of Fire. Finally, there is **one death for The Saved** and **two deaths for The Lost**. There may be A Translation for The Saved upon Christ's command, but never one for The Lost.

THE MILLENNIUM CONTINUED:

This One-Thousand-Year Reign of Christ on Earth (The Millennium) constitutes the fulfillment of The Covenant made with Israel. During this period, there will be unparalleled righteousness due to The Presence of Christ and The Absence of The Unholy Trio. Because humanity will reside in personal fellowship with Christ, this Dispensation is also known as The "Dispensation of Righteousness." It is to this end that the writer of The Book of Hebrews referred when he spoke about The Kingdom of Peace and Righteousness.

> For this Melchisedec, king of Salem, priest of the most high God, who met Abraham returning from the slaughter of the kings, and blessed him; To whom also Abraham gave a tenth part of all; first being by interpretation King of righteousness, and after that also King of Salem, which is, King of peace; Without father, without mother, without descent, having neither beginning of days, nor end of life; but made like unto the Son of God; abideth a priest continually.
>
> (Hebrews 7:1-3)

The conditions of The Millennium Dispensation will embrace Edenic physiognomies and is therefore The Second Earthly Eden.

> *The wolf also shall dwell with the lamb, and the leopard shall lie down with the kid; and the calf and the young lion and the fatling together; and a little child shall lead them. And the cow and the bear shall feed; their young ones shall lie down together: and the lion shall eat straw like the ox. And the sucking child shall play on the hole of the asp, and the weaned child shall put his hand on the cockatrice' den. They shall not hurt nor destroy in all my holy mountain: for the earth shall be full of the knowledge of the LORD, as the waters cover the sea.*
>
> *(Isaiah 11:6-9)*

Those in The Millennium will unquestionably encounter the same three tree types of The Original Eden: one to eat from, one to live from, and finally one to deceive. The difference is The Tree (Satan) that was in The Midst of The Garden of The Eden of Genesis will be in The Bottomless Pit (Abyss) until the end of The Thousand Years. The literal fruit-bearing trees will sustain them physically. Jesus is The Tree of their Spiritual Life, and even though at the end of The Millennium some will deny Him, they will not be able to deny the all-encompassing mercy that He brings. Mercy, as in the presence of Christ, prolongs the inevitable judgment; and grace, if accepted, provides relief. For those who remain with Him after the release of Satan, there is life eternal. But for those who prefer Satan, there will be a fiery battle called Gog and Magog; and for them, there is Eternal Damnation. The survivors of The Millennium will have succeeded in each of The Virtues of every Dispensation beginning with Adam. They are Innocence, Consciousness, Government, Family, Law, and Grace.

> *And when the thousand years are expired, Satan shall be loosed out of his prison, And shall go out to deceive the nations which are in the four quarters of the earth, Gog and Magog, to gather them together to battle: the number of whom is as the sand of the sea. And they went up on the breadth of the earth, and*

compassed the camp of the saints about, and the beloved city:
and fire came down from God out of heaven, and devoured
them. And the devil that deceived them was cast into the lake
of fire and brimstone, where the beast and the false prophet are,
and shall be tormented day and night for ever and ever.

(Revelation 20:7-10)

DISPENSATION 8

(The Age of Ages-Phase 6)

1. GOD THE FATHER
2. Abdication
3. Perfection
4. Solar 5
5. Dispensation of Holiness

The final dispensation is number eight, the Dispensation of Holiness, The Ultimate New Beginning. It is the final abode of The Saints with God and constitutes The Third and Final Phase of Eden. The Abdication of The Throne by The Father and The Son renders The Kingdom fully in The Spiritual Domain of El Shaddai (God Almighty).[1]

Then cometh the end, when he shall have delivered up the
kingdom to God, even the Father; when he shall have put
down all rule and all authority and power. For he must reign,
till he hath put all enemies under his feet. The last enemy that
shall be destroyed is death. For he hath put all things under
his feet. But when he saith all things are put under him, it is
manifest that he is excepted which did put all things under him.

---

[1] And when Abram was ninety years old and nine, the Lord appeared to Abram, and said unto him, I am the Almighty God; walk before me, and be thou perfect. (Genesis 17:1)

And Jesus came and spake unto them, saying, All power is given unto me in heaven and in earth.

(Matthew 28:18)

And when all things shall be subdued unto him, then shall the
Son also himself be subject unto him that put all things under
him, that God may be all in all.

(1 Corinthians 15:24-28)

Before The Fall, sin's presence adorned The Garden in The Person of Satan. Although The Inaugural Family was perfect, they had to contend with "the lust of the eye, the lust of the flesh, and the pride of life."[1] Each of those conditions fuels The Presence, Power, and Penalty of Sin. Eden Number One was closed due to the family's disobedience. Eden Number Two is reopened during The Millennium because of The Presence of Christ and The Absence of The Unholy Trio. The limit of Eden Number Two is determined by The One-Thousand-Year Sentence of Satan in The Bottomless Pit. When Satan is released, The Inhabitants of The Earth who were born during The Millennium will either rest in Grace or join Satan in his final hurrah against God. I coin the term "Eden Number Three" since New Jerusalem depicts a New Heaven and Earth without spot, blemish, or any trace of The Presence (Deception), Power (Death) or Penalty (Damnation) of sin.

And I saw a new heaven and a new earth: for the first heaven
and the first earth were passed away; and there was no more
sea. And I John saw the holy city, new Jerusalem, coming
down from God out of heaven, prepared as a bride adorned for
her husband. And I heard a great voice out of heaven saying,
Behold, the tabernacle of God is with men, and he will dwell
with them, and they shall be his people, and God himself shall
be with them, and be their God.

(Revelation 21:1-3)

At The Conclusion of Time as we know it, our existence will incorporate Glorified Bodies, which constitute both The Body of The Lord and His Bride. For a perfect view of what exactly we are to expect, there is still a veil.

---

[1] For all that is in the world, the lust of the flesh, and the lust of the eyes, and the pride of life, is not of the Father, but is of the world. (1 John 2:16)

Beloved, now are we the sons of God, and it doth not yet appear what we shall be: but we know that, when he shall appear, we shall be like him; for we shall see him as he is.

(1 John 3:2)

Although Paul's message to The Corinthians concerning The Advent of Perfection has been referenced as The Completed Works of The Bible, one might also carry the interpretation further into the events of The Abdication. Paul said:

But when that which is perfect is come, then that which is in part shall be done away.

(1 Corinthians 13:10)

For now we see through a glass, darkly; but then face to face: now I know in part; but then shall I know even as also I am known.

(1 Corinthians 13:12)

As The Apostle Paul opened his letter to The Corinthians, he shined a bright light on that which they were to expect as Christians. It yet serves as the focal point of a future that is so bright and beautiful that it can only be described as "out of this world."

But as it is written, Eye hath not seen, nor ear heard, neither have entered into the heart of man, the things which God hath prepared for them that love him.

(1 Corinthians 2:9)

CHAPTER 5

PRE-STUDY CHECK LIST

For many, The Bible is a simple reference book which is to be consulted when certain questions arise. One must not lose sight of the fact that The Bible is filled with answers to questions one would not know to ask unless they read it methodically. In the previous study of the identity of Salome, were you made aware of other discoveries not anticipated? Yes, The Bible is filled with hidden mysteries, and for that reason, we should approach it with reverence.

> *But we speak the wisdom of God in a mystery, even the hidden*
> *wisdom, which God ordained before the world unto our glory:*
> *(1 Corinthians 2:7)*

God's Word cannot be contaminated. It is Truth without any mixture of error. However, The Word of God is highly sought by those who desire to make gain of lies by counterfeiting The Truth. Supply and demand drive the commerce of the world. There is no shortage of the desire for Truth. Therefore, The Devil uses such demands to fill the markets with his perversions. There are hundreds, if not thousands, of forged bibles lining the shelves of bookstores all over the world. Take note of the many different per-versions of The Holy Bible that publishers market each year, as does the auto builders with their new additions and options.

Have you noticed that the contenders of The Theocratic Faith, Judaism, or Islamism do not tamper with their Volumes of Sacred Law (VSL)? If there is any consolation to that fact, nothing imitation is ever counterfeited. Only The Truth is subject to the attack of a lie. The Devil has staged an awesome campaign in his attempt to spread discord and false hope throughout The Universe. For The Christian who dares to know The Truth, there is hope. God's Word is within your reach, and it comes with a guarantee of authenticity. It reads:

> *The words of the Lord are pure words: as silver <u>tried</u> in a furnace of earth, purified seven times. Thou shalt keep them, O Lord, thou shalt preserve them from this generation for ever.*
>
> *(Psalm 12:6, 7)*

A wise professor once said to me "A scholar is one who knows that he knows much less of a subject matter than more."[1] Even the most accomplished Bible teacher's knowledge, when compared to the vastness of God's Knowledge, appears as the tip of a needle in the oceans. For many scholars, there is a need to recant some of the contaminated (Embedded Theology) truths once learned and to commit to an unadulterated doctrine. The Apostle Paul is one of the better examples of a man who was considered among his peers as Suma Cum Laude; yet, he counted all loss:

> *But what things were gain to me, those I counted loss for Christ. Yea doubtless, and I count all things but loss for the excellency of the knowledge of Christ Jesus my Lord: for whom I have suffered the loss of all things, and do count them but dung, that I may win Christ,*
>
> *(Philippians 3:7, 8)*

> *And I, brethren, when I came to you, came not with excellency of speech or of wisdom, declaring unto you the testimony of God. For I determined not to know any thing among you, save Jesus Christ, and him crucified. And I was with you in weakness, and in fear, and in much trembling. And my speech and my preaching was not with enticing words of man's wisdom, but in demonstration of the Spirit and of power:*
>
> *(1 Corinthians 2:1-4)*

---

[1]   The Reverend William L. McClain, Sr., Pastor and Professor of Academic Studies.

It is not enough to truly desire; one must desire Truth.[1] The former is the foundation upon which many of the unfounded, unscriptural, and deceiving unbiblical concepts is built.[2] Be aware of the wiles of The Devil. His first attempt is that of removing The Seed of Truth before it is allowed to penetrate your mind. If that fails, He will attempt to harden The Soil of Your Mind so that The Seed of Truth cannot take root. If that fails, He will sow Weeds of Conflict and Choke The Roots of Truth. Being aware of these tactics will greatly enhance one's ability to allow God's Truths to take root and produce fruit acceptable to His Will. In the theoretical sense, the aforementioned is easy to conceive. Jesus spoke of it in The Parable of The Sower. (Matthew 13:1-9) However, when it comes to applying these Truths, one must be willing to press beyond the many distractions and attractions that will bid for more of one's attention. Finally, one must be determined to reach The Pinnacle of Truth at all costs. Friends, family, and foes will likely contribute many of the distractions that must be overcome. An honest desire for The Truth will ultimately conclude with true friends, family, and even foes.

> *For whosoever shall do the will of my Father which is in heaven, the same is my brother, and sister, and mother.*
> *(Matthew 12:50)*

> *Moreover he must have a good report of them which are without; lest he fall into reproach and the snare of the devil.*
> *(1 Timothy 3:7)*

For Truth to have a chance in the lives of humanity, one must not be fearful of exposing the lie. Such were the admissions of Paul in the above Scriptures. (Philippians 3:7, 8 and 1 Corinthians 2:1-4) Every human being who desires The Truth will encounter very strong opposition. How else will there be proof of the durability of faith? Who could explain to Job the reason for his struggles? Job was a man who

---

[1]   As newborn babes, desire the sincere milk of the word, that ye may grow thereby: (1 Peter 2:2)

[2]   Beware lest any man spoil you through philosophy and vain deceit, after the tradition of men, after the rudiments of the world, and not after Christ. (Colossians 2:8)

endured a plethora of hardships; yet, through them all, he learned that if God be for you, no one will "succeed" against you.

> *But he knoweth the way that I take: when he hath tried me,*
> *I shall come forth as gold.*
>
> (Job 23:10)

> *What shall we then say to these things? If God be for us, who*
> *can be against us?*
>
> (Romans 8:31)

"To be tried or not to be tried, that is the question." John made it clear that The Church is literally picked out to be picked on:

> *Fear none of those things which thou shalt suffer: behold, the*
> *devil shall cast some of you into prison, that ye may be tried;*
> *and ye shall have tribulation ten days: be thou faithful unto*
> *death, and I will give thee a crown of life.*
>
> (Revelation 2:10)

A word about "fear versus faith." Faith does not always remove fear; it acts despite of it. The things we suffer are but matters of awareness that God's Peace for His Creation is presently being attacked by that which we refer to as consequences. However, we by faith may claim amid such attacks the inevitable "peace that surpasses all understanding."

> *And the peace of God, which passeth all understanding, shall*
> *keep your hearts and minds through Christ Jesus.*
>
> (Philippians 4:7)

Never judge a matter by the considerations of winning or losing, but by obedience to God's Word. Death is a clear example of the inevitable Enemy of Life. *(1 Corinthians 15:26)* Only those who are strong in faith may approach it fearlessly. Do not confuse fearless with emotionless. Even Jesus respected death: *"Saying, Father, if thou be willing, remove this cup from me:"* It was His human side that appealed for life in the presence of death. It was His God-side that stood the gap of obedience;

nevertheless not my will, but thine, be done." (Luke 22:42) We all are subject to fears; however, by Faith, we may do The Will of God despite them.

Believers are often under the misconception that prosperity is the mark of good favor and right relationship with God. Without a doubt, any person would be delusional to desire less. However, every soldier will soon come to know that more time must be spent in battle dress than that which is spent in formal dress. There will be far more wars than parades.

> *Wherefore take unto you the whole armour of God, that ye may*
> *be able to withstand in the evil day, and having done all, to stand.*
> *(Ephesians 6:13)*

Paul identified The Enemy as A Spiritual Enemy and not the members of the human family. If we are to be the lovers that God created us to be, then we must first inoculate ourselves through The Spiritual Grace that God freely provides. Then, and only then, will we be able to stand:

> *Stand therefore, having your loins girt about <u>with truth</u>, and*
> *having on the breastplate of righteousness; And your feet shod*
> *with the preparation of the gospel of peace; <u>Above all, taking the</u>*
> *<u>shield of faith</u>, wherewith ye shall be able to quench all the fiery*
> *darts of the wicked. And take the helmet of salvation, and the*
> *sword of the Spirit, which is the word of God: Praying always*
> *with all prayer and supplication in the Spirit, and watching*
> *thereunto with all perseverance and supplication for all saints;*
> *(Ephesians 6:14-18)*

Before sitting down to study your Bible, ensure that you have uninterrupted time to meditate on each of the words you shall read. When challenged by the fact that you do not have the luxury of such time, ask yourself this question: Am I too busy to be able to spend designated time with my Lord? If you answered "yes" due to the many responsibilities that you have, you *are* Too Busy! Comprehension is largely dependent on the time and effort applied in reading and or listening. Comprehension is multifaceted and dependent upon four language skills:[1]

1. *phonology*
2. *syntax*
3. *semantics*
4. *pragmatics*

Without explaining each of the above findings (check Glossary – Chapter 3), one may correctly assume that comprehension, in its basic sense, requires more than the sounding of words. And even with a great vocabulary, there is always the problem of comprehension when the subject matter is allegorical or figurative. Therefore, dedicate time for your study of God's Word. The Holy Spirit will either confirm your conclusions or cloud them. In either case, you will learn to compare them with that of other reputable Bible scholars.

When circumstances interfere with your plans, do not get discouraged, but rather be encouraged; it is then that you can know that The Enemy (Spiritual) is trying to prevent your blessings. Never accuse others of being The Devil when such interruptions come. It may be that The Devil is influencing such interruptions. However, it is you who control the outcome.[2] Do not allow him to sow his seeds in your field (mind). Again, The Devil's greatest weapon is the Spiritually unguarded mind of humanity. When you prove to The Enemy that you will not be easily discouraged, he will likely seek others who pose a less dedicated resistance.

> *"Submit yourselves therefore to God. Resist the devil, and he will flee from you."*
>
> *(James 4:7)*

---

[1]   According to G. E. Tompkins, author of "Literacy in the early grades: "A successful start for pre-k4 readers (3rd edition)," Boston, Pearson. p 37,

[2]   If thou doest well, shalt thou not be accepted? and if thou doest not well, sin lieth at the door. And unto thee shall be his desire, and thou shalt rule over him. (Genesis 4:7)

T. R. I. E. D.

The following acronym was selected from God's purification of His Word (Psalm 12:6) and Job's aspiration to overcome catastrophe (Job 23:10). The acronym is composed of the word "**Tried**." Any worthy consideration must withstand being *tried*. Each of the letters making up this word is used in an easy to remember check list that one might employ in their Bible study and in their outline of prayer.

THANK GOD

Thank God for preserving The Scriptures and allowing you to have access to them. Do not take for granted the fact that you have God's Personal Love Letter and that it was written expressly to you. One never forgets to hold his/her breath when free diving; likewise, one should never forget to pray before studying God's Word.

> *Be careful for nothing; but in every thing by prayer and supplication with thanksgiving let your requests be made known unto God.*
> *(Philippians 4:6)*

READ YOUR BIBLE

Read your Bible as often as time and circumstances will allow. Today there are so many resources available to those who have a desire to read The Bible. Almost every adult and many children have phones. Most of the telephones have apps or search engines that will place The Bible instantly into the palms of your hand. If the vast content of The Bible intimidates and gives rise to the question of where and/or what to read, keep in mind that everything in It is worthy. However, if you do not have a specific subject matter in mind, use this easy-to-remember reference. There are thirty-one days in the longest months of the year and thirty-one Divisions of Proverbs in The Bible. On any given day of the month, you may take that month's date and use it to decide on what Proverb to read. Okay, so today is the 15th, so I am going to read the 15th Division of The Book of Proverbs. Each Proverb is a wealth of information that will surely lead to other books and a wealth of understanding. *"The tongue of the wise useth knowledge aright: but the mouth of fools poureth out foolishness." (Proverbs 15:2)*

> *And it shall be, when he sitteth upon the throne of his kingdom, that he shall write him a copy of this law in a book out of that which is before the priests the Levites: And it shall be with him, and he shall read therein all the days of his life: that he may learn to fear the Lord his God, to keep all the words of this law and these statutes, to do them:*
>
> *(Deuteronomy 17:18, 19)*

> *All scripture is given by inspiration of God, and is profitable for doctrine, for reproof, for correction, for instruction in righteousness: That the man of God may be perfect, throughly furnished unto all good works.*
>
> *(2 Timothy 3:16, 17)*

> *Blessed is he that readeth, and they that hear the words of this prophecy, and keep those things which are written therein: for the time is at hand.*
>
> *(Revelation 1:3)*

INVITE THE HOLY GHOST

Invite The Holy Spirit to take the lead in your soul, thereby allowing you to reach the most logical point of interpretation despite personal biases or circumstances. We spend most of our developing years learning how to compete. We are rewarded with ribbons, medals, and plaques for our exceptional accomplishments. Becoming a better me is a seemingly worthy pursuit. Then I get challenged to become "a giver" instead of "a getter." I am told that I must be willing to take up my cross and to deny myself. These things are usually opposite of that which has made me successful. Did I say successful? Oh, and yes, I heard that God is not impressed with success! So, what is it that He really wants me to be?

Obedient! Yes, God wants us to be obedient, and if that is ever going to occur, then it will require the presence of The Holy Spirit and our submission. In our prayers, we must use our Will to invoke The Will of God. Give Him reign to your mind, body, and soul.

> *And be not conformed to this world: but be ye transformed by the renewing of your mind, that ye may prove what is that good, and acceptable, and perfect, will of God. For I say, through the grace given unto me, to every man that is among you, not to think of himself more highly than he ought to think; but to think soberly, according as God hath dealt to every man the measure of faith. (Romans 12:2, 3)*

The Apostle Paul spoke the following words to Timothy, Pastor of Ephesus, his Son in The Ministry:

> *Study to shew thyself approved unto God, a workman that needeth not to be ashamed, rightly dividing the word of truth.*
> *(2 Timothy 2:15)*

Studying is a very normal practice among most people. However, studying to show yourself approved unto God requires a divine approach. During the era of The Old Testament times, those who were endowed with Spiritual Knowledge were directed by "Ruach Hakodesh."[1] This means that The Holy Spirit was active in the mental and physical process of those to whom He influenced. Daniel, for the most part, is a good example of one so inspired. In The New Testament, The Holy Spirit's influence is referred to as "Comforter":

> *But the Comforter, which is the Holy Ghost, whom the Father will send in my name, he shall teach you all things, and*

---

[1] The term "holy spirit" appears three times in the Hebrew Bible: Psalm 51 refers to "Your holy spirit" (ruach kodshecha)[3] and Isaiah refers twice to "His holy spirit" (ruach kodsho).[4]

*bring all things to your remembrance, whatsoever I have said
unto you.*

(John 14:26)

Paul was telling The Teacher of The Gospel, Timothy, to become a perpetual student of The Teachings of The Holy Spirit which is *the inspiration* of "Ruach Hakodesh-The Comforter." Such may only occur with those who are "Born Again." Jesus said as much to Nicodemus with these words:

*… Verily, verily, I say unto thee, Except a man be born again,
he cannot see the kingdom of God.*

(John 3:3)

Seeing The Kingdom requires The Comforter which is not to be achieved until after one is "Born Again." Although the disciples had spent three years learning at The Feet of Christ and were divinely acknowledged for their endeavors, *"And when he had said this, he breathed on them, and saith unto them, Receive ye the Holy Ghost:"* (John 20:22), they had yet to be "Born Again." Therefore, they were forbidden to teach until after the inaugural birthing of The Church:

*"But ye shall receive power, after that the Holy Ghost is come
upon you: and ye shall be witnesses unto me both in Jerusalem,
and in all Judæa, and in Samaria, and unto the uttermost part
of the earth."*

(Acts 1:8)

Inviting The Holy Spirit is the act of surrendering ones Will to The Will of God. It is only through this act that one might accomplish an understanding that is approved of God!

*Behold, I stand at the door, and knock: if any man hear my
voice, and open the door, I will come in to him, and will sup
with him, and he with me.*

(Revelation 3:20)

EXPECT GOD TO DO

Expect God to do a wonderful work in the development of your understanding. "I cannot do any better never does any better." Every worthy undertaking begins with an idea. The mind is powerful beyond comprehension. It is the soil to the seeds of thoughts and the producer of the fruit of expectation. "I can do it!" has gotten more accomplished than "I cannot do it" ever will. God gave personal attestation to the ability of the human mind.

> *That Christ may dwell in your hearts by faith; that ye, being rooted and grounded in love, May be able to comprehend with all saints what is the breadth, and length, and depth, and height; And to know the love of Christ, which passeth knowledge, that ye might be filled with all the fulness of God.*
> *(Ephesians 3:17-19)*

Immediately after The Flood, there was a new resurgence of metro building reminiscent Enoch, the city built by Cain. Nimrod was the architect of The Tower of Babel built on location by the survivors who declared that they would not be found vulnerable to another water catastrophe. *(Genesis 11)*. While some think that the builders were motivated by the need to rise above the potential of another devastation, others would rather think that the building of the tower was due largely to the explicit motive of cultural and linguistic homogeneity mentioned in the narrative. In either case, it was the minds of humanity that succeeded in building the metropolitan prototype of every current big city skyscraper. These huge, towering buildings continue to attest to the power of human expectation and the results of mind, matter and time.

The mind is a powerful engine of motivation and drive. The only question is: Will you allow The Spirit of God to be your engineer? *"I can do all things through Christ which strengtheneth me."* (Philippians 4:13) Many of them may come by sacrifice; however, they will each be followed by undeniable blessings. Remember that it is because of your Will that God limits the things that He would rather you have. *"And he did not many mighty works there because of their unbelief."* (Matthew 13:58)

> *These things have I written unto you that believe on the name*
> *of the Son of God; that ye may know that ye have eternal*
> *life, and that ye may believe on the name of the Son of God.*
> *And this is the confidence that we have in him, that, if we ask*
> *any thing according to his will, he heareth us: And if we know*
> *that he hear us, whatsoever we ask, we know that we have the*
> *petitions that we desired of him.*
>
> (1 John 5:13-15)

After having diligently read and studied God's Word, what is it that you expect? Whatever it is, it is very probable that you will get it.

DECIDE TO APPLY

Decide to apply the things learned in a meaningful way. Set attainable goals; and by faith, trust God for *the victory* and always give Him *the glory*. "Just Do It" has become a famous slogan for a very popular athletic brand. Artist, athletes, and authors have at least one thing in common; they must each strive to attain personal satisfaction in their performance or suffer the ills of self-defeat. In his or her own right, every human being is accordingly challenged as well. Making decisions are today vastly encumbered by social media. Therefore, many would preferably reside in obscurity rather than stand up and be bold in their faith.

We are cautioned that career success is stifled by religious access. As benign as the presence of prayer is, some have made it a target and subject to courts and politics. I have decided that regardless to where prayer might not be welcomed, there is one place that it will always be welcomed. For me that place is in my heart, soul, mind, and mouth. I will not be ashamed of Him Who I desire not to be ashamed of me.

> *Whosoever therefore shall be ashamed of me and of my words*
> *in this adulterous and sinful generation; of him also shall the*
> *Son of man be ashamed, when he cometh in the glory of his*
> *Father with the holy angels.*
>
> (Mark 8:38)

1. Decide to worship The Lord publicly and privately.

   Not forsaking the assembling of ourselves together, as the manner of some is; but exhorting one another: and so much the more, as ye see the day approaching.
   (Hebrews 10:25)

2. Decide to study His Holy Word and to be tried by the things that you have learned without regret or shame.

   Study to shew thyself approved unto God, a workman that needeth not to be ashamed, rightly dividing the word of truth.
   (2 Timothy 2:15)

3. Decide today that you will become a joy to yourself; a work that God alone will perform to His and your satisfaction.

   Create in me a clean heart, O God; and renew a right spirit within me.
   (Psalm 51:10)

4. Decide today is the day. Six times in The Bible are God's people cautioned to not harden their hearts as did The House of Israel in the provocation:

   1. *Wherefore then do ye harden your hearts, as the Egyptians and Pharaoh hardened their hearts? when he had wrought wonderfully among them, did they not let the people go, and they departed?*
   (1 Samuel 6:6)
   2. *Harden not your heart, as in the provocation, and as in the day of temptation in the wilderness:*
   (Psalm 95:8)
   3. *And when Jesus knew it, he saith unto them, Why reason ye, because ye have no bread? perceive ye not yet, neither understand? have ye your heart yet hardened?*
   (Mark 8:17)

4. *Wherefore (as the Holy Ghost saith, To day if ye will hear his voice, Harden not your hearts, as in the provocation, in the day of temptation in the wilderness: When your fathers tempted me, proved me, and saw my works forty years.*
(Hebrews 3:7-9)

5. *While it is said, To day if ye will hear his voice, harden not your hearts, as in the provocation.*
(Hebrews 3:15)

6. *Again, he limiteth a certain day, saying in David, To day, after so long a time; as it is said, To day if ye will hear his voice, harden not your hearts.*
(Hebrews 4:7)

Israel questioned God's power and His decisions. They second-guessed His instructions and brought destruction upon themselves. What have you received from the Lord, that you have determined to do, that will change your life for the better? Yes, it–like some medicines–may be bitter while ingesting. But if you apply it with "**T**hanksgiving," "**R**eading" it from His Word, "**I**nviting" the comprehension of The Holy Spirit, "**E**xpecting" a mighty work, and "**D**eciding" to "Just do It!" then:

Those things, which ye have both learned, and received, and heard, and seen in me, do: and the God of peace shall be with you.

(Philippians 4:9)

Thy word have I hid in mine heart, that I might not sin against thee.

(Psalm 119:11)

CHAPTER 6

HERMENEUTICS, EXEGESIS, EPIPHANY

I can remember when I had to think for a minute to avoid confusing "Hermeneutics" with "Homiletics." While one speaks of the explanation of a text, the other speaks to the harmony or corroboration of text. In other words, The Preacher must "hermeneutic" before he can rightly "homiletic." Rightly dividing The Word of God is accomplished through obedient exegesis in the form of study. It is often the epiphany, "I got it" that brightens the heart of the diligent student of God's Word. The time that one spends learning the art of study will provide heavenly dividends.

For we must all appear before the judgment seat of Christ; that every one may receive the things done in his body, according to that he hath done, whether it be good or bad.

(2 Corinthians 5:10)

HERMENEUTICS

Hermeneutics... (/hɛrmə'nuːtɪks/ or /hɛrmə'njuːtɪks/) is the theory and methodology of text interpretation, especially the interpretation of biblical texts, wisdom literature, and philosophical texts. [1]

In the history of biblical interpretation, four major types of Hermeneutics have emerged:

---

[1] g/wiki/Christine_Hayes" \o "Christine Hayes"

1. *LITERAL*
2. *ALLEGORICAL (TYPOLOGICAL)*
3. *MORAL (TOPOLOGICAL)*
4. *MYSTICAL (ANAGOGICAL)*

Hermeneutical Schools ...

Literal:

> Encyclopedia Britannica states that "Literal" analysis means "a biblical text is to be deciphered according to the 'plain meaning' expressed by its linguistic construction and historical context." The intention of the authors is believed to correspond to the literal meaning. Literal Hermeneutics is often associated with the verbal inspiration of The Bible. While some attempt to allegorize what it means to be a Christian, The Bible speaks literally of the subject. When Jesus said, "...*Except a man be born again, he cannot see the kingdom of God." (John 3:3)* He was not giving an allegory. Paul would later remind The Saints with these words: "*Therefore if any man be in Christ, he is a new creature: old things are passed away; behold, all things are become new." (2 Corinthians 5:17 & Galatians 6:15)* To allegorize such literal truths may result in dire consequences. If one were predisposed to accept only one of the many interpretive theories, this one – "Literal"-would be the wisest choice. There are far more literal interpretations in The Bible than any of the other types.

Allegorical / Typological:

> "Allegorical" interpretation states that biblical narratives have a second level of reference that is more than the people, events and things that are explicitly mentioned. One type of Allegorical interpretation is known as Typological, where the key figures, events,

and establishments of The Old Testament are viewed as "types." In The New Testament, this can also include foreshadowing of people, objects, and events. According to this theory, readings like *Noah's Ark* could be understood by using the Ark as a "type" of Christian Church that God expected from the start. The events of Isaac's sacrifice by his father, Abraham, is also a type of God's sacrifice of His Son Jesus. Turning water to wine is a type of salvation-man becoming a New Creature. Such interpretations are not arbitrary attestations, but sound interpretations supported by Scripture. As in the last example, the water is elsewhere in The Scriptures referenced as "flesh." (John 3:5; 1 John 5:8)

Some other examples of allegories are antitypes, signs, patterns, and examples, to name a few. The pre-figurement in The OT is called the *type;* the fulfillment in The NT is called the *antitype.*

Difference between prophecies and types: "Prophecies and types both point to things future and are predictive in their natures. Types, however, are to be distinguished from prophecies in their respective forms. That is, a *type* prefigures coming reality; a *prophecy* verbally delineates the future. One is expressed in events, persons, and acts; the other is couched in words and statements" (Tan, p. 168). [1]

Moral / Topological:

"Moral" interpretation searches for moral lessons which can be understood from writings within The Bible. Allegories are often placed in this category. The many dietary prohibitions advocated by various denominations speak to such interpretations. (Romans

---

[1] Hayes, Christine (2006). "Introduction to the Old Testament

14:2) Although one's moral accomplishments should be positively affected by becoming a Christian, morality is not unique to Christianity. Many of the scholars of Philosophy preached and taught the benefits of morality.

History supports the works of men such as Socrates (470/469 – 399 BC), The Greek Philosopher, who is credited with the founding of Western Philosophy. Two of his more noted students were Plato and Xenophon. Plato's most noted student was Aristotle (Polymath), The Greek Philosopher and Scientist (384-32 BC). Aristotle was the teacher of Alexander the Great. Marcus Tullius Cicero (3 January 106 BC – 7 December 43 BC) built on the philosophies of the era and expounded the rules of morality.

Jesus did not come to His world to equip mankind for morality; such was the competency of human creation. He came to provide mankind with the ability to rise above morality and to become immortal. It is the lack of such understandings that attribute to The Jewish misconception, as well as some denominations of Christians, that Jesus was simply a teacher of God and not God. These "wannabees" may be recognized by the adorning of the flesh with uniforms and the denial of the truth concerning the "New Birth."

Mystical /Anagogical:

"Mystical" interpretation purports to explain the events of The Bible and how they relate to or predict what the future holds. This is evident in The Jewish Kabbalah, which attempts to reveal the mystical significance of the numerical values of Hebrew words and letters. In Judaism, Anagogical interpretation is also evident in

The Medieval Zohar. In Christianity, it can be seen in Mariology.

The Book of Revelation is almost entirely written of events that are futuristic, and at the same time, defining the prevailing culture of the present. Such Mystical interpretations are subject to different schools. Revelation is studied from one of the four prevailing schools: Preterism, Historicism, Idealism, and Futurism. Such varieties do not support the idea that there may be different interpretations based on opinion. Such diversity speaks to the reality that Satan has substantially clouded The Truth. Therefore, the student of such studies must be endowed and directed prayerfully by The Holy Spirit.

EXEGESIS

Exegesis... (/ˌɛksəˈdʒiːsəs/; from the Greek ἐξήγησις from ἐξηγεῖσθαι 'to lead out') is a critical explanation or interpretation of a text, particularly a religious text. Traditionally, the term was used primarily for work with The Bible. However, in modern usage, "biblical exegesis" is used for greater specificity to distinguish it from any other broader critical text explanation.[1]

Exegesis may be approached from various predetermined positions depending on ones' hermeneutical stand. The most prevalent of those are:

1. *HISTORICAL*
2. *CANONICAL*
3. *SYMBOLIC*
4. *RATIONAL*

---

[1] "https://en.wikipedia.org/wiki/Open_Yale_Courses

Historical Exegesis

Historical Exegesis examines a broad range of historical concerns beginning with the author, his timeline, and the prevailing culture. The objective is to duplicate the literary interpretation as close to the original expectations as possible.

Canonical Exegesis

Canonical Exegesis differs from Historical as the latter focuses on the community at the time of the writing; whereas the former's focus is at the time of the examination. How does and or should the present community respond to the text?

Symbolic Exegesis

Symbolic Exegesis is critical to the interpretation of The Whole Bible. The Bible is a mysterious book. Brilliant Bible scholars are diametrically opposed when it comes to the explanation of its contents. Due to the need to extract meaning from the many symbols and allegories, Biblical Symbolism is essential. Do not be dismayed by the fact that different symbols may represent the same object. As in all interpretations, be sure that they are never in violation of Biblical Context. Do not make arbitrary assumptions.

Rational Exegesis

Rational Exegesis considers the response incited by Scripture Interpretation based strictly upon the most reasonable interpretation. Decisions of obedience are made from a collection of complete or incomplete knowledge. An acceptable response to Rational Theology is "that makes sense." Because rationality is subjective, there are often disagreements depending on whose rationality overrules. While it is reasonable to consider the viability of rationality, one must be careful to search The Bible for confirmation.

FIGURE OF SPEECH

"God The Author" of language, through His use, instituted "figure of speech" as a means of attracting the reader to more in-depth understanding. Even though the larger portion of The Bible is to be interpreted literally, one would never come to a full understanding of events that speak to a time which fulfills one's need for hope and faith without *types* or *prophecies*, both better rendered figuratively.

"The ability to communicate by words is one thing that sets apart mankind from all other creatures. God is the Author of language, and no one has ever used language as precisely as God does in the Bible, including His use of figures of speech. When most people say, "a figure of speech," they are speaking in general terms of something that is not true to fact. However, genuine "figures of speech" are legitimate grammatical and lexical forms that add emphasis and feeling to what we say and write. Recognizing and properly interpreting the figures of speech in the Bible has many advantages. We can understand the true meaning of Scripture and be able to enjoy the richness of the Word of God more fully. It is important that we become at least somewhat familiar with the figures of speech in Scripture, of which there are more than 200 varieties.

The figure we are going to cover in this article is *Synecdoche* (pronounced sin-ek-de-key). It is an exchange by which the whole of something is put for only a part, or vice versa, or a genus is put for a species or vice versa. Anyone studying *Synecdoche* will soon see its similarity to the figure of speech Metonymy, and Bullinger describes it this way:

[*Synecdoche* is] a figure by which one word receives something from another which is internally associated with it by the blending of two ideas: as when a part of a thing is put by a kind of Metonymy for the whole of it, or the whole for a part. The difference between Metonymy and Synecdoche lies in this: that in Metonymy, the exchange is made between two related nouns, while in Synecdoche the exchange is made between two associated ideas.

Synecdoche is one of those figures of speech that we use every day but are not taught to be aware of it. There are hundreds of examples of *Synecdoche* in the Bible, and Bullinger has 44 pages of examples."[1]

Although there are many uses of synecdoche in Bible translations, there is also a great number of them that are removed due to translations. Such is one of many reasons why the act of translating The Bible should be restricted to a Literal rendering. Example:

"2 Kings 8:9a English Standard Version (ESV)
So Hazael went to meet him [Elisha], and took a present with him, all kinds of goods of Damascus, forty camel loads...

The Hebrew text reads that Hazael took "every good thing of Damascus" to Elisha, which, of course, is impossible. This is a *Synecdoche*-the whole for a part. Hazael took every kind of good thing. This is an example of the English versions, such as the ESV above, interpreting the verse for us rather than just translating it. That can be helpful (some think) to the beginning

---

[1] ent (Hebrew Bible) – Lecture 23

reader. But it does not give the English reader the chance to see the *Synecdoche*.

James 2:15a (KJV)

If a brother or sister be naked…

"Naked" is put by *Synecdoche* for "scantily clothed." This is a common Synecdoche in the Bible, compare John 21:7, for example, where Peter is said in the Greek to be "naked," but he would not have worked that way, especially since fishing boats on the Sea of Galilee can easily be seen from shore. Similarly, Isaiah was almost certainly not "naked" (Isa. 20:2), but he had on his inner tunic such as a mourner or even a prisoner of war would have. Many versions have replaced "naked" with "scantily clothed" or some other phrase, translating the *Synecdoche* out of the version."[1]

In the broader sense, there are countless uses of "figure of speech." One need not be a student of any to use them, either when reading or writing. It is an intuitive part of the human gene to speak and write with such eloquence. It is a fact that one might spend more time studying the art and structure of words (taxonomy) than time spent using them to compose a brilliant idea. However, it may help to be aware of the many devices that have been discovered by linguists in the use of a composition or communication.

Merriam-Webster.com posted the following list of Rhetorical devices and examples:[2]

RHETORICAL DEVICES:

- **Alliteration**

---

[1]   – Visions of the End: Daniel and Apocalyptic Literature".

[2]   Nathaniel was from Cana of Galilee and noted so in John 21:2. The Marriage was in Cana of Galilee, John 2:1.

The repetition of usually initial consonant sounds in two or more neighboring words or syllables wild and woolly, threatening throngs.

- **Anacoluthon**

Syntactical inconsistency or incoherence within a sentence especially: a shift in an unfinished sentence from one syntactic construction to another you really should have—well, what do you expect?

- **Anadiplosis**

Repetition of a prominent and usually the last word in one phrase or clause at the beginning of the next rely on his honor—honor such as his?

- **Analepsis**

A literary technique that involves interruption of the chronological sequence of events by interjection of events or scenes of earlier occurrence: flashback

- **Anaphora**

Repetition of a word or expression at the beginning of successive phrases, clauses, sentences, or verses especially for rhetorical or poetic effect we cannot dedicate—we cannot consecrate—we cannot hallow—this ground

- **Antanaclasis**

The repetition of a word within a phrase or sentence in which the second occurrence utilizes a different and sometimes contrary meaning from the first we must all hang together or most assuredly we shall all hang separately

- **Antiphrasis**

  The usually ironic or humorous use of words in senses opposite to the generally accepted meaning this giant of 3 feet 4 inches

- **Antonomasia**

  The use of a proper name to designate a member of a class (such as a Solomon for a wise ruler) OR the use of an epithet or title in place of a proper name (such as the Bard for Shakespeare)

- **Apophasis**

  The raising of an issue by claiming not to mention it we won't discuss his past crimes

- **Aporia**

  An expression of real or pretended doubt or uncertainty especially for rhetorical effect to be, or not to be: that is the question

- **Cacophony**

  Harshness in the sound of words or phrases

- **Chiasmus**

  An inverted relationship between the syntactic elements of parallel phrases working hard, or hardly working?

- **Dialogism**

  The use in a text of different tones or viewpoints, whose interaction or contradiction is important to the text's interpretation.

  Gravitation may act without contact; therefore, either some force may act without contact or gravitation is not a force

- **Dysphemism**

  The substitution of a disagreeable, offensive, or disparaging expression for an agreeable or inoffensive one Greasy spoon is a dysphemism for the word diner

- **Epistrophe**

  Repetition of a word or expression at the end of successive phrases, clauses, sentences, or verses especially for rhetorical or poetic effect of the people, by the people, for the people

- **Epizeuxis**

  Emphatic repetition [this definition is taken from the 1934 edition of Webster's Unabridged dictionary]

- **Hypallage**

  An interchange of two elements in a phrase or sentence from a more logical to a less logical relationship. You are lost to joy for joy is lost to you

- **Hyperbaton**

  A transposition or inversion of idiomatic word order judge me by my size, do you?

- **Hyperbole**

  exaggerated statements or claims not meant to be taken literally.

  "He vowed revenge with oaths and hyperboles"

- **Hypophora**

  The putting or answering of an objection or argument against the speaker's contention [this definition is taken from the 1934 edition of Webster's Unabridged dictionary]

- **Litotes**

  understatement in which an affirmative is expressed by the negative of the contrary (as in "not a bad singer" or "not unhappy")

- **Meiosis**

  The presentation of a thing with underemphasis especially in order to achieve a greater effect: UNDERSTATEMENT

- **Metaphor**

  A figure of speech in which a word or phrase literally denoting one kind of object or idea is used in place of another to suggest a likeness or analogy between them. "Drowning in money"

- **Metonymy**

A figure of speech consisting of the use of the name of one thing for that of another of which it is an attribute or with which it is associated. "Crown as used in lands belonging to the Crown"

- **Onomatopoeia**

The naming of a thing or action by a vocal imitation of the sound associated with it Buzz

- **Oxymoron**

A combination of contradictory or incongruous words cruel kindness

- **Pleonasm**

The use of more words than those necessary to denote mere sense: REDUNDANCY I saw it with my own eyes

- **Prolepsis**

The anticipation and answering of possible objections in rhetorical speech.

The representation of a thing as existing before it actually does or did so, as in he was a dead man when he entered.

- **Simile**

  A figure of speech comparing two unlike things that is often introduced by "like" or "as" cheeks like roses

- **Syllepsis**

  The use of a word in the same grammatical relation to two adjacent words in the context with one literal and the other metaphorical in sense. "She blew my nose and then she blew my mind"

- **Synecdoche**

  A figure of speech by which a part is put for the whole (such as fifty sail for fifty ships), the whole for a part (such as society for high society), the species for the genus (such as cutthroat for assassin), the genus for the species (such as a creature for a man), or the name of the material for the thing made (such as boards for stage)

- **Zeugma**

  the use of a word to modify or govern two or more words in such a way that it applies to each in a different sense or makes sense with only one (as in "opened the door and her heart to the homeless boy")

As with any Scripture, one might abuse its context by misinterpretation. Allegorical explanations are more subject to such abuse. Being careful to cross reference one's findings with concrete literal Scriptures removes such concerns.

EPIPHANY

Epiphany... Seldom used in the disciplining stage of Bible studies is the term "epiphany." An epiphany is to The Bible Student what a fish is to a fisherman. The angler anticipates his/her catch by ensuring that all necessary provisions have been properly applied before setting out into the waters. And so, it is for The Bible Student who expects to reach an inspired state of Bible Illumination. Epiphany is defined as:

1. A usually sudden manifestation or perception of the essential nature or meaning of something
2. An intuitive grasp of reality through something (as an event) usually simple and striking
3. An illuminating discovery, realization, or disclosure

In the final analysis, the epiphany is the prize that one receives from the result of properly applied Hermeneutics and Exegesis. Approach the reading of The Bible with an unselfish agenda, and you are more likely to depart from it with a wealth of knowledge, otherwise unattainable.

1. Why do you want so desperately to know what it says?
2. Are you willing to be governed by its precepts despite the consequences?

If you answered no to the latter, you are not equipped to command the former.

The Author of The Bible is non-other than God Himself. There is no fear that should hinder our efforts to conform to The Will of our Father.

> *For I reckon that the sufferings of this present time are not worthy to be compared with the glory which shall be revealed in us.*
>
> *(Romans 8:18)*

Therefore, your intentions and due diligence are pre-known. The Lord rewards those whom He knows are willing to follow through with His Divine Will.

> *For whom he did foreknow, he also did predestinate to be conformed to the image of his Son, that he might be the firstborn among many brethren. Moreover whom he did predestinate, them he also called: and whom he called, them he also justified: and whom he justified, them he also glorified.*
>
> *(Romans 8:29, 30)*

> *My sheep hear my voice, and I know them, and they follow me: And I give unto them eternal life; and they shall never perish, neither shall any man pluck them out of my hand.*
>
> *(John 10:27, 28)*

In The Bible Book of John, there is an all too familiar story generally referred to as *the first miracle* performed by Jesus. It is the infamous changing of water to wine. For most Bible Students and Teachers, the act of Christ at the marriage feast simply constitutes a mission of making our moral lives better. It is said that Jesus will take the bland water (two lives separated) and turn it into a glorious wine (two lives consummated). Notwithstanding, God at the marriage feast does just that. However, it is not that point to which this Scripture speaks. An appropriate exposition of John's account of the marriage feast is a good example of intense Bible Study. Although seldom referenced as such, Nathaniel, the disciple that met Jesus at the hands of Philip, might very well be the person whose wedding Jesus attended. How would one come to such an assumption? Work it out.[1]

For every physical or carnal application that one might interpret from God's Word, there is an equally responsible Spiritual application ready to be discovered. As a matter of fact, The Spiritual is to be known by the very presence of the physical albeit, a bit more Mystical.

---

[1] "\o "Open Yale Courses" Open Yale Courses. Yale University.
R. Carroll; M. Daniel (2002). Amos: The Prophet and His Oracles

For the invisible things of him from the creation of the world are clearly seen, being understood by the things that are made, even his eternal power and Godhead; so that they are without excuse:

(Romans 1:20)

The angler anticipates the catch by ensuring that the hook is properly baited. For The Student of The Bible, the bait may be likened unto The Glorious Gospel of Jesus Christ. Jesus is the bait. There is no other name beneath Heaven by which a man can be saved.

Neither is there salvation in any other: for there is none other name under heaven given among men, whereby we must be saved.

(Acts 4:12)

Remember those foundational truths that we earlier listed? Having a firm belief of The Truth of Jesus as Lord and His divine purpose as The Saviour is the foundation upon which all correctly interpreted studies are based.

Jesus saith unto them, Did ye never read in the scriptures, The stone which the builders rejected, the same is become the head of the corner: this is the Lord's doing, and it is marvellous in our eyes?

(Matthew 21:42)

For other foundation can no man lay than that is laid, which is Jesus Christ.

(1 Corinthians 3:11)

Here are three simple steps that The Student of The Bible may follow in search of that illusive epiphany. They are:

1. *Observation*
2. *Interpretation*
3. *Application*

Another way of looking at this approach is:

1. *what do I see?*
2. *what do I say?*
3. *what will/should I do?*

As in the previously considered acronym "T.R.I.E.D," the first step is to acknowledge your thankfulness by prayer. Prayer reminds us that The Holy Spirit is always The Teacher, and we are the disciples. Be prepared to pay close attention to His instructions.

> *Jesus answered and said unto them, Ye do err, not knowing the scriptures, nor the power of God.*
>
> *(Matthew 22:29)*

Before trying to understand the minute details, one must gain the benefits of knowing the critical facts that surround them. I liken this to a tourist who might be trekking up a trail and suddenly the guide says, "You are standing on one of the most beautiful spots in this whole valley." The tourist looks around and all that can be seen are a few rocks, some familiar trees and a continuing dirt trail. It was not until they had returned from the hike that the tourist was able to comprehend the beauty of the spot previously mentioned. From a distance, the location was adorned by the contour of a snow-capped mountain, a flowing river and beautiful vegetation.

If you want to see The Glory of The Scriptures, you must begin by simple "observation." This is that which we generally refer to as "context"-being able to see not only the verses that you are reading, but also their accompanying Truths which ultimately aid in the "interpretation." Every letter in Scripture comes together to render words which provide us with terms. The terms grow to verses which together gives paragraphs. By definition, a paragraph is a distinct section of a piece of writing, usually with a single theme and indicated by a new line, indentation, or numbering. It may also be referenced as a "passage of Scripture." The Greek definition of the same is called a Pericope: (/pəˈrɪkəpiː/; Greek περικοπή, "a cutting-out") in rhetoric, is a set of verses that forms one coherent unit or thought, suitable for public reading from a text, now usually of sacred Scripture. Paragraphs (passages-pericope) come together to reveal chapters; Chapters develop into books; Books are categorized into genres; Genres together constitute Testaments; Testaments are volumes of Sacred Law, The Bible. It must be our intention not to contradict or disturb the harmony of The Scripture, but to gain valuable insight.

As a scuba diver, one may enjoy the beauty of one of the most diverse ecosystems on Mother Earth, the coral reef. Having grown for thousands of years by tiny calcium producing organisms, a reef will have become home to countless life forms. Her color and décor are matchless in radiance and beauty. Yet, one careless diver, unable to prevent crashing into it, will destroy in a second that which may not revive in a millennium. And so, it is with Scripture. One must be patient in reading The Scriptures. Do not read in haste trying to score points based on having sounded words. Try to be in an environment that allows you to concentrate on the words you are reading. Although the new technology of Bible audio books is convenient, the observer/reader is too often drifting away on a different path of thought, while the narrator continues to sound The Words of The Scripture. Observation is best served when the reader can take his/her time and approach The Bible as though they were in personal communion with God Himself. And that is, in fact, the truth of what is occurring when one reads His Holy Word.

Hear, O Israel: The Lord our God is one Lord: And thou shalt love the Lord thy God with all thine heart, and with all thy soul, and with all thy might. And these words, which I command thee this day, shall be in thine heart: And thou shalt teach them diligently unto thy children, and shalt talk of them when thou sittest in thine house, and when thou walkest by the way, and when thou liest down, and when thou risest up. And thou shalt bind them for a sign upon thine hand, and they shall be as frontlets between thine eyes. And thou shalt write them upon the posts of thy house, and on thy gates.

(Deuteronomy 6:4-9)

Bible Study stabilizes The Believer by reinforcing the trust required to maintain faithful fellowship with The Lord. Remember, "Begin with the end in mind." Despite the circumstances, we learn that in the end, we win!

CHAPTER 7

HERMENEUTICAL ANALYSIS

THE MARRIAGE FEAST

"ONLY TRUE VIRGINS"

Our assessment Scripture is The Gospel of John, Chapter "2" Verses "1" through "11." These Scriptures provide the thread this study uses to explain many different yet required considerations when trying to reach the correct conclusion. We will examine this Scripture according to the several Schools of Interpretation as found in Hermeneutics and Exegesis. We will consider the many inclinations, and even a few desires, that often cause harm to the interpretation of Truth. *"EXAMINE EACH WORD CAREFULLY."*

And the third day there was a marriage in Cana of Galilee; and the mother of Jesus was there: And both Jesus was called, and his disciples, to the marriage. And when they wanted wine, the mother of Jesus saith unto him, They have no wine. Jesus saith unto her, Woman, what have I to do with thee? mine hour is not yet come. His mother saith unto the servants, Whatsoever he saith unto you, do it. And there were set there six waterpots of stone, after the manner of the purifying of the Jews, containing two or three firkins apiece. Jesus saith unto them, Fill the waterpots with water. And they filled them up to the brim. And he saith unto them, Draw out now, and bear unto the governor of the feast. And they bare it. When the ruler of the feast had tasted the water that was made wine, and knew not whence it was: (but the servants which drew the

water knew;) the governor of the feast called the bridegroom,
And saith unto him, Every man at the beginning doth set
forth good wine; and when men have well drunk, then that
which is worse: but thou hast kept the good wine until now.
This beginning of miracles did Jesus in Cana of Galilee, and
manifested forth his glory; and his disciples believed on him.

(John 2:1-11)

John 2:1-11 is filled with deep Spiritual Truths that are easily obtained; and at the same time, are easily omitted. Miraculously, The Bible is both logical and confounding. At the feet of Christ, the disciples became aware of this fact early in their Spiritual development:

And the disciples came, and said unto him, Why speakest
thou unto them in parables? He answered and said unto them,
Because it is given unto you to know the mysteries of the
kingdom of heaven, but to them it is not given.

(Matthew 13:10, 11)

A parable is an earthly story with a heavenly meaning. In some regards, the entire Bible might be seen as a parable. The Bible is a logical description of an invisible Spiritual existence that is encapsulated in a material/carnal environment.[1] Those who are not born again will only see the images portrayed in The Scripture relative to their earthly meaning. Jesus admonished His disciples of this fact and further proved the premise by revealing their constant failures in "interpretation" and "application." It was not until the disciples were endowed with The Holy Ghost that they were able to discern Spiritual Truths. Christ anointed the disciples at the conclusion of their training. But He did not send them out to teach until they were "born again."

---

[1] . Louisville: Westminster John Knox Press., focus on historiography H.W. W

To be or not to be born again–that is the question!

Let's detour a moment from John 2 and look at an often-misinterpreted verse of Scripture that alone would be hard to discern. If you were asked whether The Disciples of Christ were "born again" while they traveled with Him, what would your answer be? If your answer would be "yes," then read The Scripture that confirms your point. If your answer would be "no," does the following Scripture confirm the moment when the disciples became "born again?" Any biblical answer must hold true from Genesis to Revelation (Theology).

> *And when he had said this, he breathed on them, and saith unto them, Receive ye the Holy Ghost:*
>
> *(John 20:22)*

Having conflicting teachings (antithetical) often causes Christians to lose confidence in the efficacy of God's Word. Satan's tactic is to sow seeds of lies into the minds of Christians. He knows that the fruit will often render The Believer to teach and practice that which is contrary to otherwise easy to interpret Bible Truths. Teachers who teach incorrect doctrine must also find ways to support the same. What that does is create an avalanche of justifications often represented by further incorrect interpretations. The result of what is a simple explanation becomes a course of incorrect interpretations due to the chance of embarrassment caused by admission. Only those who understand that it is human to err and therefore, are willing to readily make corrections where and when corrections are found, shall be overcomers.

Let's go with the premise that John 20:22 marks the time and location that The Disciples of Christ were saved. By "saved," we mean that they received the anointing of The New Birth and became New Creatures. Such consideration would not be far-fetched if John 20:22 was the only Scripture that speaks to the salvation of the disciples and that of the world. But, if it were so, we would have to conclude that not only was Judas not saved, but also Thomas, seeing as how he was not present at the time that Jesus breathed on the others.

But Thomas, one of the twelve, called Didymus, was not with them when Jesus came.

(John 20:24)

Thomas did, later, see Jesus and mightily proclaimed Him as his Lord and his God.

And Thomas answered and said unto him, My Lord and my God.

(John 20:28)

If the disciples had become born again at the breathing of Christ, wouldn't that important event need to be represented in the life of Thomas as well? There is never a mention of Thomas having the breath of the anointing of The Holy Ghost placed upon him. But there is evidence of him being with the others at the receiving of The Holy Ghost.

And when they were come in, they went up into an upper room, where abode both Peter, and James, and John, and Andrew, Philip, and <u>Thomas</u>, Bartholomew, and Matthew, James the son of Alphaeus, and Simon Zelotes, and Judas the brother of James. These all continued with one accord in prayer and supplication, with the women, and Mary the mother of Jesus, and with his brethren.

(Acts 1:13, 14)

The next and most convincing point to the one who is not trying to prove a misguided point is the events of Pentecost. Would Christ have instructed the disciples to wait until they had received power from The Advent of The Holy Ghost if they had already been so empowered?

<u>But ye shall</u> receive power, after that the Holy Ghost is come upon you: and ye shall be witnesses unto me both in Jerusalem, and in all Judæa, and in Samaria, and unto the uttermost part of the earth.

(Acts 1:8)

The above words were spoken by a present Christ. It was the same Christ who breathed on the disciples in question. Now concerning The Holy Ghost, let's look at how Jesus explains to the disciples that He will return to them in the form of The Holy Spirit.

> *But now I go my way to him that sent me; and none of you asketh me, Whither goest thou? But because I have said these things unto you, sorrow hath filled your heart. Nevertheless, I tell you the truth; It is expedient for you that I go away: for if I go not away, the Comforter will not come unto you; but if I depart, I will send him unto you.*
>
> (John 16:5-7)

Well, *"I will send Him unto you"* may be perceived as Jesus sending to them another. However, the following verse makes it clear that The One whom the disciples were to expect is none other than Christ Himself.

> *I will not leave you comfortless: I will come to you. Yet a little while, and the world seeth me no more; but ye see me: because I live, ye shall live also. At that day ye shall know that I am in my Father, and ye in me, and I in you.*
>
> (John 14:18-20)

The belief that the disciples were saved (Born Again) at the breathing of Christ (John 20:22) is a subliminal admission of there being more than one God. Yes, Jehovah is God, and Jesus is God, and the Holy Spirit is God, and they are revealed at separate times and dispensations. But to perceive God as being three distinct personages at one time is not correct.[1] To be born again, one must be immersed into The Holy Spirit.[2] Since Jesus is God and The Holy Spirit is God, could the two be active at the same time and in the same place? Jesus said *"...for if I*

---

[1] olff, Joel und Amos (Hermeneia; Philadelphia: Fortress Press, 1977), p. 215. P. Carny, 'Doxologies: A Scientific Myth', Hebrew Studies 18 (1977), pp. 149–59 (157) J. Radine, The Book of Amos

[2] in Emergent Judah (Tübingen: Mohr Siebeck, 2010) D.R. Hillers, 'Treaty-Curses and the Old Testament Prophets' (unpublished PhD diss

go not away, the Comforter will not come..." Jesus was explaining to the disciples the imperativeness of His departure, which they struggled to understand.

Jesus brought to the minds of the disciples The Testament of The Father (Jehovah-God), The Testament of The Son (Jesus-God), and The Testament of The Holy Ghost (Spirit-God).

> *In the last day, that great day of the feast, Jesus stood and cried, saying, If any man thirst, let him come unto me, and drink. He that believeth on me, as the scripture hath said, out of his belly shall flow rivers of living water. (But this spake he of the Spirit, which they that believe on him should receive: for the Holy Ghost was not yet given; because that Jesus was not yet glorified.*"
>
> (John 7:37-39)

The glorification that Jesus spoke of was that which He personally held with The Father in the beginning. He laid down His glory for the love of humanity[1] and would pick it up again after His resurrection.

> *And now, O Father, glorify thou me with thine own self with the glory which I had with thee before the world was.*
>
> (John 17:5)

If The Lord Had Baptized them with The Holy Ghost in John 20:22, then they apparently had lost it by Acts 1:5?

> *And, being assembled together with them, commanded them that they should not depart from Jerusalem, but wait for the promise of the Father, which, saith he, ye have heard of me. For John truly baptized with water; but ye shall be baptized with the Holy Ghost not many days hence.*
>
> (Acts 1:4, 5)

---

[1]   ertation); Rome Pontical Biblical Institute, 1964

No, that is not the case. However, those who would rather believe that one can lose his/her salvation may use such incorrect interpretations trying to prove that assumption. Jesus did just as he promised in John 16:5–7; He departed and then He returned in The Person of The Holy Ghost.

> *Even the Spirit of truth; whom the world cannot receive, because it seeth him not, neither knoweth him; but ye know him; for he dwelleth with you, and shall be in you."*
>
> *(John 14:17)*

It was not until the disciples were baptized (Born Again) in The Spirit that they were to have the power to carry out The Commission. That power is the living presence of God in their souls. If God were living in the souls of the disciples in John 20: 22, then there must be at least two Gods since Jesus was standing there.

> *But ye shall receive power, after that the Holy Ghost is come upon you: and ye shall be witnesses unto me both in Jerusalem, and in all Judaea, and in Samaria, and unto the uttermost part of the earth.*
>
> *(Acts 1:8)*

> *And when he had spoken these things, while they beheld, he was taken up; and a cloud received him out of their sight.*
>
> *(Acts 1:9)*

> *And when the day of Pentecost was fully come, they were all with one accord in one place. And suddenly there came a sound from heaven as of a rushing mighty wind, and it filled all the house where they were sitting. And there appeared unto them cloven tongues like as of fire, and it sat upon each of them. And they were all filled with the Holy Ghost, and began to speak with other tongues, as the Spirit gave them utterance.*
>
> *(Acts 2:1-4)*

Jesus' breath on the disciples marked the conclusion of the earthly teachings they had received. Thomas' experience proved to be the same, albeit, received by the mere sight of The Risen Saviour. The disciples, like all who have lived since the departure of Jesus, were/are saved only by the reality of The New Birth. Such is The Dispensation of Grace and was not instituted until after Christ's departure to Heaven and the return of The Holy Ghost. In the lives of those who are not yet saved, The Holy Spirit works by convicting them of their sins.

And when he is come, he will reprove the world of sin, and of righteousness, and of judgment:

(John 16:8)

The Lost, without the intervention of The Holy Spirit, could never be saved. This little detour was meant to provide you with a clear understanding of how one must apply The Entire Bible in the explanation of just one verse. Taken alone, one verse may do detrimental things to the perception of the reader. That is why it is so important and blessed to be a part of a Bible Preaching and Teaching Church. To have teachers who do not compromise Truth for the sake of acceptance is indispensable. Now before going further, did you know that the disciples were not born-again during Christ's earthly tenure?

ANALYTICAL SCHOOLS OF HERMENEUTICS

John's Gospel stands out among The Four Gospels. The three which precede John are generally referred to as The Synoptic Gospels. Synoptic describes The Gospels of Matthew, Mark and Luke as telling the story of Jesus Christ's life and ministry from a similar structure and point of view. Although each of the four books lives in the genre of "Gospel," John speaks more specifically to Christ's Godship. John begins with Jesus as The "Word," whereas the others speak to His genealogy. It is helpful for the reader to be aware that Scripture may be interpreted from one or more of the following.

WHICH PATH AM I ABOUT TO TAKE?

ANALYZING SCRIPTURES

Okay, so you open your Bible and begin reading a passage of Scripture. Answer this question: Is the sense of what you read easy to understand? If it is, then you have your "interpretation." On the other hand, are you left meditating and questioning The Scripture due to a plethora of unanswered questions? If so, then you must prayerfully analyze The Scripture in search of The Truth. Being mindful of the different biblical approaches provides flexibility during the "observation." The reader may look at one passage from several different viewpoints.

As an example, take The Scripture we are using, John 2:1-11: Why did Jesus choose the creation of wine as His first recorded miracle? Although some have attempted to justify the consumption of wine based on this event, such is not the message that Jesus was conveying. One's logical response to Jesus' act should lead to questions like, why wine? To reach the correct answer, one must proceed down the following path:

HERMENEUTICAL ANALYSIS: L.H/C.T.S.

LEXICAL/SYNTACTICAL
HISTORICAL/CULTURAL
CONTEXTUAL
THEOLOGICAL
SPECIAL LITERARY

Carefully consider each of the following analytical points throughout the study of the passage:

LEXICAL/SYNTACTICAL ANALYSIS:[1]

The units of analysis in Lexical Semantics are **lexical units** which include, not only words, but also sub-words or sub-units such as affixes

---

[1] G. Cox, The 'Hymn' of Amos: An Ancient Flood Narrative. Journal for the Study of the Old Testament Vol 38.1 (2013): pp. 81–108

and even compound words and phrases. Lexical units make up the catalogue of words in a language, the lexicon. Lexical Semantics looks at how the meaning of the lexical units correlates with the structure of the language or syntax. This is referred to as "syntax-semantic interface."

Syntax is the set of rules, principles, and processes that govern the structure of sentences in a given language, specifically word order. The term "syntax" is also used to refer to the study of such principles and processes. The goal of many syntacticians is to discover the syntactic rules common to all languages. A Lexical/Syntactical Analysis will reveal the basis from which a more in-depth understanding may be reached.

What does it say?

Simply removing or placing a comma may change the meaning of a sentence completely. Such is not only true for the writer, but also for the reader. Without paying close attention to each punctuation, one's interpretation may take on a whole new meaning.

I remember my dad saying to me that children should not be a part of The Church. He was studying the following verse:

> "But Jesus called them unto him, and said, Suffer little children to come unto me, and forbid them not: for of such is the kingdom of God." (Luke 18:16)

Although the above Scripture does not forbid children, it may be perceived as such with a small adjustment to mental punctuation:

> "But Jesus called them unto him, and said, Suffer little children to come unto me and forbid them, not for of such is the kingdom of God." (Luke, As you See It)

How would you interpret the following?

Let's eat grandpa. (Someone should warn grandpa!)

Maybe they meant: Let's eat, Grandpa.

Let's get the hot plate of food and cool it. (Why get it hot, just wait until it cools off!)

Maybe they meant: Let's get the hot plate, and cool it.

Without a doubt, we must follow the academic laws of writing if we intend to convey our message correctly. Equally important is our need to read correctly, if the message is to be interpreted correctly. Our Father has given His Word without any mixture of error. Therefore, it is up to us, with the guidance of The Holy Spirit, to apply it correctly.

> *Verily I say unto you Whosoever shall not receive the kingdom of God, as a little child shall in no wise enter therein. (Luke, As he saw It)*

The above is speaking to those who shall not receive The Kingdom of God. They are included with little children who also will not enter Heaven. With a simple replacement of proper punctuation, the meaning changes completely:

> *"Verily I say unto you, Whosoever shall not receive the kingdom of God as a little child shall in no wise enter therein." (Luke 18:17)*

The placement of one comma changed the meaning entirely. Before attempting to understand *what* it means, answer these questions:

o *What does it say?*
o *Is your answer rational?*
o *Does it agree with all that you know about The Bible?*
o *Do you believe what you just read?*
o *Should you believe it?*

These are but a few simple questions that will aid you in furthering your study and coming away with The Truth.

Because of one's failure to take into consideration the grammatical structure of a sentence, centuries of wrong interpretations may follow.

Take, as an example, the commonly stated "Five-Fold Ministry." Most established Bible colleges and scholars will readily identify them as:

1. *Apostles*
2. *Prophets*
3. *Evangelists*
4. *Pastors*
5. *Teachers*

If the above list was to be interpreted as read, The Scripture referencing it should read as follows:

> *"And he gave some, apostles; and some, prophets; and some, evangelists; and some, pastors; and some, teachers;"* ~~(Ephesians 4:11)~~

The punctuation used in The Bible treats the reference to the pastor and teacher as one. In the above rendering, the semi colon that follows each of the nouns is inserted after the word "pastors." Therefore, The Office of Pastor and Teacher is divided. However, the below rendering from The Bible renders The Office of "Pastor and Teacher" as one:

> *"And he gave some, apostles; and some, prophets; and some, evangelists; and some, pastors and teachers;"* (Ephesians 4:11)

To confirm the matter concerning the "Four-Fold Ministry," one need only to discover the true reference to The Office of The Pastor. The following cross references shall confirm that The Pastor's Office is synonymous with *teaching*:

> *"And I will give you pastors according to mine heart, which shall feed you with knowledge and understanding."* (Jeremiah 3:15)

> *"Therefore thus saith the Lord God of Israel against the pastors that feed my people; Ye have scattered my flock, and driven*

them away, and have not visited them: behold, I will visit upon you the evil of your doings, saith the Lord." (Jeremiah 23:2)

"A bishop then must be blameless, the husband of one wife, vigilant, sober, of good behaviour, given to hospitality, apt to teach;" (1 Timothy 3:2)

Throughout The Scripture, the theme for authority rest in the ability of one to teach. In the following verse, it is affirmed that God does not subject the role of pastoring to women. The words/phrase "teach," "authority," and "over the man" are the clues. These are references to one being The Under Shepherd of The Flock. It is not to be interpreted that a woman may not teach a man, as is proven in the fact that Timothy was taught by his mother and grandmother (2 Timothy 1:5).

"But I suffer not a woman to teach, nor to usurp authority over the man, but to be in silence." (1 Timothy 2:12)

The correct listing of The Bible Ministries is 4-Fold:

1. *Apostles*
2. *Prophets*
3. *Evangelists*
4. *Pastors and teachers*

A common mistake by Bible scholars is the tendency *to read into* The Bible rather than *read from* The Bible. Do not forget that The Bible *speaks*; It does *not hear*. Being sure of the etymology (exegesis) of the words and punctuations will provide an initial understanding based on the current rules of literary interpretation. However, one must not stop at this juncture.

Simple observation:

What do the words say about **then, now, and later**? Are the words applicable to the original recipients, current readers, and/or future communities? Any reference to The Great Tribulation would be applicable only to those who shall exist immediately following The Rapture.

One of the major rejections of The Early Church Doctrine by The Reformers was its insistence on elevating the opinion of magistrates to be equal with that of The Scriptures. Such became the impetus of The Protestant Revolution. Martin Luther is noted for his rejection of The Church's dogma when found to be in contention with that of The Bible.

Scholars as well as The Reformers have agreed upon The Five Solae as being essential to the correct "interpretation" and "application" of God's Word!

FIVE SOLAE:

1) Sola gratia: "Alone"
   - o Salvation is made possible only by *grace,* and that the faith and works of men are secondary means that have their origins in and are sustained by *grace.*
2) *Sola fide:* "Alone"
   - o The doctrine asserts that it is on the basis of their *faith* that Believers are forgiven their transgressions of The Law of God, rather than on the basis of good works which they have done.
3) Solus Christus: "Alone"
   - o Salvation is by faith in *Christ* alone, through the atoning work of *Christ* alone, apart from individual works, and that *Christ* is the only mediator between God and man. It holds that salvation cannot be obtained without *Christ.*
4) Sola Scriptura: "Alone"
   - o Christian *Scripture* is the sole, infallible source of authority for Christian faith and practice.
5) *Sole Deo gloria:* "Alone"
   - o As a doctrine, it means that everything is done for *God's Glory* to the exclusion of mankind's self-glorification and pride. Christians are to be motivated and inspired by *God's Glory,* and not their own.

These Five Solae are considered by some Protestant groups to be the theological pillars of "The Reformation."[1] The key implication of the principle same authority as The Scriptures themselves. Hence, The Ecclesiastical Authority is viewed as subject to correction by The Scriptures, even by an individual member of The Church.

Martin Luther said, "a simple layman armed with Scripture is greater than the mightiest pope without it." The intention of The Reformation was to correct what he (Martin Luther) asserted to be the errors of The Catholic Church by appeal to the uniqueness of The Bible's textual authority. Catholic doctrine is based in sacred tradition, as well as Scripture. Sola Scriptura rejected the assertion that infallible authority was given to the magisterium to interpret both Scripture and tradition.[2]

Sola Scriptura, however, does not ignore Christian history, tradition, or The Church when seeking to understand The Bible. Rather, it sees The Church as The Bible's interpreter, the regula fidei (embodied in the ecumenical creeds) as the interpretive context, and Scripture as the only final authority in matters of faith and practice.[3] As Luther said, "The true rule is this: God's Word shall establish articles of faith, and no one else, not even an angel can do so."[4]

---

[1]   ll rights reserved.
Some Rights Reserved (2009-2018) by Ancient History Encyclopedia Limited, a non-profit organization registered in the UK.
Study to shew thyself approved unto God, a workman that needeth not to be ashamed, rightly dividing the word of truth. (2 Timothy 2:15)
From Wikipedia, the free encyclopedia
https://en.wikipedia.org/wiki/Syncretism
When the morning stars sang together, and all the sons of God shouted for joy? (Job 38:7)
[2]   I will ascend above the heights of the clouds; I will be like the most High. (Isaiah 14:14)
And he said unto them, I beheld Satan as lightning fall from heaven. (Luke 10:18)
"They that see thee shall narrowly look upon thee, and consider thee, saying, Is this the man that made the earth to tremble, that did shake kingdoms; That made the world as a wilderness, and destroyed the cities thereof; that opened not the house of his prison
[3]   ers? Isaiah 14:16-17 By the multitude of thy merchandise they have filled the midst of thee with violence, and thou hast sinned: t
[4]   ...therefore I will cast thee as profane out of the mountain of God: and I will destroy thee, O covering cherub, from the midst of the stones of fire. (Ezekiel 28:16)

HISTORICAL/CULTURAL ANALYSIS:

In The Schools of Systematic Studies, there are several different approaches to Bible criticism. For those of us who have accepted The Bible to be Verbal Plenary Inspired (VPI), a study in Historical/Cultural background is rather simple. We are simply attempting to understand the time in and of which the author wrote. In some cases, due to VPI, the author and the time of which he wrote were not the same. A clear example of this is The Book of Genesis. In Genesis, Moses wrote about a time filled with events that he was too young to have witnessed. Some of the critics would like to believe that Moses wrote from information passed down by The Elders, but The Bible speaks otherwise. Human knowledge of The Creation Week only began on The Sixth Day. However, Moses wrote about an Age before Dispensations (Genesis 1:1).

On the other hand, as Moses penned The Book of Exodus, it is evident that much of that which he wrote is contemporary to his time. One must progress toward The Historical/Cultural Analysis of The Scripture. Although words speak for themselves, they are often used in a context that may obliterate its Literal Interpretation.

> *And again I say unto you, It is easier for a camel to go through the eye of a needle, than for a rich man to enter into the kingdom of God.*
>
> *(Matthew 19:24)*

To interpret this verse literally means that wealth is a sure detriment to salvation. So, the reader must initially try this verse by each of the conditions from which Scripture canonization is applied. Did Jesus die for the salvation of all, or a select few?

> *That whosoever believeth in him should not perish, but have eternal life.*
>
> *(John 3:15)*

Interpreted in context, neither Matthew 19:24 nor John 3:15 is in conflict.

o   Simple observation: When reading about customs, classes, and special groups, one will gain a healthy insight into the conditions current during the time being written about. Words like "Pharisee" or "legions" are best understood by historical reference outside of The Bible, i.e., extra-Biblical study.

CONTEXTUAL ANALYSIS:

Using Contextual Analysis to evaluate texts english.unl.edu
By; Stephen C. Behrendt – Spring 2008

"A **contextual analysis** is simply an analysis of a text (in whatever medium, including multi-media) that helps us to assess that text within the context of its historical and cultural setting, but also in terms of its textuality – or the qualities that characterize the text as a text. A contextual analysis combines features of formal analysis with features of "cultural archeology," or the systematic study of social, political, economic, philosophical, religious, and aesthetic conditions that were (or can be assumed to have been) in place at the time and place when the text was created. While this may sound complicated, it is deceptively simple: it means "situating" the text within the milieu of its times and assessing the roles of author, readers (intended and actual), and "commentators" (critics, both professional and otherwise) in the reception of the text.

A contextual analysis can proceed along many lines, depending upon how complex one wishes to make the analysis. But it generally includes several key questions:

1. **What does the text reveal about itself as a text?**
    – Describe (or characterize) the language (the words, or vocabulary) and the rhetoric (how the words are

arranged to achieve some purpose). These are the primary components of style.

2. **What does the text tell us about its apparent intended audience(s)?**
   – What sort of reader does the author seem to have envisioned, as demonstrated by the text's language and rhetoric?

   – What sort of qualifications does the text appear to require of its intended reader(s)? How can we tell?

   – What sort of readers appear to be excluded from the text's intended audiences? How can we tell?

   – Is there, perhaps, more than one intended audience?

3. **What seems to have been the author's intention?** Why did the author write this text? And why did the author write this text in this particular way, as opposed to other ways in which the text might have been written?
   – Remember that any text is the result of deliberate decisions by the author. The author has chosen to write (or paint, or whatever) with these particular words and has therefore chosen not to use other words that she or he might have used. So we need to consider:

   – what the author said (the words that have been selected);

   – what the author did not say (the words that were not selected); and

   – how the author said it (as opposed to other ways it might or could have been said).

4. **What is the occasion for this text?** That is, is it written in response to:

 − some particular, specific contemporary incident or event?

 − some more "general" observation by the author about human affairs and/or experiences?

 − some definable set of cultural circumstances?

5. **Is the text intended as some sort of call to − or for − action?**
 − If so, by whom? And why?

 − And also, if so, what action(s) does the author want the reader(s) to take?

6. **Is the text intended rather as some sort of call to − or for − reflection or consideration rather than direct action?**
 − If so, what does the author seem to wish the reader to think about and to conclude or decide?

 − Why does the author wish the readers to do this? What is to be gained, and by whom?

7. **Can we identify any non-textual circumstances that affected the creation and reception of the text?**
 − Such circumstances include historical or political events, economic factors, cultural practices, and intellectual or aesthetic issues, as well as the particular circumstances of the author's own life."

What Does the Context Include when applied to Scripture interpretation?

"It is important to understand what is meant by "context" when using it to interpret a passage of Scripture. The context of a passage includes all the following things:

a)   The verses immediately before and after the passage.

b)   The paragraph and book in which the passage appears.

c)   Other books by this author, as well as the overall message of the entire Bible.

d)   The cultural environment of the time when the passage was written.

e)   The historical period (dispensation) of "Progressive Revelation" during which the passage was written."

Robert Gundry, Survey of the New Testament

SIMPLE OBSERVATION:

> *Verily I say unto you, There be some standing here, which shall not taste of death, till they see the Son of man coming in his kingdom."*
>
> *(Matthew 16:28)*

Some have questioned The Kingdom of God-the Millennium-suspiciously due to the apparent deaths of the three disciples who accompanied Jesus when He made the above statement. To question The Kingdom based on this one statement is to take this statement out of context. John's life experience certainly led him to the very Throne of God. The Book of Revelation attests to that fact. One's need to always satisfy an opinion based on personal experiences may lead to incorrect "interpretations."

THEOLOGICAL ANALYSIS:

One should consider The Theological Process before settling on a specific "interpretation." Keep in mind that one verse seldom constitutes Theology. Take for instance The Bible's reference to Spiritual gifts; they are listed in Romans, Ephesians and 1 Corinthians. Before settling on a conclusive explanation of Spiritual gifts, one should examine all that The Bible has to say on the subject.

Faith in God's Word is the essential ingredient in advancing ones' knowledge through wisdom to understanding. Faith is blind trust. It may require one, in certain circumstances, to act without understanding. Keep in mind that understanding, in this case, means that one might not know the outcome of the act. But never should there be a question as to why, or what is expected.

The Bible helps us to bridge the gap between reason and faith. Appropriately applied, there is really no conflict between the two. Reasoning is a God-given ability and God expects us to act upon it. (Isaiah 1:18) Essentially, The Bible is the conduit to faith. (Romans 10:17) One must reason that all human endeavors are charted and approved or disapproved through the writings of The Scriptures. Notwithstanding, God, through the presence of The Holy Spirit, speaks to our souls concerning His Will for our lives collectively, as well as individually. It is during those moments when reasoning seems to be a challenge that we turn to The Bible for confirmation, *"These were more noble than those in Thessalonica, in that they received the word with all readiness of mind, and searched the scriptures daily, whether those things were so."* (Acts 17:11)

While "faith," as a term, speaks of ones' trust-whether in matter, person, or God-it is only in God that we should not question or analyze His ability to do even those things which we consider impossible. When one is acting on the instructions of God, it is reasonable beyond a shadow of doubt.

Finally, biblical faith supports, without question, that the thing spoken shall occur without the possibility of failure. So, when The Bible proclaims faith as the substance of hope, it is not suggesting that faith should leave us hoping as though it might not happen. Biblical faith is rational assurance that the thing hoped for, although not yet fulfilled, is as assured as it would be if you were holding it in your hands. It is through the study of The Bible, from Genesis to Revelation, that we find it reasonable to apply utmost faith in all that God speaks.

A. *EMBEDDED THEOLOGY:*

"Embedded Theology, by definition, is what we gather implicitly from our church surroundings. It is our first understanding of the faith and the subsequent actions and practices that it entails – those things that have been learned and reinforced by the examples of our environments. Some would describe embedded theology as being like a Christian cultural heritage or the presuppositions and assumed beliefs that one holds."[1]

Think about the new convert who is told to repent, convert, and receive The New Birth. Shortly after confirming that these vital steps have been accomplished, the new brother/sister is directed to a verse of Scripture that confirms their new life in Christ.

> *For whosoever shall call upon the name of the Lord shall be saved.*
>
> *(Romans 10:13)*

Next, they are presented a few questions that will help their verification:

- *Did you call on the name of the Lord?*
- *Do you trust that God has done what He said He would do?*
- *Are you saved?*

Without any real biblical understanding, The New Saint in Christ goes out happy and rejoicing. If we were to place the theology of The New Believer in a category, it would be that of Embedded Theology. Why? Because everything, correct or not, that The New Convert knows is based on the witness of those who are endeared and held in high esteem, exclusive of The Bible.

---

[1] The prophets prophesy falsely, and the priests bear rule by their means; and my people love to have it so: and what will ye do in the end thereof? (Jeremiah 5:31)

When the members of a church receive all their Christian training based on church association, Embedded Theology is uncorroborated. Many of the beliefs and practices of the embedded culture are achieved through the most childish means of assimilation. It is safe to say that every human being utilizes an intuitive unexplainable gift that reaches, like a flower responding to the rays of the sun, for the presence of The Creator. However, there is an invisible barrier affecting human intellect that comes from the root of The Tree of The Knowledge of Good and Evil. Satan, as He did to our fore-parents (Adam and Eve), persuades the mind through soothing "interpretations" that poison the soul.

For example, the very first human sin involved the eating of a fruit. Is it possible that "the forbidden fruit" was an apple? If you answered "YES," and I argued that it was a banana, it is safe to say that we might both agree that it is possible that either you or I am correct.

But what if I look you squarely in the eye and respond "NO, it is absolutely, positively impossible that the fruit was an apple!" How would it make you feel? If the feelings or emotions tend to reach a level of annoyance or strong disagreement, it is because of Embedded Theology. Your opinion of your answer is apparently influenced by your association with those that you hold to be Fellow Believers. Without a doubt, the witness and "interpretations" of others is essential to the spreading of The Gospel. However, dependence on others, without personally searching The Scriptures for confirmation, is the primary cause for many misguided institutions.

> *Therefore leaving the principles of the doctrine of Christ, let us go on unto perfection; not laying again the foundation of repentance from dead works, and of faith toward God, Of the doctrine of baptisms, and of laying on of hands, and of resurrection of the dead, and of eternal judgment.*
>
> *(Hebrews 6:1, 2)*

B. *DELIBERATIVE THEOLOGY*

The second type of theology can be referred to as Deliberative Theology. It is "the understanding of faith that emerges from a process of carefully reflecting upon embedded theological convictions." Deliberative Theology includes a critical search of Bible Truths with the courage to be willing to discover inappropriate and or dangerous philosophical traits that damage the witness and truthfulness of The Local Church. Peace is a virtue that appeals without persuading. Being comfortable with untruths has greatly inhibited The Ministry of The Church. Of such peace Jesus said, *"Think not that I am come to send peace on earth: I came not to send peace, but a sword." (Matthew 10:34)*

One of the many notable quotes of the statesman, Thomas Paine is,

> *"A long habit of not thinking a thing wrong, gives it a superficial appearance of being right, and raises at first a formidable outcry in defense of custom. But the tumult soon subsides. Time makes more converts than reason."*

The vast array of denominations attests to the fact that Embedded Theology is very much alive and too many of those who depend solely upon it are not.[1] Regardless to what philosophy or theology that one holds, it is from the very Word of God, as provided in The Bible, that we shall be judged.

> *Blessed is he that readeth, and they that hear the words of this prophecy, and keep those things which are written therein: for the time is at hand.*
>
> *(Revelation 1:3)*

> *And I saw the dead, small and great, stand before God; and the books were opened: and another book was opened, which is the book of life: and the dead were judged out of those things which were written in the books, according to their works.*
>
> *(Revelation 20:12)*

Deliberative Theology is the will to see "the elephant in the living room" and then to follow-up with actions to remove it. If you agreed

---

[1] midst of the stones of fire." (Ezekiel 28:16)

Genesis 3:2-4 And the woman said unto the serpent, We may eat of the fruit of the trees of the garden: But of the fruit of the tree which is in the midst of the

above that an apple could have possibly been the fruit of our demise, let's take another look with the intent of seeing through the eyes of Scripture rather than culture.

> *And out of the ground made the Lord God to grow every tree that is pleasant to the sight, and good for food; the tree of life also in the midst of the garden, and the tree of knowledge of good and evil.*
>
> (Genesis 2:9)

Notice above that The Lord God made trees pleasant to sight and good for food from the ground; The Tree of Life *"also in the midst of the garden"*, and *"the tree of knowledge of good and evil."*

The editable fruit were of trees that were grown from the ground with roots buried deep, anchoring them to a permanent location. Not so for the *"tree of life"* or *"the tree of the knowledge of good and evil"*. The word *"midst,"* as illustrated below, may be interpreted in one or more of the four listed definitions:

o The middle position or part; the center: in the midst of the desert.

o A position of proximity to others: a stranger in our midst.

o The condition of being surrounded or beset by something: in the midst of all of our problems.

o A period of time approximately in the middle of a continuing condition or act: in the midst of the war.

To use the "tree of life" as a model with which the word "midst" may be understood brings us to the awareness of a movable presence in and among The Garden. Such would define the presence of The Lord (Tree of Life) and Satan (Tree of Knowledge of Good and Evil)-Tree, a symbol of their presence and viability, as a type of substance conveying life and/or death-not a vegetable substance of human consumption.

In which of the three categories will you find the apple? Is it from the edibles of the ground? Is it from The Tree of Life? Is it the fruit of The Tree of The Knowledge of Good and Evil? This is the answer coming from Eve:

Eve clearly distinguished the consumable fruit as a product of the "trees" of The Garden. But there was only one tree from which they were not to touch or eat from.

> *And the woman said unto the serpent, We may eat of the fruit*
> *of the trees of the garden: But of the fruit of the tree which is*
> *in the midst of the garden, God hath said, Ye shall not eat of*
> *it, neither shall ye touch it, lest ye die.*
>
> *(Genesis 3:2, 3)*

It was the tree that we listed above in the third category, *"the tree of knowledge of good and evil."* No, the apple could not have been the fruit of disobedience. It was, and remains to this day, an edible fruit that God intended to be consumed by human beings.

> *And God said, Behold, I have given you every herb bearing*
> *seed, which is upon the face of all the earth, and every tree,*
> *in the which is the fruit of a tree yielding seed; to you it shall*
> *be for meat.*
>
> *(Genesis 1:29)*

Adam's apple, and the thousands of visual cues that support The Embedded Theology of The Fall of Humanity, serves to prove how deeply affected humanity is due to the lack of Deliberative Theology. When faith meets understanding, it is only because one has dared questioned "why" rather than simply following the who, what, when, and where! Remember, faith makes sense, and that is reasonable.

C. REFLECTIVE THEOLOGY

Theological Reflections are responses to events, theoretical or practical, that may be related to something biblical or Spiritual. Most sermons include a great deal of associations that are to be considered for the purpose of encouraging faith or obedience. What you do with the knowledge you possess reflects upon your theology. The human logic system responds easily to visual cues. Leaders are often the catalyst of Embedded Theology and, therefore, every word spoken should be appropriately deliberated before reaching a conclusion.

The very popular, but incorrect, interpretation·of "Glossolalia" (speaking in tongue) as a sign of salvation may be the result of Reflective Theological responses. On April 17, 1906, during the apex of the ministry of William Seymour's teachings of tongues, the Los Angeles Daily Times sent a reporter to Seymour's revival:

> *On April 17, The Los Angeles Daily Times sent a reporter to the revival. In his article the next day, he baffooned the meeting and the pastor, calling the worshippers "a new sect of fanatics" and Seymour "an old exhorter." He mocked their glossolalia as "weird babel of tongues." More important than the critical opinions expressed by the reporter was the providential timing of his visit. The article was published on the same day as the great earthquake in San Fransciso. Southern Californians, already gripped with fear, learned of a revival where doomsday prophecies were common.[1]*

The fact of the earthquake being associated with the "dooms day" preaching and the need to speak in tongues (Glossolalia) reflected upon the peoples' interpretations of The Scriptures resulting in a worldwide movement. Today, Pentecostalism, as a movement, has found itself in many different denominations of Christianity. Does the timing or opinion of the pastors prove the "interpretations" to be correct?

> *That seeing they may see, and not perceive; and hearing they may hear, and not understand; lest at any time they should be converted, and their sins should be forgiven them.*
>
> *(Mark 4:12)*

Did anyone care to associate the earthquake with God's disapproval of the movement? In either case, the tool used would be Reflective Theology.

---

[1] I have planted, Apollos watered; but God gave the increase. (1 Corinthians 3:6)

SPECIAL LITERARY ANALYSIS:

The Bible contains books categorized initially by Testaments, then broken down into several different Genres. Understanding the genres will help in the appropriate application of The Scripture in question.

Simple Observation: When reading a book from The Old Testament Prophets, one would do well to anticipate God's message as that which confirms His control of future events and His personal manifestation in Earth.

Prophecy:

Let not them that are mine enemies wrongfully rejoice over me: neither let them wink with the eye that hate me without a cause.

(Psalm 35:19)

New Testament Prophecy goes deeply into the Spiritual fulfillment of Old Testament Prophecy.

But this cometh to pass, that the word might be fulfilled that is written in their law, They hated me without a cause.

(John 15:25)

Bible genres are Law, History, Poetry, Prophecy, Gospels, and Epistles. The genres should be interpreted based on The Testament in which they are located. That prevents incorrect explanations.

Simple observation:

I form the light, and create darkness: I make peace, and create evil: I the Lord do all these things.

(Isaiah 45:7)

So, what are we to think about evil? Should we dismiss it since God said He created it? No! We must search the other Scriptures and confirm God's message in context with His divine purpose. The Creator of The

Will of man is responsible for every act perpetrated by The Creature. God does not alibi His omnipotence by projecting the problems of the world as being beyond His control. All things occur based on God's Permissive Will. However, the foregone fact does not relieve the world of its responsibility to conform to The Divine Will of God. With responsibility comes consequences; therefore, everyone should beware:

> But he that shall blaspheme against the Holy Ghost hath never forgiveness, but is in danger of eternal damnation:
>
> (Mark 3:29)

Does the observation:

1. Reveal every fact completely?
2. Is it figurative (can I receive a deeper meaning from this Scripture)?
3. Does it provide a moral compass that I will use to navigate my actions?
4. Does it reach the supernatural (Spiritual realm)?

Even if your "observation" says that it does not, that of The Early Church Fathers agreed with each expectation.

The Council of Laodicea (A.D.363-ccclxiii), The Council of Hippo (A.D. 393-cccxciii) and the Council of Carthage (A.D. 397-cccxcvii) agreed on the following conditions of The New Testament.

1. Each book had to have been written by an Apostle or a close associate (Mark/Peter, Luke/Paul).
2. Each book had to be accepted by The Body of Christ at large.
3. Each book had to contain consistency of doctrine and orthodox teaching.
4. Each book had to bear evidence of high moral and Spiritual values reflecting the work of The Holy Spirit.

The Canon of Scripture by F. F. Bruce and Logos Bible Software

The Muratorian Canon (also called the Muratorian Fragment) is an ancient list of New Testament books–the oldest such list we have found. The original document, which was probably written in Greek, is dated to about A.D. 180 and lists 22 of the 27 books that were later included in The New Testament. This Canon was discovered by Italian Historian Ludovico Muratori in the Ambrosian Library in Northern Italy and was published by him in 1740. A common theme in the books accepted as canonical in The New Testament is:

1. Jesus is repeatedly referred to as "Lord." (Romans 10:9; Acts 2:36; Jude 17)
2. Jesus is equated with God. (John 1: 1-3; 20:28 Philippians 2:6-8)
3. Jesus took on human flesh. (John 1:14; 1 John 4:2)
4. Jesus died in the place of the sinners. (1 Corinthians 15:3)
5. Jesus was raised bodily from the dead. (Luke 24: 36-40; Acts 1:3; 2:24-35; 1 Corinthians 15:4)
6. Forgiveness of sin is only found through "Faith" in Him (John 6:47; Acts 13:38, 39; Galatians 2:15, 16)

The Muratorian Canon by F. F. Bruce and Logos Bible Software

Scripture "observation" provides us with an awareness (knowledge). However, alone, it does not give us the authority to explain appropriately (wisdom) the contents of the message. Such skills are the results of a careful and sincere deliberative study of the passage being considered. As learning is defined as a change in behavior, one must not stop at the ability to explain The Scripture, but must seek the ability to live (understand) The Scripture.

The mere discovery of an airplane constitutes knowledge and enables one to direct another to its location. But, having never seen one operate makes it impossible to explain its purpose. However, after observing the vehicle takeoff and land, one's knowledge would advance to an "interpretation" of its purpose, i.e., wisdom. To learn all that is required to safely operate the airplane places the person in the category of understanding. We must not stop at the initial "observation" of the Scripture or even the academic accomplishment of its wisdom, but prayerfully advance our study in search of the "application" (understanding). Do it!

CHAPTER 8

KNOWLEDGE "TO SEE" (OBSERVATION)

In the next three chapters, we shall look closer at Embedded, Deliberative and Reflective Theology. Each has been given a reference to Knowledge, Wisdom and Understanding. What do I see? What do I say? What do I do? We must answer these important questions before gaining the benefits of Bible "Interpretation."

STEP ONE: BIBLE METHODOLOGY

"Knowledge" What do I see? (Embedded Theology)

The High Recon:

Helicopter pilots are known for their ability to land their crafts in offsite locations. Having the ability to take off and land vertically makes the helicopter very versatile. However, when landing in an unapproved location, the pilot's first concern is the unknown danger lurking below. So, the pilot will circle the intended landing zone, paying close attention to the topography, to detect potential dangers. Once the pilot feels reasonably assured that the intended landing zone (LZ) is free of obstacles, a careful descent follows.

For The Bible scholar, the high recon is a general "observation" of the text in consideration. Before getting too deeply into the "interpretation" phase, the student will answer a few general questions.

After reading John 2:1-11, take time to answer the following questions:

1. What Testament?
2. What Genre?
3. Who is the Author?
4. What Chapter?
5. What Subject area?
6. What Paragraph?
7. Is it a repeated theme?

1. What Testament?
The New Testament

2. What Genre?
Gospel

3. Who is the Author?
John

4. What Chapter?
2:1-11

5. What is the Subject Area?
Marriage Feast

6. What are the various Paragraphs?
Examine The Scriptures for indications of the subject matter. Editors will sometimes use a pilcrow ("¶") at the beginning of a paragraph. If there are subtopics depicted or listed, give them consideration.

7. Is it a Repeated Theme?
The institution of Marriage is one of the most reoccurring themes in The Bible.

Having studied each of the foregone considerations, the verification of the frequency of the subject matter concludes the general "observation" (High Recon).

Your initial "observation" will almost always reveal a moral perceptible lesson. Using Scripture as an ethical compass to navigate through the maze of time is the first step in *obedience*. However, to land upon The Spiritual significance of The Scriptures, one must seek to descend deeper. Bible scholars are never surprised to learn that a previously interpreted thought concerning a passage of Scripture reveals a deeper truth, unseen for years.

The Low Recon

After the high recon, the helicopter pilot descends to a low recon. As the craft gets closer to the surface, the pilot can see things that were previously obscured or hidden. The lower altitude will allow for the detection of obstructions that were invisible from the higher recon altitude. Human quest penetrates the darkness. The advent of high-power lights (HPL), infrared (IR), and night vision goggles (NVG) enhanced the pilot's ability to see otherwise unseen obstacles. These discoveries simply allow the pilot to see that which was previously unseen during certain low light conditions. From the high recon, the tree in the landing zone (LZ) is easily seen. But not until up close is the protruding branch detectable.

Such is the logic of Bible "Observation." The initial "observation" will reveal those general facts. But a closer look at them may reveal a deeper awareness. For the pilot, certain conditions-night operations (obscured LZs)-require the aid of advanced optics (HPL-IR-NVG). For the student of The Bible, it is The Holy Ghost which always serves as advanced optics. Any literate human being may read The Bible (high recon). But only those who are filled with The Holy Ghost (unction) shall deeply discern its meaning (low recon).

> *But ye have an unction from the Holy One, and ye know all things. I have not written unto you because ye know not the truth, but because ye know it, and that no lie is of the truth.*
> *(1 John 2:20, 21)*

A quick reference of The Scriptures being considered has satisfied the high recon. We have a general idea what this Scripture is about. Our desire to know more is enhanced by the presence of The Holy Spirit. He is helping us to penetrate the veil of darkness with Spiritually Enhanced Illumination. Encyclopedias, Dictionaries, Concordances, and other extra-biblical works are the tools of every well-informed student of God's Word. It is from the proper use of these resources that the student can make good the low recon, i.e., close "observation."

In The Bible, a man from Ethiopia of great authority (a Eunuch), had traveled to Jerusalem to worship Jehovah. On his return home, he read a passage of Scripture from Isaiah 53:

> *He was oppressed, and he was afflicted, yet he opened not his mouth: he is brought as a lamb to the slaughter, and as a sheep before her shearers is dumb, so he openeth not his mouth. He was taken from prison and from judgment: and who shall declare his generation? for he was cut off out of the land of the living: for the transgression of my people was he stricken. And he made his grave with the wicked, and with the rich in his death; because he had done no violence, neither was any deceit in his mouth.*
>
> *(Isaiah 53:7-9)*

He was more than capable of reading and comprehending the literal words (Literary/Syntactical). However, he could not interpret its mystical (Contextual Analytics) meaning. Also note The Holy Spirit's role as the orchestrator of the events that brought Wisdom and Understanding to the otherwise vague "observation."

> *"And the angel of the Lord spake unto Philip, saying, Arise, and go toward the south unto the way that goeth down from Jerusalem unto Gaza, which is desert."*
>
> *(Acts 8:26)*

Philip was apparently motivated by obedience without a clue of that which he was about to become involved (Divine Appointment).

And he arose and went: and, behold, a man of Ethiopia, an eunuch of great authority under Candace queen of the Ethiopians, who had the charge of all her treasure, and had come to Jerusalem for to worship,

(Acts 8:27)

We might note at this moment that even Philip found himself observing The Eunuch from afar. He was taking part in his own high recon of the situation.

Was returning and sitting in his chariot read Esaias the prophet.
(Acts 8:28)

Philip did not approach the man until instructed by The Spirit to do so.

Then the Spirit said unto Philip, Go near, and join thyself to this chariot.

(Acts 8:29)

It was at that moment that Philip moved decisively toward the chariot and initiated a conversation that led to a divine epiphany for The Eunuch.

And Philip ran thither to him, and heard him read the prophet Esaias, and said, Understandest thou what thou readest?
(Acts 8:30)

Even the answer that Philip received from the man speaks of the work of The Holy Spirit, convicting our hearts to the desire of "the sincere milk" of The Word of God.

And he said, How can I, except some man should guide me? And he desired Philip that he would come up and sit with him.
(Acts 8:31)

The man that desired guidance from Philip is a type of us all. There are moments when, due to lack of Knowledge, we will require the careful guidance of those that are more experienced in the ways and words of our Lord (Ephesians 4:11, 12). The endless volumes of literary work that remains at our disposal speak to the due diligence and Godly scholarship of those that preceded us on this path of Knowledge, Wisdom and Understanding.

All are beholden on the support gained from the labor of others. Therefore, there should be a willingness to advance the cause, with the support of those who come after. Although The Scriptures, read from The Book of Isaiah, spoke of an occasion that might have been confused for any number of worldly events, Philip, using a now New Testament "interpretation," opened the man's Knowledge to the full and applicable "interpretation" thereof.

> Then Philip opened his mouth, and began at the same scripture, and preached unto him Jesus.
>
> (Acts 8:35)

Using the same Scripture, (Old Testament), Philip raised the man's consciousness from the literal "letter of the law" to the applicable (New Testament) "Spirit of The Law." It is also apparent that the man was directed by an established means by which the Jewish culture needed to comply, in the process of acknowledging Jesus as their Lord and Saviour, i.e., being Born Again. Note that Philip associated The Eunuch's salvation with The Ordinance of Baptism. Such is biblically required for those that are recanting Judaism. Although clearly not a member of The National House of Israel, The Eunuch was a confessed worshipper of Judaism (proselyte). Therefore he would, by necessity, have to comply with the mandate to Jews.

> Therefore let all the house of Israel know assuredly, that God hath made that same Jesus, whom ye have crucified, both Lord and Christ. Now when they heard this, they were pricked in their heart, and said unto Peter and to the rest of the apostles, Men and brethren, what shall we do? Then Peter said unto

them, Repent, and be baptized every one of you in the name of Jesus Christ for the remission of sins, and ye shall receive the gift of the Holy Ghost.

(Acts 2:36-38)

During their trek in the desert, they came upon a pool of water large enough to facilitate a baptism. Such is clearly a miracle, as is this entire Divine Appointment.

And as they went on their way, they came unto a certain water: and the eunuch said, See, here is water; what doth hinder me to be baptized? And Philip said, If thou believest with all thine heart, thou mayest. And he answered and said, I believe that Jesus Christ is the Son of God.

(Acts 8:36, 37)

Philip carried out his commission and was immediately removed from the man's presence. He had done all that God intended for the time being.[1]

And he commanded the chariot to stand still: and they went down both into the water, both Philip and the eunuch; and he baptized him. And when they were come up out of the water, the Spirit of the Lord caught away Philip, that the eunuch saw him no more: and he went on his way rejoicing.

(Acts 8:38, 39)

This beautiful passage of Scripture is just one of many examples in The Bible of how The Lord makes His Truths available to those who diligently seek Him.

Another such passage is the event revealed by John Mark of a blind man who encountered Jesus during His travels.

---

[1]

And these shall go away into everlasting punishment: but the righteous into life eternal. (Matthew 25:46)
And God blessed Noah and his sons, and said unto

And he took the blind man by the hand, and led him out of
the town; and when he had spit on his eyes, and put his hands
upon him, he asked him if he saw ought. And he looked up,
and said, I see men as trees, walking. After that he put his
hands again upon his eyes, and made him look up: and he was
restored, and saw every man clearly.

(Mark 8:23-25)

The man was *"blind"* and therefore he saw nothing. However, after his initial encounter with Jesus, he saw men as trees. Our first "observation" reveals a blind man. We may liken this condition to that of "dead eyes." As we look closer, we observe the man's encounter with Jesus, which made it possible for him to see, albeit not clearly.

The mere fact that the man received sight may be seen as the man receiving life. Since Jesus is The Creator, *all life* is a result of His Power. However, *such life* is not that which is required for one to have a relationship with God. Due to sin, man must be "born again." The initial life of humanity comes with a Will, and one must be willing to surrender that Will to the calling of Christ, if Relationship is to be received.

The man confessed that he was able to see. However, he stated that he saw men, not as men, but as trees. This is the condition of humanity when absent of The Spiritual Eyes that every "born-again" person receives. Our Spiritual Eyes open the moment we become New Creatures (Born Again). But even they must be cultured by an increasing acuity.

Beloved, now are we the sons of God, and it doth not yet
appear what we shall be: but we know that, when he shall
appear, we shall be like him; for we shall see him as he is.

(1 John 3:2)

"*After that he put his hands again upon his eyes and made him look up:*
and he was restored, and saw every man clearly." The word "again" deserves close attention in this passage. The Lord "again" touched the man and "made" him look up and he was "re"-stored, and "saw" every man

"clearly." At this point, The Lord reopened that which He alone had previously opened. Life is due to the creative power of God alone. However, if Eternal Life is to be received, one must be willing to receive the "New (re) Birth."

The initial "observation" (high recon) reveals the literal meaning of the words revealed by The Scriptures. Any literate person may receive a logical "interpretation" of them. However, for one to associate this Scripture with The New Birth, a closer "observation" (low recon) is required. And since such "understanding" must penetrate the darkness (HPL-IR-NVG), The Anointing (unction) of The Holy Spirit is a must. Prayer is the student's personal reminder that every study of God's Word should follow The Light of The Holy Spirit.

> *But the Comforter, which is the Holy Ghost, whom the Father will send in my name, he shall teach you all things, and bring all things to your remembrance, whatsoever I have said unto you.*
>
> *(John 14:26)*

Because the man referenced his sight of men as trees, it offers the student an even deeper opportunity to uncover Spiritual Truths. The man apparently knew the difference between trees and men. Therefore, it goes without saying, that although he had received sight, there was need for a clearer view.

Since The Bible is God's Word, every utterance of It has the power to enlighten. Some, unlike the blind man, will stop at the first "observation" of light and find themselves stumbling through life with half-baked (Embedded) ideas. Answering the call to prayerful (Deliberative) study, will remove the scales from one's Spiritual Sight revealing The Glorious Light (Reflective).

The concerns of the low recon are much the same as those of the high recon; it's just that we approach them more carefully.

OBSERVATION 1: WHAT GENRE?

From the "observation" platform, one must carefully consider The Scripture that is about to be challenged. Imagine going SCUBA (Self-Contained Breathing Apparatus) diving in an unfamiliar location. Would it not be prudent to ask around and to determine if there are any concerns that might enhance one's safety before aimlessly penetrating the depths of the water?

There are several different genres of Scripture, and each bears its own peculiar purpose. One should not expect to read and comprehend The Book of Revelation as one would the writings of The Apostle Paul. Whereas The Revelation speaks to Eschatology (The Study of End Times), Paul's Epistles (Formal Letters) speak more to the structure, doctrine, and teachings of the local assembly. So before diving into The Scripture, make it your business to know from which genre it speaks.

A word of caution: genres may change momentarily during your read. One must be alert for these occasions during the low recon. As an example, The Book of Revelation is prophetic. The first chapter immediately attests to that fact.[1] However, Chapters 2 and 3 read more like an Epistle. Such consideration may also be seen in The Book of Genesis, which falls under the genre of Historical Narrative/Epic. But Chapter 3 verse 15 may be categorized as Gospel. Pray for Spiritual Illumination as you look closer at The Scriptures. Even Paul had his eschatological moments.[2]

---

[1] them, Be fruitful, and multiply, and replenish the earth. (Genesis 9:1)
And Cain knew his wife; and she conceived, and bare Enoch: and he builded a city, and called the name of the city, after the name of his son, Enoch. (Genesis 4:17)
And they said, Go to, let us build us a city and a tower, whose top may reach unto heaven; and let us make us a name, lest we be scattered abroad upon the face of the whole earth. (Genesis 11:4)
As newborn babes, desire the sincere milk of the word, that ye may grow thereby: (1 Peter 2:2)

[2] SCHOOL OF EDUCATION AND COMMUNICATION Jönköping University English 61-90 hp C-essay 15 hp, Linguistics Tutor: Mattias Jakobsson Examiner: Mari-Ann Berg, Eila Hedvall

BSERVATION 2: WHO IS THE AUTHOR?

Who the author is might be confusing when only considering the title of the book. Although The Book of Luke was written by Dr. Luke, The Book of Ruth was reportedly written by Samuel. As in the case of the latter, the book itself does not specify the author; therefore, tradition has done so. Although The Book of Hebrews does not specify its' author, most scholars attribute authorship to the Apostle Paul. One important benefit of knowing the author is the ability to comprehend the era in which the book was written.

Knowing the history of the author will aid in the specific matters that veiled the time in which the author wrote.

When you read about the tax collector, it is advisable to search the conditions upon which taxes were levied. It will help you to understand the plight of the people and the prevailing rules of government. Such knowledge will greatly assist one's familiarization with the prevailing culture at that time. It will also help prevent taking The Scriptures out of context, which results in unfounded doctrinal applications.

> *Many will say to me in that day, Lord, Lord, have we not prophesied in thy name? and in thy name have cast out devils? and in thy name done many wonderful works? And then will I profess unto them, I never knew you: depart from me, ye that work iniquity.*
>
> *(Matthew 7:22, 23)*

OBSERVATION 3: WHO IS THE INTENDED AUDIENCE?

Praying for the insight to know to whom the particular Scripture was speaking will prevent many out of context "interpretations." Who is the intended audience? As simple as it may appear, the word "thou," for example, must be positively identified before one can correctly interpret the intended audience. "In the King James Version from 1611 there are eight different forms of personal pronouns for second person: the singular forms thou, thee, thy, thine and the corresponding plural forms ye, you, your and yours. Because of linguistic changes in the English language the number of the second person pronouns has declined during the centuries. Accordingly, in the New King James Version from 1990 these eight earlier pronouns are represented by only three pronouns: you, your, yours.[1]

And thou shalt speak unto him, and put words in his mouth: and I will be with thy mouth, and with his mouth, and will teach you what ye shall do.

(Exodus 4:15) KJV

Now you shall speak to him and put the words in his mouth. And I will be with your mouth and with his mouth, and I will teach you what you shall do.

(Exodus 4:15) New King James (NKJV)

From a literary perspective, the KJV is clear as to who is the intended audience. The first and last "you" of the NKJV, as an example, may be interpreted either singular or plural by the casual observer. Not so in the KJV, as the "thou" speaks specifically to one person and the "ye" specifically to more than one.

Many of the unfounded denominations of Christianity are a result of Scripture that was taken out of context and doctrinally applied. For example, The Seventh Day Adventist Church attempts to apply the following Scripture as a Christian rule:

Remember the sabbath day, to keep it holy. Six days shalt thou labour, and do all thy work: But the seventh day is the sabbath of the Lord thy God: in it thou shalt not do any work, thou, nor thy son, nor thy daughter, thy manservant, nor thy maidservant, nor thy cattle, nor thy stranger that is within thy gates:

(Exodus 20:8-10)

Denying or failing to apply this passage in perspective is a result of poor Theological Analytics, Historical/Cultural Analytics, as well

---

[1] Copyright © 2021 Spirit & Truth via

as Contextual Analytics. The following New Testament explanation to Jews concerning such should have made it clear that Sabbath Day Worship, as vital as it is to Judaism, is not a mandatory doctrine in Christianity. It was observed by Jews that The Disciples of Jesus did unacceptable toils on The Sabbath. This was their inquiry:

> *And the Pharisees said unto him, Behold, why do they on the sabbath day that which is not lawful?*
>
> *(Mark 2:24)*

An important, but easily overlooked, "observation" is the answer to the question: who are "they"? The answer is given in the preceding verse ... "*his disciples*" ... (Mark 2:23). The Disciples of Christ (The Church) are no longer under "The Letter of The Law," but "The Spirit of The Law." What is the purpose of the law? Christ explained as much with these words:

> *And he said unto them, The sabbath was made for man, and not man for the sabbath: Therefore the Son of man is Lord also of the sabbath.*
>
> *(Mark 2:27, 28)*

The Apostle Paul, once a Pharisee, understood the difference between The Letter of Judaism and The Spirit of Christianity, and explained as much to The Colossians:

> *Let no man therefore judge you in meat, or in drink, or in respect of an holyday, or of the new moon, **or of the sabbath days**:*
>
> *(Colossians 2:16)*

Christ's remarks are completely disregarded by The Seventh Day Adventist, or maybe simply misinterpreted. In either case, the denomination is one of syncretic persuasion.

God's Spirit shines all over The Letter of The Sabbath but remains hidden from those who refuse The Light of Christ. Any literate person may read The Scripture in question and assume "keeping The Sabbath" to be an applicable law. However, the reader that is endowed with The Light of Christ (Holy Ghost) will see, as finally did the blind man, clearly.

> *Having the understanding darkened, being alienated from the*
> *life of God through the ignorance that is in them, because of*
> *the blindness of their heart:*
>
> *(Ephesians 4:18)*

The Law is an essential tool for the maturation of humanity for the fulfillment of The Mission of God. However, The Present Dispensation, The Ecclesiastical, is well-endowed with The Spiritual attributes required to carry out the final stage of this Age. Paul's frustration of Christians who demonstrated such weak "interpretations" are found in these words: *"Are ye so foolish? Having begun in the Spirit, are ye now made perfect by the flesh?" (Galatians 3:3)* The ability to apply appropriately "The Letter of The Law" helps one's Knowledge of the "application" of The Spirit of The Law." To misunderstand the two may result in one's failure to allow Christ His rightful position of being their personal Lord.

> *Therefore the Jews sought the more to kill him, because he not*
> *only had broken the sabbath, but said also that God was his*
> *Father, making himself equal with God.*
>
> *(John 5:18)*

Know the audience and time of the message. Correctly interpret the writer's intent and apply it with respect for Christ's role as The Present King of Kings. (Matthew 28:18)

OBSERVATION 4: WHAT IS THE GEOGRAPHICAL LOCATION OF THE BOOK?

Knowing the location from which the book speaks is important because the book may be speaking about a location that is different from that of its author. Probably the best example of this is The Book of Genesis. Moses is the author. Yet he wrote about the events of Eden, the earthly Paradise of God. Moses (the author) and Eden (the place) were separated by over two thousand years. Therefore, the consideration of Moses' era alone will not facilitate one's awareness of the physical settings of Eden. Now add to the fact that Moses wrote about events that only God could have known, and one's acceptance of Verbal Plenary Inspiration (VPI) is a given. Through VPI, the faith in God's Word as being divine is easily accepted.

The following Scripture might be studied without consideration of geography. That could prevent one from seeing the mystical act of God and an all too important factor for a Jew converting to Christianity:

> *And the angel of the Lord spake unto Philip, saying, Arise, and go toward the south unto the way that goeth down from Jerusalem unto Gaza, which is desert.*
>
> *(Acts 8:26)*

If so, what very important "observation" might be over-looked? The words *"which is desert."* An important aspect of a desert is its absence of water. However, in the case of Philip, there was enough water to facilitate a baptism. The early Jewish Converts were required to be baptised before receiving the gift of The Holy Spirit. The Eunuch (a Jewish proselyte) was under the mandate of his Jewish brethren.

> *Therefore let all the house of Israel know assuredly, that God hath made that same Jesus, whom ye have crucified, both Lord and Christ.*
>
> *(Acts 2:36)*

In response to Peter's preaching of Jesus Christ as Lord, The Jews asked:

> *"Now when they heard this, they were pricked in their heart, and said unto Peter and to the rest of the apostles, Men and brethren, what shall we do?*
>
> *(Acts 2:37)*

Peter's response:

Then Peter said unto them, Repent, and be baptized every one of you in the name of Jesus Christ for the remission of sins, and ye shall receive the gift of the Holy Ghost.

(Acts 2:38)

Despite the Eunuch's circumstances, God made it possible for him to repent and to be baptized.

And as they went on their way, they came unto a certain water: and the eunuch said, See, here is water; what doth hinder me to be baptized?

(Acts 8:36)

An all too important lesson might be learned from the events involving The Eunuch: Christ is The Way of Salvation, despite the circumstances.

"And Philip said, If thou believest with all thine heart, thou mayest. And he answered and said, I believe that Jesus Christ is the Son of God. And he commanded the chariot to stand still: and they went down both into the water, both Philip and the eunuch; and he baptized him."

(Acts 8:37, 38)

Recalling the importance of every word, when trying to understand Scripture, proves here to be most vital. Cross-referencing the inaugural baptism of Jews with that of Gentiles shows a distinct difference in the order of The Baptism of The Holy Ghost. Such shall be covered more in detail in Chapter 11. Taking the time required to orient oneself with the topography in which The Scripture represents will afford valuable dividends in *correctly* "interpreting" The Scripture.

OBSERVATION 5: WHAT ARE THE MOST NOTABLE EVENTS OCCURRING?

The Bible has many memorable events that reveal notable episodes. The Creation, The Fall of Man, The First Murder, The Angels Assaults on Humanity, The Flood, The Tower of Babel, etc. are only a few. Are these episodes to be considered as narratives or historical? Narratives provide insight into the lives and characters of The Bible. Historical "observations" give the reader the awareness of the prevailing culture of times past.

In as few words as you can utter, answer the question–Why was this book written? The Book of Judges, as an example, chronicles the use of Judges who were divinely inspired to lead God's people in times of trouble. Its main premise is the exposure of the people's disobedience followed by petitions of mercy which usually led to their exoneration. Once the people were free of their oppressors, they returned to their unfaithful ways, thereby continuing the downward spiral.

A more in-depth look at this trend points to the DNA (deoxyribonucleic acid) of evil that every human being must overcome by The Death, Burial, and Resurrection of Jesus The Christ. Use every available resource to acquaint yourself with the special literary tools needed to correctly place The Scripture being considered in the appropriate genre. It greatly enhances one's ability to properly assimilate its meaning.

OBSERVATION 6: WHAT ARE THE MOST IMPORTANT REPEATED WORDS AND PHRASES?

REPETITION

Repetition of words and phrases is a long time employed stratagem of writers who are attempting to establish a memorable point. Most song writers will add a familiar hook in their lyrics. It is the hook and the melody that keeps the audience interested.

Martin Luther King's speech, "I Have a Dream," is remembered most by the repeating of the phrase "I have a dream." Before each of Dr. King's notable renderings, he began by emphasizing that he had a dream. Look at the following excerpts from his speech.

And even though we face the difficulties of today and tomorrow, *I still have a dream* deeply rooted in the American dream.

I have a dream that one day this nation will rise up and live out the true meaning of its creed: "We hold these truths to be self-evident, that all men are created equal."

I have a dream that one day on the red hills of Georgia, the sons of former slaves and the sons of former slave owners will be able to sit down together at the table of brotherhood.

I have a dream that one day even the state of Mississippi, a state sweltering with the heat of injustice, sweltering with the heat of oppression, will be transformed into an oasis of freedom and justice.

I have a dream that my four children will one day live in a nation where they will not be judged by the color of their skin but by the content of their character.

I have a dream today!

Although memorable and profound, the above words are but an example of God's original use of repetition as means of emphasizing a more important point. God instituted language as a means of not only communicating, but also documenting. Only humans can read, write, and speak in a universal tongue. God instituted a literary type of beauty with the art of composition. Where He intended emphasis is clearly seen in the use of repetition and parallelism. Repetition and parallelism are forms of biblical poetry that weave the reader into the seams of the message.

Today, one need only to repeat sayings such as "Just Do It" or "Salt Life" and people get the point. In The Book of Deuteronomy, God established the code of authenticity. In The Ancient World, a thing was considered valid only if it were corroborated by two or three witnesses.

One witness shall not rise up against a man for any iniquity, or for any sin, in any sin that he sinneth: at the mouth of two witnesses, or at the mouth of three witnesses, shall the matter be established.

(Deuteronomy 19:15)

The Gospels are eyewitness accounts of The Life of Jesus The Christ. There are four different, yet collaborative, accounts of The Life of Jesus. The Lord provided the synoptic (3) agreement, plus one additional (John's Gospel) witness that went beyond Jesus' earthly pedigree to His Heavenly Deity. Jesus is the most important person in The Bible. All other Scriptures, either directly or indirectly, relate to the importance of Jesus.

And beginning at Moses and all the prophets, he expounded unto them in all the scriptures the things concerning himself.

(Luke 24:27)

For had ye believed Moses, ye would have believed me: for he wrote of me. But if ye believe not his writings, how shall ye believe my words?

(John 5:46, 47)

There are also smaller points of repetition. "Verily, verily" and "holy, holy, holy" are two examples. Repetition of a word or phrase draws attention to the importance placed on the matter being revealed. Also note below the capitalization of "Verily" and "Except" as each is preceded by a comma. Such "observation" places exceptional importance and consideration to the point being made. In this case, failure to comply would result in eternal damnation!

Jesus answered and said unto him, Verily, verily, I say unto thee, Except a man be born again, he cannot see the kingdom of God.

(John 3:3)

And the four beasts had each of them six wings about him; and they were full of eyes within: and they rest not day and night, saying, Holy, holy, holy, Lord God Almighty, which was, and is, and is to come.

(Revelation 4:8)

Repetition focuses on the semantics (meaning) of the subject matter. There are several types of repetition depending on where exactly in the sentence the repeated words appear.

It is not uncommon for a speaker to say that he/she is using a "figure of speech" (Synecdoche) or "rhetoric" when attempting to clarify a point. God, in His infinite wisdom, simply used them to emphasize those points that He determined to be more important to His reader.

ANADIPLOSIS:

Repetition of the last word or phrase of one line as the first word of the next. ("rely on his honor—honor such as his?")

Anadiplosis is from the Greek prefix ana (again) and diploun (to double) or diplous (double) and is the very first figure of speech used in The Bible.

> *1. In the beginning God created the heaven __and the earth. 2.__*
> *__And the earth__ ... (Genesis 1:1, 2)*

Notice that in verse 1, The Scripture speaks of both Heaven and Earth. However, in verse 2, it speaks only of The Earth. Emphasis is placed on The Earth as the major reference to which most of Genesis shall apply. It is vitally important that humanity understand its role in God's cosmos. Therefore, God opens His Book with a breakdown of that which affected the habitation of humanity.

Article By Spirit & Truth
Anadiplosis

"This article will cover the figure Anadiplosis, which is the repetition of the same word or words at the end of one sentence and the beginning of the next, or at the end of one phrase and the beginning of the next. Anadiplosis is from the Greek prefix ana, again, and diploun, to double, or diplous, double, and it is the very first figure of speech used in the Bible.

Genesis 1:1 and 2 (KJV)

(1) In the beginning God created the heaven **and the earth**.
(2) And the earth was without form, and void; and darkness was upon the face of the deep...

Notice that <u>Genesis 1:1</u> refers to both the heaven and the earth, but the second verse refers only to the earth. Thus there is a clear emphasis on the earth and God's relation to it, which we see all throughout early Genesis. When it comes to the Passover lamb, Anadiplosis places a special emphasis on the lamb, the "flock animal" that was to be slain. It is worth noting that although almost all versions of the Bible read "lamb" in verses 4 and 5 of <u>Exodus 12</u>, the Hebrew word she does not mean "lamb," but is the generic word for an animal from the flock, and can refer to a sheep or a goat.

<u>**Exodus 12:4**</u> **and 5 (KJV)**
(4) And if the household be too little for the lamb [lit. "a flock animal"], let him and his neighbor next unto his house take it according to the number of the souls; every man according to his eating shall make your count for **the lamb ["the flock animal"]**.

(5) Your lamb ["a flock animal"] shall be without blemish, a male of the first year: ye shall take it out from the sheep, or from the goats:

By repeating the "flock animal" at the end and beginning of the sentence, God places his emphasis on the importance of its part in the Passover. Furthermore, the figure of speech is even clearer in Hebrew than in English because the word "your" does not appear at the front of verse 5 in the Hebrew text, but occurs later in the verse. Unfortunately for Bible students, many modern versions lose the emphasis that the figure of speech brings to the text because they translate it right out of the Bible.

For example, look at the NIV:

Exodus 12:4 and 5

(4) If any household is too small for a whole lamb, they must share one with their nearest neighbor, having taken into account the number of people there are. You are to determine the amount of **lamb** needed in accordance with what each person will eat.

(5) The **animals** you choose must be year-old males without defect, and you may take them from the sheep or the goats.

First and most obviously, there is no Anadiplosis in the NIV at all. The noun "flock animal," has been moved from the end of verse 4 into the middle of the verse, where it is translated as "lamb." Second, although the Hebrew word ending verse 4 and starting verse 5 is the same singular noun, the NIV translates it "lamb" in verse 4 and "animals" in verse 5.

Given that the Anadiplosis emphasizes the flock animal, the lamb, we must ask, "Why would God emphasize the animal in the first place?" The answer to that lies in the whole concept of the Passover and the importance of the shedding of blood. Think about it. God did not need to have the Israelites shed the blood of a Passover lamb to ensure their protection, as evidenced by the fact that in 10 plagues upon Egypt, the fourth was swarms of flies, but God protected the Israelites from the flies such that there were no flies where the Israelites lived (Exod. 8:22). The fifth plague was the death of Egyptian livestock, but no Israelite livestock died (Exod. 9:4-7). The seventh plague was hail, but no hail fell where the Israelites lived (Exod. 9:26). The ninth was darkness over the land of Egypt for three days, but there was light where the Israelites lived (Exod. 10:23).

So after protecting the Israelites from the brunt of the plagues without them having to do anything for their own protection, why does God have them kill a flock animal, a lamb or a goat, in order to be protected from the last plague? The answer is that the death of the lamb or goat, and the putting blood on the doorposts, points to the life and death of Jesus, who is called "our Passover" in 1 Corinthians 5:7."[1]

Attempting to rewrite that which God has written, dangerously impacts the exegesis He intended.

ANAPHORA:

Repetition of a word or phrase at the beginning of several subsequent clauses or phrases. (Lincoln's "we cannot dedicate—we cannot consecrate—we cannot hallow—this ground")

Most Bible readers are soon attracted to a passage referred to as The Beatitudes. Jesus uses anaphora to capture the reader's attention and to convey a string of assurances:

---

[1]Beware lest any man spoil you through philosophy and vain deceit, after the tradition

3 Blessed are the poor in spirit: for theirs is the kingdom of heaven.

4 Blessed are they that mourn: for they shall be comforted.

5 Blessed are the meek: for they shall inherit the earth.

6 Blessed are they which do hunger and thirst after righteousness: for they shall be filled.

7 Blessed are the merciful: for they shall obtain mercy.

8 Blessed are the pure in heart: for they shall see God.

9 Blessed are the peacemakers: for they shall be called the children of God.

10 Blessed are they which are persecuted for righteousness' sake: for theirs is the kingdom of heaven.

(Matthew 5:3-11)

11 Blessed are ye, when men shall revile you, and persecute you, and shall say all manner of evil against you falsely, for my sake.

There are far more who are familiar with The Beatitudes as blessings than are those who have memorized them. Therefore, The Lord's Words do exactly what He determined the anaphora to do; they reassure the reader of Jesus as being The "Blessing."

The Ten Commandments are another passage where anaphora is used. "Thou shalt, Thou shalt not," Exodus 20. If one were to query the average Bible student concerning The Ten Commandments, the findings will prove that there are far more who are aware of them than are those who can recite them. God, by the repeated use of, "Thou Shalt," emphasizes His superiority and man's duty to comply with His Will.

Also, there is Ecclesiastes 3:1-8 which repeatedly emphasizes "There is a time." The word "time" appears in The Bible nearly 750 times. Without saying, time is important to the mission of which each of God's Creatures must endure. For humanity, God has appointed a time for every conceivable event as a portal to Judgement and ultimately to Eternity. That there is "a time" is firmly implanted in the minds of Bible students because of the emphasis made in Ecclesiastes 3.

EPISTROPHE:

Repetition of the same word at the end of every line or phrase.

An epistrophe is the opposite of an anaphora in that the latter repeats the words at the beginning of a sentence or clause, whereas the former repeats the words at the end of the sentence or clause. Think of them as bookends beginning with "A" and ending with "E."

"We are familiar with Epistrophe in Lincoln's Gettysburg Address, which speaks of "...that government of the people, by the people, and for the people, shall not perish from the earth." Lincoln wanted "the people" to know that government is for them and not against them.

Paul's address to the people of Rome was equally assuring as to the protection afforded them by God:

...If God is for us, who can be against us? (Romans 8:31)

The repeated use of the word "us" emphasizes God's protection in all matters. It brings assurance to the reader.

Note the emphasis placed on the repeated words of the following:

(Psalm 118:10-12) (KJV)
(10) All nations compassed me about: but <u>in the name of the LORD will I destroy them.</u>

(11) They compassed me about; yea, they compassed me about: but <u>in the name of the LORD I will destroy them.</u>

(12) They compassed me about like bees; they are quenched as the fire of thorns: for <u>in the name of the LORD I will destroy them.</u>

This is God's repeated emphasis that the victory belongs to Him. "In His name" implies that The Enemy must be His enemy and the response has to be in His Will. Look closely at the above Scriptures and see if you can reason repetitions of other classifications.

The following New Testament references place emphasis on the word "child." The literal meaning is self-evident; however, the allegorical meaning may speak of the child as an adult unsaved, and a man as the saved.

When I was a child, I spake as a child, I understood as a child, I thought as a child: but when I became a man, I put away childish things.

(1 Corinthians 13:11) (KJV)

As a student of The Bible, one should examine closely The Scriptures for those embedded repetitions that enlighten the reader to a more vivid understanding.

SYMPLOCE:

Combination of anaphora and epistrophe. Repetition is both at the beginning and at the end. ("When there is talk of hatred, let us stand up and talk against it. When there is talk of violence, let us stand up and talk against it." — Bill Clinton)

Symploce adds emphasis on both ends of the statement or clause. The redundancies draw the reader deeply into the full meaning.

Their land also is full of silver and gold, neither is there any end of their treasures; their land is also full of horses, neither is there any end of their chariots:

(Isaiah 2:7)

Their land also is full of idols; they worship the work of their
own hands, that which their own fingers have made:

(Isaiah 2:8)

The Apostle Paul used Symploce to emphasize the truth of The
Resurrection. By doing so, he helps his reader to accept, appreciate
and understand, by faith, an event that must occur in the life of The
Believer.

(1 Corinthians 15:42-44)

42 So also is the resurrection of the dead. It is sown in
corruption; it is raised in incorruption:

43 It is sown in dishonour; it is raised in glory: it is sown in
weakness; it is raised in power:

44 It is sown a natural body; it is raised a spiritual body. There
is a natural body, and there is a spiritual body.

The consecutive repeating of the words "sown" and "raised" leaves
The Believer with a firm reassurance of life after death. The importance
of The Spiritual Life, although often denied, is that on which Paul
wanted The Corinthians to focus.

Symploce was also used by Paul to bring clarity to a misinterpretation
that exists until this present time:

What is it then? I will pray with the spirit, and I will pray
with the understanding also: I will sing with the spirit, and I
will sing with the understanding also.

(1 Corinthians 14:15)

Here the two words "spirit" and "understanding" are emphasized to
help the reader appreciate the importance of intelligible sound. Whether
"praying" or "singing," both a method of praise, one must invoke with
understanding rather than confusion. As previously mentioned, there is
yet confusion relative to the appropriate understanding of Glossolalia.

However, it is so because of one's lack of understanding the semantics of linguistics. Paul used the above Symploce with intent to bring clarity to: *"For if I pray in an unknown tongue, my spirit prayeth, but my understanding is unfruitful." (1 Corinthians 14:14)* As concluded in the Symploce of verse 15, understanding is that which God gives to one's Spiritual insight or unction.

POLYPTOTON:

Polyptoton is the repetition of the same word with the same meaning, but in a different case, mood, tense, person, degree, number, gender, etc.[1] *(as in Tennyson's "my own heart's heart, and ownest own, farewell")*

Polyptoton places emphasis by replaying, albeit in a different tense, the same root word. Observe how each expression, by use of polyptoton, brings out the vivid expression of the statement.

> *Numbers 16:30. "But if the Lord make a new thing." Hebrew, create a creation: i.e., do something wonderful.*
>
> *1 Samuel 4:5.- "All Israel shouted with a great shout": i.e., with a very loud and prolonged or sustained cry.*
>
> *2 Samuel 12:16.- "And David fasted," lit., fasted a fast: i.e., completely or truly fasted.*
>
> *2 Samuel 13:36.- "And all his servants wept very sore." In Hebrew the figure is "wept a great weeping greatly."*
>
> *1 Kings 1:40.- "The people piped with pipes, and rejoiced with great joy": i.e., their joy scarcely knew bounds.*
>
> *2 Kings 4:13.- "Thou hast been careful for us with all this care": i.e., exceedingly careful.*

---

2 Kings 13:14.- "Now Elisha was fallen sick of his sickness":
i.e., was exceeding sick so that he died.

Polyptoton is used throughout The Bible in both Testaments. It makes that which is clear even clearer due to the repeated reference of the affected verb, noun or adverb.

(Matthew 7:1, 2)
1. Judge not, that ye be not judged. 2. For with what judgment
ye judge, ye shall be judged: and with what measure ye mete,
it shall be measured to you again.

"Polyptoton may be used with the variant form of an active and passive verb to signify the performance of a single action by one and to the other. An effective repetition of the inflectional ending of a word merely ties the wording of a sentence together in such form that denotes the same reciprocal relationship."[1]

"He that hath ears to hear, let him hear." (Matthew 11:15)

(Elijah and John the Baptist)

"Who hath ears to hear, let him hear." (Matthew 13:9) (The
parable of the sower)

The various classifications of repetition, with adequate study, will surely enhance the reader's ability to "hear" with greater emphases the message of The Word of God.

---

[1] In Judaism, Holy Spirit" Holy Spirit (Hebrew: רוח הקודש, ruach ha-kodesh) refers to the divine force, quality, and influence of God over the universe or over God's creatures, in given contexts. Alan Unterman the death of the cross.

OBSERVATION 7: IS THERE ANY PARALLELISM TO BE CONSIDERED?

PARALLELISM[1]

Parallelism is another method used in grammar which reinforces a point by two different but agreeable renderings. While Repetition focuses on meaning (semantics), Parallelism focuses more on structure (syntax). In Hebrew writings, there are several different types of Parallelism.

The main thrust of Parallelism is the corroborated rendering of Bible Truths emphasized redundantly. One should be mindful of Parallelism normally found in paragraphs exemplified through corresponding words, terms, phrases or even verses. The second or successive statement(s) add to the initial rendering. There are three main types of Parallelisms: Synonymous, Antithetical, and Synthetic.

SYNONYMOUS:

As the name implies, this type has the second or parallel line saying about the same thing as the first—for emphasis. Proverbs is especially full of these. Be vigilant for the conjunction "and."

> *In the way of righteousness is life; and in the pathway thereof there is no death. (Proverbs 12:28)*

> *I am the rose of Sharon, and the lily of the valleys. (Song of Songs 2:1)*

The following words of Jesus, misinterpreted, have led some to teach that water baptism is inferred in Jesus' conversation with Nicodemus.

> *Jesus answered and said unto him, Verily, verily, I say unto thee, Except a man be born again, he cannot see the kingdom of God.*
>
> *(John 3:3)*

---

[1]

The words "born again" apparently struck Nicodemus as an impossible event among humanity. Therefore, focusing entirely on the human limitation, *"Nicodemus saith unto him, How can a man be born when he is old? can he enter the second time into his mother's womb, and be born?"* (John 3:4)

> *Jesus answered, Verily, verily, I say unto thee, Except a man be born of water and of the Spirit, he cannot enter into the kingdom of God.*
>
> (John 3:5)

By repeating the words, "Verily, verily" (anaphora), Jesus is signaling the divine importance of the message. One might never come to the knowledge of Sarah's age when she conceived Isaac without any collateral damage. But not so concerning The New Birth. "Verily, verily" and "Except" should leave no doubt of the emphatic requirement in the response of Christ. Jesus was undoubtably speaking to Nicodemus concerning the prerequisite of Salvation. Verse 6 serves as a Synonymous Parallelism of verse 5.

> *That which is born of the flesh is flesh; and that which is born of the Spirit is spirit.*
>
> (John 3:6)

The point made clear is that the word "water" in verse "5" is an allegorical rendering explained in verse "6" as "flesh." The word "Spirit" in verse "5" is repeated (emphasizing its importance) in verse "6." In the big picture, Jesus was simply explaining to Nicodemus that to be born again was not a matter of *physical birth*, as Nicodemus had intimated, but a *Spiritual birth*!

Implying that "born of water" means to be baptized may certainly be taught as a literal image of a Spiritual Truth. However, it is not that of which Jesus spoke to Nicodemus. One may use the words of The Apostle Paul for such renderings with perfect impunity:

Therefore we are buried with him by baptism into death: that like as Christ was raised up from the dead by the glory of the Father, even so we also should walk in newness of life.

(Romans 6:4)

Buried with him in baptism, wherein also ye are risen with him through the faith of the operation of God, who hath raised him from the dead.

(Colossians 2:12)

As immersed represents the embryo prior to the physical birth (water), it also represents the soul prior to The Spiritual Birth (Spirit). *"That which is flesh is flesh and that which is Spirit is Spirit."* Therefore, we must conclude that Jesus was telling Nicodemus that he had to be born again Spiritually and not physically. In this rendering the reader must make the connection without the use of a conjunction.

ANTITHETIC:

Antithetic Parallelism is a means by which a point is made by using contrasting views that arrive at the same conclusion. It is another means by which a point is made more than once in a statement. Such persistence speaks to the seriousness of the point being made. Be aware of the conjunction "but-than" between the phrases.

This type puts two lines "against" each other that form a contrast:

For the Lord knoweth the way of the righteous: but the way of the ungodly shall perish.

(Psalm 1:6)

Hatred stirreth up strifes: but love covereth all sins.

(Proverbs 10:12)

It is better to dwell in a corner of the housetop, than with a brawling woman in a wide house.

(Proverbs 21:9)

He that keepeth the commandment keepeth his own soul; but
he that despiseth his ways shall die.

(Proverbs 19:16)

"*He that keepeth the commandment*" is the opposite of "*he that despiseth his ways*". The result is life or death, which is also a contrast or Antithetical. The reader may use both renderings as a means by which their own actions, or lack of the same, may be considered. However, the author's purpose in the use of contrasting renderings is that of warning the reader to not choose the latter (death).

In the following verse, the reader is not only provided a contrasting view, but also an allegory. The words "heart" and "right & left" speak of a deeper meaning than the literal terms imply. Initial "observation" may lead one to any number of conjectures. But the proper "interpretation" speaks of an essential need for one who desires to be saved.

A wise man's heart is at his right hand; but a fool's heart at
his left.

(Ecclesiastes 10:2)

The word "heart" in this case speaks of the whole being of a person: "*And God, which knoweth the hearts, bare them witness, giving them the Holy Ghost, even as he did unto us;*" *(Acts 15:8)* The "right hand" verses the "left" hand may be seen in: "*And he shall set the sheep on his right hand, but the goats on the left.*" *(Matthew 25:33)* You may have noticed that the mentioning of the right and left in Matthew is also Antithetical. One leads to life while the other means death. It is also noteworthy that the "right hand" speaks of The Love of God while the left speaks of His Justice; so, heart-love and mind-justice. One should bid for God's Love and not His Justice. The choice either way (contrast) will lead to a critical end.

SYNTHETIC:

Since Synthetic Parallelism is considered no Parallelism, why is it considered? It is another means by which the author generates an awareness of an all-important point. The point being made is singular, but the reader is brought to it through several different perspectives. The use of Repetition of meaning reinforces the point. One sure consideration of Synthetic Parallelism is the fact that it is neither Synonymous nor Antithetical. Although that might sound rhetorical, and if so, it is because it is.

The second line of poetry builds up (synthesis is Greek for "putting together") the thought in the first line:

> *The Lord is my shepherd;*
> *I shall not want.*
> *(Psalm 23:1)*

> *Keep thy heart with all diligence;*
> *for out of it are the issues of life.*
> *(Proverbs 4:23)*

> *"An high look, and a proud heart, and the plowing of the*
> *wicked, is sin."*
> *(Proverbs 21:4)*

Rather than speaking expressly of the same nature, albeit in a different tone, the author speaks about a progression of events which conclude in sin.

- *The high and mighty attitude*
- *A heart filled with pride*
- *A selfish walk*

These are several of the ingredients of a life of sin. Of course, they are not Synonymous nor are they Antithetical. The author is either repeating, albeit in different words, or contrasting the same rendering.

But they are generated terms that magnify by means of communication, a point that is absolutely required if one is to shun evil.

Another type of Synthetic Parallelism brings the reader to a point of "observation" where an action is compared to another action of greater or lesser consequences.

> *"The sacrifice of the wicked is abomination: how much more,*
> *when he bringeth it with a wicked mind?"*
>
> *(Proverbs 21:27)*

At face value, the clause *"The sacrifice of the wicked is abomination"* should cause one to be admonished of their evil ways. Just the word "abomination" (exceptionally loathsome, hateful, sinful, wicked...) is enough to perk the reader's interest. However, the author adds to one's consideration a question: *"how much more, when he bringeth it with a wicked mind?"* As bad as an abomination is, the reader is forced to consider that there is something worse i.e., *"when he bringeth it with a wicked mind?"* It is here, through the understanding of Parallelisms, that the reader may calculate the difference between sin and iniquity. The former, any act against The Will of God, even without knowledge; but the latter, an intentional act against God's Will. As you can see, the latter is greater than the former.

Parallelism, as a study, includes other classifications with either general or specificity focus.

FORMAL:[1]

This type is parallel in form only; the two (or more) lines don't contrast, expand, or emphasize. It is just two lines of poetry put together to express a thought or theme:

> *Yet have I set my king*
> *upon my holy hill of Zion. (Psalm 2:6)*

---

[1] Genesis 2:1-2 Thus the heavens and the earth were finished, and all the host of them. And on the seventh day God ended his work which he had made; and he rested on the seventh day from all his work which he had made.

In Formal Parallelism, sometimes termed Synthetic Parallelism, the two lines have a formal relationship defined by rhythm or line length. But the A-line is semantically continued in the B-line. The couplet contains only one complete sentence, not two coordinated sentences, as in the other types of Parallelism. Counting the words in the following translation works. However, some Hebrew translations to English require more words than the original.

> *Many there be which say of my soul,*
> *There is no help for him in God. Selah. (Psalm 3:2)*

Hebrew poetry seems to be governed by a basic balance between the lines of a couplet (or triplet) whereby each line has the same number of word units. Most couplets have three major stressed word units in each line resulting in a 3 + 3 pattern.

EMBLEMATIC:

Emblematic Parallelism always compares the first line to the next. But it is not to be confused with Synonymous Parallelism. The lines in Emblematic Parallelism are reliant on each other, unlike Synonymous. Synonymous Parallelism does not make comparisons, but repeats a similar concept.

Emblematic Parallelism generally uses similes or metaphors to compare one thing to another. In this proverb:

> *A word fitly spoken is like apples of gold in pictures of silver*
> *(Proverbs 25:11)*

This Parallelism weaves beauty into the adage, and the poetry is richer because of the device that is being used.

If Proverbs 25:11 were written in Synonymous Parallelism, it would read:

> "A word fitly spoken is a phrase said at the right time."

A figure of speech in the first line of poetry illustrates the content of the second line:

> *As the hart panteth after the water brooks, so panteth my soul after thee, O God.*
>
> *(Psalm 42:1)*

> *As a jewel of gold in a swine's snout, so is a fair woman which is without discretion.*
>
> *(Proverbs 11:22)*

Another example of Emblematic Parallelism is found in Proverbs 27:15:

> *A continual dropping in a very rainy day and a contentious woman are alike*

This couplet compares a repetitive annoyance with a spouse who picks fights. The emblem, or symbol, in this couplet is a continual drip. One may feel trapped in his house on a rainy day, just as he may feel trapped in an argument. Many emblematic devices are found in The Proverbs because they teach lessons through lively word choice.

Proverbs 27:17 is one of the more popular proverbs:

> *Iron sharpeneth iron; so a man sharpeneth the countenance of his friend.*

The emblem in this proverb is iron, which becomes stronger and more useful when sharpened with another iron. This is compared to a person who becomes stronger and more useful when in a relationship with a friend. The proverb is teaching that humans are made better when sharing life with each other. We all can become sharper in spirit when we are friends with other believers.

As you read The Bible, especially The Hebrew Old Testament, take your time and look for the frequent uses of Parallelism. The authors were heavily dependent on them for emphasis. Because of the broad use of different types of Synthetic Parallelism, the best approach at discovering it is by elimination. Most often, if it is Parallelism-but not Synonymous (formal) or Antithetical-then it is Synthetic.

To which of the three categories, Synonymous, Antithetical or Synthetic does the following verse belong?

> *"It is better to hear the rebuke of the wise, than for a man to hear the song of fools."*

> *(Ecclesiastes 7:5)*

First "observation" is "better than." The author is not expounding by rendering a point to be made clearer the second time around, therefore not Synonymous. Although there is a strong temptation to associate "better to hear the rebuke of the wise" than "to hear the song of fools" as Antithetical, it is not so. For example, "to hear the rebuke of the wise *leads to life*", but "to hear the song of fools *leads to death*", would be Antithetical. However, Ecclesiastes 7:5 speaks of a thing that is simply <u>better than</u> another thing. Any graduation of a point-better than, worse than, more than, or less than-are Synthetic Parallelisms.

Learning to look for Parallelism is a major leap towards a deeper understanding of Bible Truths. The reader, by awareness of their use, will immediately become more analytical as a student.

OBSERVATION 8: HOW AM I GOING TO PUT WHAT I HAVE GLEANED TO PRACTICAL USE?

There is a phase of Bible study that is referred to as "Application." We are not there yet. We are still in the "Observation" phase. However, each answer to the questions hereto considered should be self-indicting. Am I able to receive the truth of my "observation" without clouding it with my previous opinions? No one ever goes into a gold mine with intentions of depositing gold. So, when you go into The Bible, never go in with the intent of proving your point or finding your opinion. The Bible speaks, but it does not listen! If you say what it says and mean what it means, you will be the happier for it.

So shall my word be that goeth forth out of my mouth: it shall not return unto me void, but it shall accomplish that which I please, and it shall prosper in the thing whereto I sent it.

(Isaiah 55:11)

Exposition John 2:1-11

A closer look at our Scripture, John "2," reveals an important "observation" that was not considered during the high recon. It is the first word in verse 1 of Chapter "2"-"And." The conjunction "and" at the beginning of a sentence signals a "U-Turn," appealing to the reader to be aware of The Scripture preceding it. What information prior to Chapter "2" is essential to the understanding? Following the "And" opening, the 2nd Chapter is a reference to a number of days. The first step is to carefully read the entire 1st Chapter looking for a connection to the reference of days. To this point, whenever you come across the often-used term "therefore," ask yourself the question: what is it there for?

At the conclusion of Chapter One, it is discovered that several days were significant in the events of The Lord's coming. Each of them was referenced chronologically. We conclude that upon opening the Second Chapter, one's attention to the "And" is actually a continuation of a succession of events rather than a beginning.

And the third day there was a marriage in Cana of Galilee; and the mother of Jesus was there:

(John 2:1)

What is significant about the "third day?" Here are the things we observed while reading Chapter "1" beginning with the first reference to a day.

The next day John seeth Jesus coming unto him, and saith, Behold the Lamb of God, which taketh away the sin of the world.

(John 1:29)

"The next day" is interpreted as the **second (next)** day following the initial appearance of Jesus.

> ➤ *Two days have passed:*

> *Again the next day after John stood, and two of his disciples;*
> *The day that Jesus began to appoint His Disciples.*
>
> > *(John 1:35)*

"Again the next day," is the day after the 2nd day, therefore, the **third** day.

> ➤ *Three days have passed:*

> *The day following Jesus would go forth into Galilee, and findeth Philip, and saith unto him, Follow me.*
>
> > *(John 1:43)*

"The day following," is the day after the 3rd therefore, the **fourth** day.

> ➤ *Four days have passed:*

> *And the third day there was a marriage in Cana of Galilee; and the mother of Jesus was there:*
>
> > *(John 2:1)*

"And the third day," is three days after the 4th day which constitutes the **Seventh** day.

> ➤ *Seven days have passed:*

Considering the number of days to be seven opens a multitude of possibilities in Bible study. The number seven should be no surprise to The Bible Student with its abundant uses throughout The Scriptures. Seven, or a derivative thereof, is "repeated" over 500 times in The Bible. It often represents a meaning much deeper than the number itself. So, this fact alone should prompt the student's curiosity and desire to search for (low recon) a more specific Spiritual "Application." It is at this juncture that the study will lend itself to "interpretation." Notwithstanding, note that initially, one must question the literacy of The Scripture.

The first four days "and" three more days to The Marriage Feast constitute seven days. God's initial use of the number seven is found in the act of bringing to life The Dispensations. The world, as we know it, was completed for human habitation in six days with specific instructions on how and why to honor the seventh day.[1] The initial Sabbath spoke to the need for physical rest and worship. The Marriage Feast occurs on the seventh day, and the inference speaks of The Sabbath of Eternal Rest.

Literally speaking, changing water to wine is impossible. That fact alone should expose the student to the need to plunge deeper in search of the reason for it to be a possibility, albeit Spiritual. *"And Jesus looking upon them saith, With men it is impossible, but not with God: for with God all things are possible." (Mark 10:27)* Considering The Words of Christ, it appears that the impossible nature of the event is meant to make one aware of The Presence and Power of God. Jesus was not only speaking of His Divinity, but demonstrating That Truth (His Divinity) through an otherwise impossible feat.

Since the preponderance of Bible "Interpretation" is Literal, the "Observation" Phase reveals, without further analysis, The Truth, as intended. However, beyond the literal world of carnal "interpretation," there is a Spiritual world of even greater relevance. *"And I, brethren, could not speak unto you as unto spiritual, but as unto carnal, even as unto babes in Christ. I have fed you with milk, and not with meat: for hitherto ye were not able to bear it, neither yet now are ye able." (1 Corinthians 3:1, 2)* Therefore, one limits his or her understanding of "The Spirit of The Law" if it is only "The Letter of That Law" that is searched. In our "Interpretation Phase," we must take a closer look (through Spiritual microscopes) at each of the objects gleaned in the "observation"-the number seven, the pot, the water, and the wine, to name a few.

---

[1] John 3:29 He that hath the bride is the bridegroom: but the friend of the bridegroom, which standeth and heareth him, rejoiceth greatly because of the bridegroom's voice: this my joy therefore is fulfilled.

Having appropriately studied The Scripture in the "Observation" Phase exposes one to endless views of Bible stories and events. But, to apply these facts appropriately in life plans, and things anticipated in the future, one must advance their "Observation" to "Interpretation."

CHAPTER 9

WISDOM "TO SPEAK" (INTERPRETATION)

Step Two: Bible Methodology

"Wisdom" What do I say? (Deliberative Theology)

"Interpretation" is the phase of study where meaning is associated with the Scripture being considered. It is the phase of study that one is most likely to remember when the particular text is being discussed. It is from this phase whereby the opinion becomes fact.

The Marriage now takes on the complexion of Spirituality rather than carnality.[1] To the uninitiated, the story reveals a normal occurrence. However, it is associated with a most magnificent event; the changing of water to wine. There are a number of events contained in John 2:1-11 that one might spend hours researching – to add to our previous considerations: the size of the pots, the volumes of water, also the unawareness of the governor. However, we will focus on the time (Bema), the water (flesh), and the wine (Spirit).

The ability to reach a deeper understanding from the initial "observation" is challenged by one's exhaustive Bible knowledge (Theology). Having a broad awareness of the various genres and their contributions to the overall message will often aid one's search of Spiritual meaning from an otherwise Literal understanding. John's teachings are deep and mystical, requiring the observer to be familiar

---

[1] Every man's work shall be made manifest: for the day shall declare it, because it shall be revealed by fire; and the fire shall try every man's work of what sort it is.

with God's plans for Jews, Gentiles and The Church. After all he is The Apostle chosen by Jesus to reveal the mysteries of Eschatology. Having said that, let's consider the events that will aid our "interpretation" of The Scripture at hand.

BEMA

Before expounding on The Bema, one must understand how we logically arrived at its "interpretation." The number "7" speaks to finality. The Marriage Ceremony concludes with a seven-day event. At the conclusion thereof, The Marriage is finally consummated, and The Bride and The Groom are husband and wife in the home of The Groom's father. Think about what we have just gleaned. Jesus came to this world for His Bride! He will gather Her to His Father's House (Heaven) for seven years to conclude The Marriage Ceremony. She, likened to The Jewish Wife, must be proven to The Father to be pure and chaste. *"That he might present it to himself a glorious church, not having spot, or wrinkle, or any such thing; but that it should be holy and without blemish." (Ephesians 5:27)* Having been acclaimed a virgin, she inherits all that was promised by her husband's estate. *"And while they went to buy, the bridegroom came; and they that were ready went in with him to the marriage: and the door was shut." (Matthew 25:10)*

One's knowledge of the expected Second Coming of Christ opens volumes of questions around this highly anticipated Prophecy. One of the many approaches may begin with the question of "When shall these things be?" *"And as he sat upon the mount of Olives, the disciples came unto him privately, saying, Tell us, when shall these things be? and what shall be the sign of thy coming, and of the end of the world?" (Matthew 24:3)*

The Bema is the title given to The Judgment of The Saints.[1] It will occur in Heaven after The Rapture of The Church.[2] During this

---

[1]   1 Thessalonians 4:16-17 For the Lord himself shall descend from heaven with a shout, with the voice of the archangel, and with the trump of God: and the dead in Christ shall rise first: Then we which are alive and remain shall be caught up together with them in the clouds, to meet the Lord in the air: and so shall we ever be with the Lord.

[2]   And if any man shall take away from the words of the book of this prophecy, God shall take away his part out of the book of life, and out of the holy city, and from the things which are written in this book. (Revelation 22:19)

time, The Nations will encounter The Tribulation, which will last for seven years. The seven years are known as Daniel's 70th Week. Think for a minute about the term "70th Week." Before expounding on what is meant by "70th" Week, you need to know when the calculation of weeks began.

Daniel's Seventy Weeks is not something that you are likely to have remembered from your childhood Sunday School days. So, do not get frustrated if this is your first academic approach to it. Simply buckle down and get ready to add to your Bible experience this all-important fact concerning The End Times (Eschatology). Note at this juncture you are about to add a study of Daniel 9 to your search of The Spiritual Truth revealed in our study of John Chapter 2. Through this part of the study, you will enjoy revealing in The New Testament that which is concealed in The Old Testament.

QUESTION: "WHAT ARE THE SEVENTY WEEKS OF DANIEL?"

Seventy weeks are determined upon thy people and upon thy holy city, to finish the transgression, and to make an end of sins, and to make reconciliation for iniquity, and to bring in everlasting righteousness, and to seal up the vision and prophecy, and to anoint the most Holy.

(Daniel 9:24)

Answer: The Seventy Weeks of Daniel is God's prophetic map of the destiny of Jesus Christ. Christ's First Advent was not a coincidence. Jehovah revealed to Daniel the exact circumstances and consequences that ushered in the physical presence of The True and Living God. Daniel, like you and me, struggled with the understanding of Scriptures. God sent His Messenger, Gabriel, to console Daniel in his quest to understand the plight of Israel.

THE DIVISIONS OF THE 70 WEEKS

For one to understand the "70" Weeks, one must first understand Week One. The Bible Student must use all available resources to research the "70" Weeks in context.

The Seventy Weeks of which Gabriel spoke in verse 24 constitute seventy-sevens. "70 X 7" equals "490." We interpreted the weeks to represent years and concluded that Gabriel was speaking of "490" years. How did we know to make weeks synonymous with years? Time and study revealed it. Over the years, scholars like you have searched The Scriptures trying to make sense of Truths hidden from the view of common logic. What did they discover? After searching the events revolving around Jesus' coming, they observed a striking correlation with history and Daniel's writings.

> *Know therefore and understand, that from the going forth of the commandment to restore and to build Jerusalem unto the Messiah the Prince shall be seven weeks, and threescore and two weeks: the street shall be built again, and the wall, even in troublous times.*
>
> *(Daniel 9:25)*

The clock began at the time of the command to *"restore and to build Jerusalem."* To calculate, by use of the reports of The Prophets and the agreement of history, that then places Jesus' triumphal entry into Jerusalem to be "483" years from the time of the decree to rebuild.

The Prophecy goes on to divide the "490" years into three smaller units: one of "49" years, one of "434" years, and one of "7" years. The final period of seven years is split at "3.5" years.

49 YEARS:

We know from history that the command to "restore and rebuild Jerusalem" was given by King Artaxerxes of Persia c. 445 B.C. (see Nehemiah 2:1-8) The first period of 49 years (seven "sevens") is the time required to rebuild The Holy City, *"the street shall be built again, and the wall, even in troublous times."* (Daniel 9:25) This rebuilding is also chronicled in The Book of Nehemiah.

434 YEARS:

Verse 25 says, (paraphrasing) *From the time the word goes out to restore and rebuild Jerusalem until the Anointed One (The Ruler) comes, there will be seven "sevens," and sixty-two "sevens."* Seven "sevens" is 49 (XLIX) years, and sixty-two "sevens" is another 434 (CDXXXIV) years. These numbers give historians all the proof they should desire to confirm the events which support Daniel's Prophecy. Four Hundred and eighty-three years (CDLXXXIII) till The Coming of The Savior was The Message God gave to the world.

Keep in mind that for Daniel, this message was still a bit enigmatic. God's Word is timed and often will not be fully understood until the time is right. Jesus, when preparing to leave His Disciples, cautioned them that though He had shared many Truths, they were stilled limited in their ability to interpret.

> *I have yet many things to say unto you, but ye cannot bear them now.*
>
> *(John 16:12)*

7 YEARS:

The seven years that Daniel saw were split in the middle. These years are yet to be. They speak to that which we know as The Tribulation. The first half, consisting of 3.5 years, will represent a rather harmonious period and will immediately follow The Rapture of The Church. During this time, there will be An Evangelic Movement that shall include, Moses, Elijah and all saved converts.

> *And I will give power unto my two witnesses, and they shall prophesy a thousand two hundred and threescore days, clothed in sackcloth.*
>
> *(Revelation 11:3)*

It is during this period that The House of Israel shall gain favor from The Antichrist and will reinstitute their Temple of Worship. However,

The Temple will suffer desecration and Jews shall be persecuted more violently than ever before in history. God will hide The People of Israel for the final 3.5 years, which constitute The Great Tribulation.

> *And the woman fled into the wilderness, where she hath a place prepared of God, that they should feed her there a thousand two hundred and threescore days.*
>
> *(Revelation 12:6)*

The Tribulation will end in Armageddon, The Holy War against Satan and His army. Our victorious Lord will judge The Nations and set up His Millennium Kingdom.

> *And I saw heaven opened, and behold a white horse; and he that sat upon him was called Faithful and True, and in righteousness he doth judge and make war.*
>
> *(Revelation 19:11)*

At the end of the 70th Week, The Dispensation of Righteousness (Millennium) will commence. During The Millennium, Jews will witness the fulfillment of The Covenants that they have longed for. Every Soul born into The Millennium will, at the end thereof, choose between Christ and Satan.

49 years = From the decree to build, until completion
434 years = Until Christ's Triumphal entry into Jerusalem
? years = Until the Church is Raptured
7 years = Tribulation

490 YEARS END OF THE 70TH WEEK

Daniel is told the divine purpose of The Prophecy in verse 24. Daniel was not only given the number of years, but also the reason for them:

1. *to finish the transgression*

2. *and to make an end of sins*
3. *and to make reconciliation for iniquity*
4. *and to bring in everlasting righteousness*
5. *and to seal up the vision and prophecy*
6. *and to anoint the most Holy*
    (Daniel 9:24)

Each of the aforementioned events speaks to God's plan to heal the world of sin and iniquity. You may search each of the events by cross referencing Scriptures that illuminate them:

1. *"To finish the transgression"* speaks to The Coming of Jesus. The ultimate transgression was The Crucifixion of Jesus. Every disobedient act is against God. Therefore, only God could bring an end to that which every human being possesses at birth, "sin."

    > *There is none greater in this house than I; neither hath he kept back any thing from me but thee, because thou art his wife: how then can I do this great wickedness, and sin against God?*
    > *(Genesis 39:9)*

    > *Against thee, thee only, have I sinned, and done this evil in thy sight: that thou mightest be justified when thou speakest, and be clear when thou judgest.*
    > *(Psalm 51:4)*

2. *"To make an end of sins"* would speak to the abolition of the damnation of sin. Sin prevented even The Saved Ones, during The Dispensations preceding The Coming of Christ, from going to Heaven. Until Christ was resurrected, Paradise, for all who departed life, was in The Earth. No one could go to The Home of God until He had justly removed the sting of death and received victory over the grave. Jesus' death paid the ransom for sin, and His resurrection reconciled for iniquity. After Jesus' resurrection, Paradise was moved from the heart of The Earth to His Heavenly Home.

And no man hath ascended up to heaven, but he that came down from heaven, even the Son of man which is in heaven.

(John 3:13)

And the graves were opened; and many bodies of the saints which slept arose, And came out of the graves after his resurrection, and went into the holy city, and appeared unto many.

(Matthew 27:52, 53)

3. *"To make reconciliation for iniquity:"* Jesus' blood paid the debt that humanity owed from generation to generation. Jesus (God) became man, which made Him a member of the human family, and therefore heir to the debt of sin. His purpose in life was to die in payment for the sins of His people; thereby removing the animosity that existed between God and Man.

    Whom God hath set forth to be a propitiation through faith in his blood, to declare his righteousness for the remission of sins that are past, through the forbearance of God; To declare, I say, at this time his righteousness: that he might be just, and the justifier of him which believeth in Jesus.

    (Romans 3:25, 26)

4. *"Everlasting righteousness"* speaks of The Advent of Christ's Second Coming. Then He will judge the world and establish His Kingdom on Earth as it is in Heaven.

    And before him shall be gathered all nations: and he shall separate them one from another, as a shepherd divideth his sheep from the goats:

    (Matthew 25:32)

Immediately following The Judgments of The Nations, Jesus will set up His Righteous Kingdom, The Millennium. I speak of this event as The Second Earthly Eden, which by definition is Paradise (a place of open fellowship with The Lord). The Millennium is the 1000-Year reign of Christ during a time when The Unholy Trio, consisting of Satan, Anti-Christ, and False Prophet, will be properly disposed.

> *And the beast was taken, and with him the false prophet that wrought miracles before him, with which he deceived them that had received the mark of the beast, and them that worshipped his image. These both were cast alive into a lake of fire burning with brimstone.*
>
> *(Revelation 19:20)*

> *And he laid hold on the dragon, that old serpent, which is the Devil, and Satan, and bound him a thousand years,*
>
> *(Revelation 20:2)*

> *Blessed and holy is he that hath part in the first resurrection: on such the second death hath no power, but they shall be priests of God and of Christ, and shall reign with him a thousand years.*
>
> *(Revelation 20:6)*

5. *"To seal up the vision and the prophecy"* is the consummation of God's plan for humanity. Daniel was informed of the limitations applied to The Prophecy of the human host. As Jesus is the ultimate fulfillment, there is no longer a need to anticipate His Coming after He has come. Today, those who consider themselves prophets apparently do not know that The Lord's Book is complete.[1] In The Old Testament Era, there were false prophets. However, in The New Testament Era there are false teachers. Prophets received "revelation" and wrote through "inspiration." Now that The Bible is complete, Pastors minister through the anointing of "illumination."

   > *But there <u>were false prophets</u> also among the people, <u>even as there shall be false teachers among you</u>, who privily shall bring in damnable heresies, even denying the Lord that bought them, and bring upon themselves swift destruction.*
   >
   > *(2 Peter 2:1)*

---

[1] Matthew 25:9 But the wise answered, saying, Not so; lest there be not enough for us and you: but go ye rather to them that sell, and buy for yourselves.

> *God, who at sundry times and in divers manners spake in time*
> *past unto the fathers by the prophets, Hath in these last days*
> *spoken unto us by his Son, whom he hath appointed heir of*
> *all things, by whom also he made the worlds;*
>
> *(Hebrews 1:1, 2)*

6. *"And to anoint the most Holy"* is the abdication of The Throne spoken of by The Apostle Paul. It is the mark of a completed assignment. Just as God in six days completed the world for the habitation of mankind, He submits to Daniel Six Phases of the completion of man for preparation for the habitation of Heaven.

> *And when all things shall be subdued unto him, then shall the*
> *Son also himself be subject unto him that put all things under*
> *him, that God may be all in all.*
>
> *(1 Corinthians 15:28)*

In only a few short verses, Daniel was given a vision that has troubled scholars for centuries. However, such was the dilemma of all prophets as they were given information that even they were not able to fully understand.

> *And these all, having obtained a good report through faith,*
> *received not the promise: God having provided some better*
> *thing for us, that they without us should not be made perfect.*
>
> *(Hebrews 11:39, 40)*

The writer of Hebrews was acknowledging the agreement between The Prophets of The Old Testament and The Apostles of The New Testament. It is through such studies that we are able to distinguish between The Jews, The Gentiles and The Church. Jesus' purpose is simply salvation. Only God can save. Confusion concerning The Triune Presence of God is dispelled if one would consider Jehovah as God, Jesus as God, and The Holy Spirit as God. Never think of either as one of the others. Jesus is not Jehovah, nor is He The Holy Spirit. Each of The Persons is God. God is never in conflict with Himself. Therefore, when Jesus (God) was discussing with His Disciples His plan to come to them as The Comforter (Holy Spirit-God), He stressed the necessity to first depart as The God-Man.

> *Nevertheless I tell you the truth; It is expedient for you that I go away: for if I go not away, the Comforter will not come unto you; but if I depart, I will send him unto you.*
>
> *(John 16:7)*

In the final analysis, Daniel was given a glimpse of The Dispensation of Holiness (The Perfect Dispensation), New Jerusalem. It is the ultimate fulfillment of The Kingdom of God here on Earth. Here referred to as The Third and Final Eden depicted by The Scriptures.

> *And I saw a new heaven and a new earth: for the first heaven and the first earth were passed away; and there was no more sea. And I John saw the holy city, new Jerusalem, coming down from God out of heaven, prepared as a bride adorned for her husband. And I heard a great voice out of heaven saying, Behold, the tabernacle of God is with men, and he will dwell with them, and they shall be his people, and God himself shall be with them, and be their God.*
>
> *(Revelation 21:1-3)*

Daniel 9:26 speaks of the events relating to Jesus' death, departure and destiny. Just as John stated above in Chapter 16:7, the Lord's "cut-off" (Daniel 9:26) is a major part of God's plan to reconcile His people. He would accomplish this through the indwelling of The Holy Spirit. This is also a time when Spiritual evil will advance its tactics against humanity. So much so that Paul stated clearly to The Ephesians that the fight is against a Spiritual enemy of great prowess.

> *For we wrestle not against flesh and blood, but against principalities, against powers, against the rulers of the darkness of this world, against spiritual wickedness in high places.*
>
> *(Ephesians 6:12)*

And after threescore and two weeks shall Messiah be cut off, but not for himself: and the people of the prince that shall come shall destroy the city and the sanctuary; and the end thereof shall be with a flood, and unto the end of the war desolations are determined.

(Daniel 9:26)

a. Daniel was informed of the impending Tribulation following The Rapture of The Church
b. Daniel was told how the matter with Antiochus would play out
c. Daniel was told of the trials of Israel during The Dark Period between Malachi and Matthew
d. Daniel was told of The Crucifixion of Christ for the salvation of the world

Theology is never a product of one verse, but one Bible. The paragraph in which Daniel 9:26 resides ends with:

"And he shall confirm the covenant with many for one week: and in the midst of the week he shall cause the sacrifice and the oblation to cease, and for the overspreading of abominations he shall make it desolate, even until the consummation, and that determined shall be poured upon the desolate."

(Daniel 9:27)

THE CRUCIFIXION

And after threescore and two weeks shall Messiah be cut off ... "And he began to teach them, that the Son of man must suffer many things, and be rejected of the elders, and of the chief priests, and scribes, and be killed, and after three days rise again." (Mark 8:31)

The Church (gap)

... but not for himself ...

"For I would not, brethren, that ye should be ignorant of this mystery, lest ye should be wise in your own conceits; that blindness in part is happened to Israel, until the fulness of the Gentiles be come in." (Romans 11:25)

The Antichrist

... and the people of the prince that shall come shall destroy the city and the sanctuary; ...

"Let no man deceive you by any means: for that day shall not come, except there come a falling away first, and that man of sin be revealed, the son of perdition;" (2 Thessalonians 2:3)

The Great Tribulation

... and the end thereof shall be with a flood, ...

"And the serpent cast out of his mouth water as a flood after the woman, that he might cause her to be carried away of the flood." (Revelation 12:15)

The Terminus

... and unto the end of the war desolations are determined.

And the devil that deceived them was cast into the lake of fire and brimstone, where the beast and the false prophet are, and shall be tormented day and night for ever and ever. And I saw a great white throne, and him that sat on it, from whose face the earth and the heaven fled away; and there was found no place for them. And I saw the dead, small and great, stand before God; and the books were opened: and another book was opened, which is the book of life: and the dead were judged out of those things which were written in the books, according to their works. And the sea gave up the dead which were in it; and death and hell delivered up the dead which were in them: and they were judged every man according to their works. And death and hell were cast into the lake of fire. This is the second death. And whosoever was not found written in the book of life was cast into the lake of fire.

(Revelation 20:10-15)

A life lesson may be learned by conditioning oneself to not stop with what appears to be the right answer at the exclusion of other possible answers that may be more appropriate.

Daniel saw great Tribulation in the future of his people. He saw a flood much like the deluge that claimed the lives of all but eight humans. How do these things fit into the vision of Daniel? The 69 Weeks took us right up to Christ's Triumphal Entry into Jerusalem. But what happens after that point? The 70th Week is a period that comes at a time beyond the cliffs of the 69th Week. We are presently residing in The Valley that separates these two points.

Today, Jews, as a religion, have yet to accept Jesus as God. The reason is because they cannot reconcile the events around Christ's life as being a fulfillment of that which they interpret to be prophecy. If The Jew were to accept John the Baptist as having been in The Spirit of Elijah, then where is the victory that was to follow his coming?

And ye shall tread down the wicked; for they shall be ashes under the soles of your feet in the day that I shall do this, saith the Lord of hosts.

(Malachi 4:3)

The "ashes" stated above is a symbolic reference to "the goat" on The Left Hand of Christ at The Judgment of The Nations; following which shall be The Millennial Kingdom (The Dispensation of Righteousness) and the fulfillment of The Covenant mentioned in Malachi 4:3. Imagine Jews, at The Birth of Christ, accepting Him as their Saviour. Because God is The God of fulfilled promises, the course of the world would have taken a course where Gentiles would increasingly find the gap of salvation widening. Also, since the ultimate fulfilment of God's Covenant would require Him to occupy The Earthily Throne, such would require an Edenic-Type Dispensation without the much-needed evangelism presently employed. As you can see, the present plan of God speaks to His love and virtue, *"For God so loved the world, that he gave his only begotten Son, that whosoever believeth in him should not perish, but have everlasting life. (John 3:16)*

The Jews are to this day living in a state of dependence that only confirms for them that the promise of world greatness is yet to come. As they refuse to acknowledge the light of The New Testament (Jesus), they continue to live in a state of Spiritual darkness. Such darkness, however, is not entirely due to their apathy, seeing as how God suffered it to be so.

> *I say then, Hath God cast away his people? God forbid. For I also am an Israelite, of the seed of Abraham, of the tribe of Benjamin.*
>
> *(Romans 11:1)*

> *Now if the fall of them be the riches of the world, and the diminishing of them the riches of the Gentiles; how much more their fulness?*
>
> *(Romans 11:12)*

> *As concerning the gospel, they are enemies for your sakes: but as touching the election, they are beloved for the fathers' sakes.*
>
> *(Romans 11:28)*

Such confusion speaks to the inclination of Jews to look at the world through egotistical eyes. God came to the world to save the world (John 3:16) inclusive of Jews, but not exclusively. Jews are champions of the fact that there is but one God. They are simply blind to the fact that Jesus *is* God manifested flesh. *(1 Timothy 3:16)*

Yes, The Valley in which we now reside is The Valley of Grace, which calls all men to accept Jesus as God. He is The Savior of the world. It is the time of The Holy Spirit (God), The "You Testament." God resides in the souls of them who accept Him.

The 70th Week shall encounter catastrophic events that will remove all doubt as to who Jesus is. We specifically refer to the 70th Week as The Week of The Tribulation. By our calculations of the times previously considered, we must see the final week as 7 years. Those seven years are to be split in the middle. The Book of Revelation was written almost in its entirety to bring understanding to this most important phase of God's plan for humanity. All of humanity is classified into one of three categories: Jew, Gentile and Church. *"Give none offence, neither to the Jews, nor to the Gentiles, nor to the church of God:" (1 Corinthians 10:32)*

JEWS:

Jews will make a pact with The Enemies of God during The Tribulation. However, at Satan's expulsion from Heaven, fierce assaults will be launched against Jews, including The Desecration of The Temple. Satan will use His power to attempt the destruction of Jews by the unleashing of a flood. Yet, God will cause The Earth to open and to swallow the waters, thereby saving The Jews. Jews will literally be housed safely from the assaults of Satan during the final 3.5 years of The Tribulation. However, A Remnant of them shall witness the atrocities of that era.

> *And to the woman were given two wings of a great eagle, that she might fly into the wilderness, into her place, where she is nourished for a time, and times, and half a time, from the face of the serpent. And the serpent cast out of his mouth water as a flood after the woman, that he might cause her to be carried away of the flood. And the earth helped the woman, and the earth opened her mouth, and swallowed up the flood which the dragon cast out of his mouth. And the dragon was wroth*

with the woman, and went to make war with the remnant of her seed, which keep the commandments of God, and have the testimony of Jesus Christ.

(Revelation 12:14-17)

NATIONS-GENTILES:

The events of The Rapture will put The Nations on notice as to who God is. There shall be a mass exodus of children of every culture. Families all over the globe will awaken to the absence of their children and then The Words of Jesus will begin to sink in.

But Jesus said, Suffer little children, and forbid them not, to come unto me: for of such is the kingdom of heaven.

(Matthew 19:14)

CHURCH:

The Church will be raptured to Heaven where She shall be judged (Bema) and fitted with Her glorious body.

Then we which are alive and remain shall be caught up together with them in the clouds, to meet the Lord in the air: and so shall we ever be with the Lord.

(1 Thessalonians 4:17)

And while they went to buy, the bridegroom came; and they that were ready went in with him to the marriage: and the door was shut.

(Matthew 25:10)

Daniel's Prophecy is so exactly calculated chronologically that some have considered it to have been written after the events that it depicts. Rather than acknowledge the perfection of God and His omniscience, scoffers waddle in human philosophy. God's plans cannot be upset.

Declaring the end from the beginning, and from ancient times the things that are not yet done, saying, My counsel shall stand, and I will do all my pleasure:

(Isaiah 46:10)

Behold, I come quickly: blessed is he that keepeth the sayings of the prophecy of this book.

(Revelation 22:7)

There is no shortcut to learning. One must be prepared to invest quality time in the understanding of God's Word. Each of the previous steps was an example of how one must meditate with expectation of reaching an epiphany. With the help of the understanding of Daniel's Prophecy, we are able to perceive the seven-day event depicted in John Chapter-2 allegorically as the seven years or the 70th Week. As we have studied, these seven years in Heaven run concurrent with the seven years of desolation. Think of the consequences of the seven years to be relative to Water-Flesh or Wine-Spirit. They shall each reside at the same time. However, for The Water, there is Tribulation;[1] and for The Wine, there is The Bema.[2]

WATER AND WINE

Water versus Wine: Water speaks of the physical existence of humanity. In the chapter that follows The Marriage Feast of John, Jesus references "water" to The Flesh Birth. He also elevates our understanding of the need to be Born Again. The New Birth is The Spiritual Birth. For there to be a Spiritual Birth, there is by necessity the need to have first been physical.

Howbeit that was not first which is spiritual, but that which is natural; and afterward that which is spiritual.

(1 Corinthians 15:46)

---

[1] Matthew 25:10 And while they went to buy, the bridegroom came; and they that were ready went in with him to the marriage: and the door was shut.

[2] In the Bible they are referred to as Epistles.

Jesus answered and said unto him, Verily, verily, I say unto thee, Except a man be born <u>again</u>, he cannot see the kingdom of God.

(John 3:3)

Jesus answered, Verily, verily, I say unto thee, Except a man be born of water <u>and</u> of the Spirit, he cannot enter into the kingdom of God. That which is born of the flesh is flesh; and that which is born of the Spirit is spirit.

(John 3:5, 6)

And there are three that bear witness in earth, the Spirit, and the water, and the blood: and these three agree in one.

(1 John 5:8)

The water with which Jesus instructed the servants to fill the pots represents physical beings. The pots were large enough to baptize a body. The act that rendered the water to become wine was a creative act. Such is to be interpreted as a re-creation, first water then wine; first the physical man, then the Spiritual man born in the pot of carnality. Imagine the result of a human left submerged in a pot of water-"Death"-

Jesus said unto him, Let the dead bury their dead: but go thou and preach the kingdom of God.

(Luke 9:60)

Then imagine a human rising from the water alive after death-"Resurrection"-

Jesus said unto her, I am the resurrection, and the life: he that believeth in me, though he were dead (water), yet shall he live (wine):

(John 11:25)

Through prayerful consideration of God's Word, the world is at best a temporary period or transition to something eternal. Although

Scriptures point clearly to the understanding of such, only those who have need, "eternal life," may know it.

> *Jesus answered them, I told you, and ye believed not: the works that I do in my Father's name, they bear witness of me. But ye believe not, because ye are not of my sheep, as I said unto you. My sheep hear my voice, and I know them, and they follow me: And I give unto them eternal life; and they shall never perish, neither shall any man pluck them out of my hand. My Father, which gave them me, is greater than all; and no man is able to pluck them out of my Father's hand. I and my Father are one.*
> *(John 10:25-30)*

CHAPTER 10

UNDERSTANDING "TO DO" (APPLICATION)

Step Three: Bible Methodology

"Understanding" What do I do? (Reflective Theology)

Having reached a conclusion in your study, you must seek the means by which you shall employ the things you have learned. Having Knowledge and Wisdom without "application" is like standing on a train track observing an approaching high-speed locomotive with no intent of stepping off the tracks. Such action constitutes lack of Understanding or worse, idiocy. In either case, one can expect imminent doom, death and destruction.

Remember Embedded Theology and Deliberative Theology? Now we are going to add Reflective Theology. Through these, Eternal Depths Reached (EDR), one may land upon an unprecedented epiphany.

Reflective Theology, as a study, is not so well defined academically or ecclesiastically. However, as a practice, it defines culture based on the opinions of Pastor/Teachers. Churches tend to publish their opinions under the word "Fellowship." Fellowship is maintained by an approved set of rules and rituals often found in documents labeled as Constitutions, Policies and Procedures, Rules of Decorum, or some other official document.[1] In either case, members of church congregations are led to

---

[1] Hebrews 11:1 Now faith is the substance of things hoped for, the evidence of things not seen.

self-examine themselves and to hopefully find their actions in concert with God's Will. Do you agree that you are growing in The Faith by Knowledge and complying in works by Actions?

> *But let a man examine himself, and so let him eat of that bread, and drink of that cup.*
>
> *(1 Corinthians 11:28)*

Although the ordinance of Communion is symbolic of "fellowship" made possible by The "New Birth," inappropriate "application," according to God's Word, has resulted in sickness and death. *"For he that eateth and drinketh unworthily, eateth and drinketh damnation to himself, not discerning the Lord's body. For this cause many are weak and sickly among you, and many sleep." (1 Corinthians 11:29, 30)*

Some have substituted the bread and wine for the substance of The "Word of God." Like The Baptism, The Communion is to be observed while gathered with other Believers (Church) in The House of The Lord. *"What? have ye not houses to eat and to drink in? or despise ye the church of God, and shame them that have not? What shall I say to you? shall I praise you in this? I praise you not. (1 Corinthians 11:22)* Many who are yet struggling to understand this Truth are insisting on taking Communion in their own homes, not realizing the significance of taking it in The House of the Lord.

WHAT DOES IT MEAN TO ME?

Assurance:

It confirms my faith in Christ and the efficacy of His being. Christ is my Lord, and He loves me without measure.

Heaven is a place, and I am sure to get there one day.

Action:

I must respect The Lord's Mission by emulating His love and His purpose.

Accountability:

I must seek to grow in faith by searching His Word for instruction. I must exhibit growth and development firmly and with steadfastness. I must give account for the things that are done in the flesh. Actions have consequences.

Over the course of this study, you should be able to measure your growth in areas of biblical compliance as well as growth in study habits. Answer the following questions:

    I.   *Have you established a designated time to read and study your Bible?*

    II.   *Are you pleasantly surprised at some of the discoveries that you have found during your self-studies?*

    III.   *Are you finding personal conclusions based solely on your private interpretation of The Scriptures?*

    IV.   *Do you feel less intimidated as you open your Bible to read?*

    V.   *Are you feeling more competent to assist others in Bible understanding?*

    VI.   *Do you understand the connection, as well as the disconnect, between The Old and The New Testament?*

    VII.   *Does it make sense that Scripture may be taken out of context?*

If you answered "no" to any of the above, then focus on answering the question: Why? Any answer that supports a reason for you not being able to say "yes" is an answer that should be placed at the top of your list for Observation, Interpretation and Application. In other words, eliminate the cause for the reason that inhibits your personal Spiritual growth. Once a matter has been concluded, it is time to move on to something more challenging. Growth is measured by a continued challenge requiring deeper understanding, i.e., "Application."

Therefore leaving the principles of the doctrine of Christ, let us go on unto perfection; not laying again the foundation of repentance from dead works, and of faith toward God, Of the doctrine of baptisms, and of laying on of hands, and of resurrection of the dead, and of eternal judgment.

(Hebrews 6:1, 2)

REWARDS ARE ETERNAL.

CHAPTER 11

BAPTISM

A THESIS OF CHRISTIAN BAPTISM

A Thesis is, when correctly composed, an epiphany of one's research proving or asserting an otherwise controversial subject. Included is a comprehensive examination of the term "El Shaddai." Baptism is the visible reference to an invisible phenomenon essential to Salvation.

To Be Or Not To Be

Baptism (BEING BURIED IN WATER), as a doctrine (TEACHING), has been defined in many ways; most of them contradicting each other. For some, it is believed to be essential to Salvation (BEING ABLE TO LIVE ETERNALLY IN HEAVEN WITH THE LORD), while for others it is not. Parents, of some children, are instructed to have their children baptized at an age as early as eight (8) days old, while others are told that children are not to be baptized at any age. It is confusing to say the least. However, to clearly understand water baptism, one must focus on *the why* and not so much *the what*. Yet, "the what" should not be totally disregarded as it plays a significant role in the understanding of this ordinance (ORAL LAW/ BOUNDARIES).

The foundation to such understanding is The Truth concerning what is represented by an ordinance. Ordinances are instructions that, when carried out correctly, will reveal a Spiritual Truth which is otherwise invisible. Therefore, care must be applied when attempting to understand something that is without physical substance, thereby invisible. Faith (Hebrews 11:1)[1] is the only logical means to accomplish such. Faith, being the product of God's Word, requires study (Romans 10:17, 2 Timothy 2:15).[2] We shall begin with the understanding of children being subjected to the religious act of baptism.

PEDOBAPTIST/ANABAPTIST

Churches perform ritual baptisms by four different methods (Sprinkling-Aspersion, Pouring-Affusion, Total or Partial-Submerging) and for different purposes (Salvation, cleansing-Spiritual washing away of sin, or even Membership). One must query The Church's reason and methodology before being assured of the full meaning applied in the baptism.

PEDOBAPTIST

Pedobaptist are those who believe that infants are to be baptized to ensure their Salvation. Example: Some believe that the act of water baptism for children (Pedobaptism) is required as a confirmation that they are the recipients of the faith and grace of the believing parents, which affords them a passport to Heaven should their lives come to an end. The fact that children are affected by the conduct and traits of their guardians is not a condition requiring baptism. When parents are taught that water baptism is required for the child to inherit Eternal Life, it supposes that to not do so results in Eternal Damnation. That is absurd! Any person who dies before the Age of Accountability is assured of being at home with the Lord.[3]

---

[1] Romans 10:17 So then faith cometh by hearing, and hearing by the word of God.

2 Timothy 2:15 Study to shew thyself approved unto God, a workman that needeth not to be

ashamed, rightly dividing the word of truth.

[2] Mark 10:14 But when Jesus saw it, he was much displeased, and said unto them, Suffer the little children to come unto me, and forbid them not: for of such is the kingdom of God.

[3] For what man knoweth the things of a man, save the spirit of man which is in him? even so the things of God knoweth no man, but the Spirit of God. Now we have received,

Some churches use The Doctrine of Water Baptism as a type of initiation required before one may take part in any of the church's ministries. As we shall see later, appropriately applied, such is true. However, it is applicable only to those who have reached the "age of accountability" (self-emancipation), and then only once in their Christian journey, regardless to how many different congregations they may join.

ANABAPTIST

Baptizing an individual after their Confession of Faith, which follows a previous "infant baptism" of said person, is by some considered to be Anabaptist. The Anabaptist Movement dates back to The Protestant Reformers of the 16th century. Ulrich Zwingli, believed by many to be The Father of The Movement, rejected the baptism of infants (Pedobaptism practiced by Catholicism). He taught that, unless one was baptized as an adult, they would not go to Heaven, i.e., Anabaptist (therefore, the need to be "baptized again" in defiance of a previous infant or child baptism).

However, one may conclude that any baptism that was not administered to a "self-emancipated" or accountable party who had confessed their faith in Jesus, was not a Scriptural Baptism. Therefore, one who administers the appropriate baptism is not agreeing with the Anabaptist teaching, albeit may be performed after concluding that a previous baptism was unscriptural. But is agreeing with The Bible's teaching of baptism, which only occurs once in the life of a Believer and is associated with The Spiritual Baptism (New Birth) of The Holy Ghost.

Many of those who teach infant baptism, and most of those who do not, agree that the first word in Salvation is "repent." *"And he came into all the country about Jordan, preaching the baptism of repentance for the remission of sins;" (Luke 3:3)* Think for a moment about the act of Repentance. It is defined as "a heartfelt sorrow." It is normally associated with Conversion, "the act of turning to Christ." Christ's

---

not the spirit of the world, but the spirit which is of God; that we might know the things that are freely given to us of God. 1 Corinthians 2:11-12

instruction concerning the need to convert reveals the circumstances which render the affected party as one who has surrendered his/her Will, which places them, in a Spiritual sense, back in the dependent role of a child: *"And said, Verily I say unto you, Except ye be converted, and become as little children, ye shall not enter into the kingdom of heaven." (Matthew 18:3)* To become "as a child" suggests that the one to whom the message is stated "is not a child." However, the appropriate understanding of the role of the child vs. adult helps one to understand the role of Christian vs. Christ.

Children are not left to their own undeveloped Will, and therefore are subject to the provisions of their guardians. The innocence of a child is God's hallmark of Salvation. Jesus' representation of the candidates for Salvation is *"children"*-*"But Jesus called them unto him, and said, Suffer little children to come unto me, and forbid them not: **for of such is the kingdom of God." (Luke 18:16)***

The purpose of adults, when it comes to parenthood, is extremely important. Without exception, a child's challenges are relative to the conditions afforded them by their parents. Therefore, parents are instructed to bring-up their children in admonition of The Lord, *"Train up a child in the way he should go: and when he is old, he will not depart from it." (Proverbs 22:6)* As it shall be revealed later, to introduce a child to baptism before the child reaches adulthood may do more damage to their understanding of the "right way."

As essential as the water baptism is, it is not an act that renders Salvation. Jesus confirmed as much on many different occasions and with many different words. However, the most graphic event was The Salvation of The Malefactor (Convicted Criminal) on The Cross: *"And Jesus said unto him, Verily I say unto thee, To day shalt thou be with me in paradise." (Luke 23:43)* The one who many refer to as "The Thief" was not afforded the opportunity to be water-baptized. But was, according to God's Word, Saved (Spiritually Saved & With The Lord in Heaven).

REPENT/CONVERT-CHILD PROOF

Repentance is the first word in Salvation (Matthew 3:2, Mark 1:15, Luke 3:3). For The Believer, it requires a Conversion (surrender of a Will) which opens The Door to Christ and permits The Spiritual Baptism of The New Birth (Regeneration).

Repentance requires one to acknowledge The Spirit's conviction of being Lost. It stands to reason that before one may admit being Lost, one must first set-out on a journey with a destination in mind. Imagine as a child being told that during the summer break from school, the family is going to Granny's house for vacation. Granny lives hundreds or maybe thousands of miles away. How many children, without their parents, would be able to make the trip? None! But, with the children in tow, the parents load up their chosen means of transportation, and not too long thereafter the family is sitting at Granny's table enjoying a wonderful meal.

So it is with the children of the world should God choose to bring them home before the "age of accountability" (the age at which one is free to decide one's destiny). They are safely ushered into The Ever-Loving Hands of The Father. To think that they needed to make preparation for Heaven makes less sense than thinking that they could make preparation for the trip to Granny's.

It is not until the child has reached the "age of accountability" that Christ requires a decision of faith. There is a constant knock on the heart of every person (Repent/Conviction) that signals their need to hear The Lord's plea for their Salvation. It is one's personal Persuasion that Christ seeks: *"Behold, I stand at the door, and knock: if any man hear my voice, and open the door, I will come in to him, and will sup with him, and he with me." (Revelation 3:20)* Although the words "if any man" are to be understood as "any human," it is not to be understood as "any human child." Any human child is provided The Saving Grace of God until reaching the "Age of Accountability." To this fact, Jesus said: ... ***for of such is the kingdom of God." (Luke 18:16)*** Paul distinguished between the acts of children and adults when he wrote: *"When I was a child, I spake as a child, I understood as a child, I thought as a child: but when I became a man, I put away childish things." (1 Corinthians 13:11)*

Peter expanded the point by the use of the idiom "newborn babes": *"As newborn babes, desire the sincere milk of the word, that ye may grow thereby:" (1 Peter 2:2)* To be "<u>as</u> newborn babes" suggests that one is not a "newborn babe." However, the attributes of absolute trust and faith required to survive in the flesh by the newborn babe must now be extended to Jesus for survival in The Spirit by the newborn soul. This reference to survival is not to be understood as being Saved. Saved is that which the "new-born soul" is, having accepted Jesus as God. This survival speaks of the many challenges that face The New Convert.

When I was a boy, my dad, up until 1957, did not have a vehicle. Therefore he would walk to and from work every working day, unless he was able to catch a ride with someone going his way. What would you imagine his response to be if one day he returned from work and found sitting in the yard a brand-new automobile that was a gift from me? Yes, I am old. But let me assure you, that in 1957, I was in elementary school.

To add to the above point, what would a parent need to be before prescribing a potentially deadly drug to their child?

I can tell you emphatically that things would have been going downhill quickly in the McClain household if I had tried to convince my dad that I had acquired an automobile. And it stands to reason that one should be a doctor before writing prescriptions. How many parents, who insist that their children should be baptized, are true teachers of The Word? What would you expect to be my dad's response if I were grown and gainfully employed, and the same circumstances revealed a new car in the yard as a gift from me? Yes, he would have been proud, grateful, and happy.

And, if anyone were to ask where his son got the car, he would probably answer, as did the parents of the blind man that had received his sight from Christ:

> *"But by what means he now seeth, we know not; or who hath opened his eyes, we know not: he is of age; ask him: he shall speak for himself."*
>
> (John 9:21)

The same response should one have when they hear their grown child say, "I am born again!"

As a child, I repented often at the believed consequence of a belt whipping because of committing some undesirable act. That which followed my "Repentance" was not a total surrendering of my "Will" (Conversion), but a powerful reminder of the consequences of my actions. The same also occurs in the life of adults. However, the guardian and disciplinarian is The Lord.

It is sometimes confusing as to the condition of a child's heart when it is obvious that the child's actions (Fruit) suggest that Repentance is, for the child, a reality. Do not confuse yourself with the question of whether a child can repent. They certainly can. However, the Repentance required for Salvation to be possible must be followed by a Conversion of "Will." Conversion for a child is as possible for the child as a day on the town is for a prisoner in shackles and chains locked in a dungeon. The child cannot give its "Will" to Christ because it has not been relieved from the "Will" of its guardian(s). Therefore, the child who is presented to The Church for the purpose of being baptized would be making an unwarranted confession of the personal surrender of a "Will" that he/she does not have full control of. Compare the difference in the situation of giving my dad a car as a child, and giving him a car as his "grown" child.

BELIEVER'S (SCRIPTURAL) BAPTISM

What is and **what is not** The Truth concerning Water Baptism as it relates to The Saved? The one who responds to The Conviction of The Holy Spirit by Repenting and Converting is Regenerated by God. The word "Regenerated" implies Re-Created. The New Birth, as it is sometimes referred, has baffled many. Some think it to be a simple rethinking of a matter, while others a future event for which we desire. To make it undeniably clear, Jesus left us His dialogue with a Pharisee (Jewish Religious Leader) by the name of Nicodemus. Nicodemus was to understand that before one could claim Heavenly Membership, one must become a New Creation.

> There was a man of the Pharisees, named Nicodemus, a ruler
> of the Jews: The same came to Jesus by night, and said unto
> him, Rabbi, we know that thou art a teacher come from God:
> for no man can do these miracles that thou doest, except God

be with him. Jesus answered and said unto him, Verily, verily,
I say unto thee, Except a man be born again, he cannot see
the kingdom of God.

(John 3:1-3)

Nicodemus represented any intelligent person hearing the words of one that he held to be able to perform miracles. He was simply unsure of himself as to how such a thing was to occur. To be specific he responded:

... *"How can a man be born when he is old? can he enter the second time into his mother's womb, and be born?"*

(John 3:4)

The Lord's reply is a repeat of the very thing previously stated:

"Jesus answered, Verily, verily, I say unto thee, Except a man be born of water and of the Spirit, he cannot enter into the kingdom of God. That which is born of the flesh is flesh; and that which is born of the Spirit is spirit."

(John 3:5, 6)

There are two births represented in Christ's words to Nicodemus.

1. *The Water-Birth (Physical)*
2. *The Spiritual-Birth (Spiritual)*

Just as one enters life through the birthing process of water-flesh, one must enter Eternal Life through the birthing process of Spirit-Spirit. The flesh birth renders one to be a member of the human family with all its faculties. The Spiritual Birth renders one to be a member of God's family with all its faculties. Such is the meaning of the words "Spiritual Baptism, gift of The Holy Ghost, and born of Spirit-Spirit."

The Apostle Paul spoke to the Corinthians:

"Therefore if any man be in Christ, he is a new creature: old things are passed away; behold, all things are become new."

(2 Corinthians 5:17)"

All things are become new" implies a continuous process of Spiritual growth in the human body. The authority of The Spirit of The Man (Flesh) and/or The Spirit of The World (Satan) is constantly being crucified by The Spirit of God in The Soul of The Born-Again Believer:[1]

I protest by your rejoicing which I have in Christ Jesus our Lord, I die daily.

(1 Corinthians 15:31)

I am crucified with Christ: nevertheless I live; yet not I, but Christ liveth in me: <u>and the life which I now live in the flesh</u> I live by the faith of the Son of God, who loved me, and gave himself for me. I do not frustrate the grace of God: for if righteousness come by the law, then Christ is dead in vain.

(Galatians 2:20, 21)

As previously stated, being able to appreciate the reality of The New Birth opens one's understanding as to why a child does not need to be water baptized, and an adult only in obedient recognition of The Spiritual Truth of Salvation. Water Baptism is a public confession of The Truth concerning Jesus Christ as God. And that He died for the payment of sin which all of humanity inherited from Adam, The Father of Humanity.

"But not as the offence, so also is the free gift. For if through the offence of one many be dead, much more the grace of God, and the gift by grace, which is by one man, Jesus Christ, hath abounded unto many."

(Romans 5:15)

---

[1] Behold, I stand at the door, and knock: if any man hear my voice, and open the door, I will come in to him, and will sup with him, and he with me. (Revelation 3:20)

Yes, Born-Again Believers maintain control of their actions.[1] However, final authority always works in favor of God's Will in their lives.

> *"And we know that all things work together for good to them that love God, to them who are the called according to his purpose."*
>
> *(Romans 8:28)*

With The Penalty of Sin (Damnation) removed, The Believer may navigate through The Presence of Sin (Temptation) by The Faith of Christ which assures a safe arrival in Heaven when The Power of Sin (Death) has come to fruition.

DO NOT REPENT YOUR REPENTANCE

As Saved adults, we shall also encounter situations and circumstances that are not efficacious (capable of having the desired effect or result) to the appropriate behavior of Believers. In such cases, we too shall have need to repent again and again. Paul in his message to the people of Corinth wrote:

> *"For godly sorrow worketh repentance to salvation not to be repented of: but the sorrow of the world worketh death."*
>
> *(2 Corinthians 7:10)*

Paul was speaking of the sorrow that grieves the heart of many, including Christians. To include Christians is to say that those who are eternally Saved, must still contend with the pains of the perversions of the world (sin). Therefore The Saved will find need to respond in a positive way to the Repentance provoked by such pains.

The Holy Spirit makes us aware of the cause when our hearts are filled with sorrow, thereby rendering comfort in the process of being healed. Paul's inference of turning away, "not to be repented of," is an

---

[1] 1 John 1:9 If we confess our sins, he is faithful and just to forgive us our sins, and to cleanse us from all unrighteousness.

act of confession/agreement whereby the affected is encouraged to make a better choice, and to not repent or feel sorrow for the grief.[1] The end of the grief for The Saved is Joy. (Romans 8:28)

Paul concludes this message with the consequences of "worldly grief" which has the same sense of awareness, but leads ultimately to devastation.

BAPTISM BY ANY OTHER WORD

The words "urban dictionary" give license for anyone to give their personal definition of a previously established word or term. It is said that, "Peckham started Urban Dictionary in 1999 when he was a freshman at California Polytechnic State University. Among the first definitions on the site was "the man," which the site now defines this way: "The man is the head of 'the establishment' put in place to 'bring us down."[2]

Well, redefining words began long before 1999. "The meaning of the word Baptism is rarely argued otherwise. However, it too is affected by metonymy.[3] Affusion (pouring) and aspersion (sprinkling) are the best-known culprits. Even those who practice sprinkling will agree with the literal meaning of the word baptism. In fact, John Calvin, considered to be at the heart of the Presbyterian church, who sprinkles instead of submerging, said that 'the word *baptize* means to immerse' and 'it is certain that immersion was the practice of the early church.'[4]

---

[1]   Street Smart: Urban Dictionary-The New York Times

[2]   the substitution of the name of an attribute or adjunct for that of the thing meant, for example suit for business executive, or the track for horse racing.

[3]   John Calvin (1509–1564) wrote that "it is evident that the term baptise means to immerse, and that this was the form used by the primitive Church", but in the same context (Institutes of the Christian Religion IV, xv, 19),[111] using the same verb "immerse", but indicating that it does not necessarily mean immersing "wholly", he also wrote: "Whether the person who is baptised be wholly immersed, and whether thrice or once, or whether water be only poured or sprinkled upon him, is of no importance; Churches ought to be left at liberty in this respect, to act according to the difference of countries." Modern, professional lexicography defines βαπτίζω as dip, plunge or immerse, while giving examples of its use for merely partial immersion.[112]

[4]   2006-2018. Truth411.com / Jacob Abshire (www.t411.com, www.truth411.com, and jacobabshire.com). All text on jacobabshire.com, t411.com, and truth411.com may be

Outside the Bible, ancient Greek literature agrees. Even the Roman Catholic Church practiced immersion until the 14th century (except in unusual cases). So, the meaning of the word settles the score."[1] Since there is no English equivalent to properly translate Baptizo, the word is brought over from the Greek, transliterated by simply changing the last alphabet from "o" to "e."

In Hebrew, it is referred to as a MIKVEH-an immersion. Basically, "it is an immersion into another substance," for the purpose of being saturated by it. Such is the inference of turning water to wine. (John 2:1-11) Although the act is a miracle of creation, it is observed by one substance being immersed into the existence of another. Probably, in The New Testament, the main reason that The House of Israel (Jews) is required to be baptized *prior* to receiving The Holy Spirit, and The Gentiles required to being baptized *after* receiving The Holy Spirit is because Jews, unlike Gentiles, were already using the baptism as a means of purification.

Paul included in his message to the people of Corinth a note concerning The Salvation that God afforded Israel at the hand of Moses:

> *"And were all baptized unto Moses in the cloud and in the sea;*
> *And did all eat the same spiritual meat; And did all drink the*
> *same spiritual drink: for they drank of that spiritual Rock that*
> *followed them: and that Rock was Christ."*
>
> *(1 Corinthians 10:2-4)*

The message gave them hope and assurance that God completely ingulfs His people from that which otherwise would destroy them. Paul added that all who were inundated did eat and drink from The Rock of Christ. Before this event, God saved eight (Noah's family) people in The Ark of Safety. While all others were baptized into their death.

Joshua became the new Moses as he was to complete the mission which Moses began, delivering the people safely home. Again, God

---

reproduced and distributed at will, providing text has not been edited and is properly cited.

[1] Every man's work shall be made manifest: for the day shall declare it, because it shall be revealed by fire; and the fire shall try every man's work of what sort it is. (1 Corinthians 3:13)

instituted a baptism which would see the people through the waters of the Jordan:

"And as they that bare the ark were come unto Jordan, and the feet of the priests that bare the ark were dipped in the brim of the water, (for Jordan overfloweth all his banks all the time of harvest,) That the waters which came down from above stood and rose up upon an heap very far from the city Adam, that is beside Zaretan: and those that came down toward the sea of the plain, even the salt sea, failed, and were cut off: and the people passed over right against Jericho."

(Joshua 3:15, 16)

The writer to The Hebrews also notes more than one baptism:

"Therefore leaving the principles of the doctrine of Christ, let us go on unto perfection; not laying again the foundation of repentance from dead works, and of faith toward God, Of the doctrine of baptisms, and of laying on of hands, and of resurrection of the dead, and of eternal judgment."

(Hebrews 6:1, 2)

The word "baptisms" is used implying more than one. However, The Spiritual Baptism is singular: *"One Lord, one faith, one baptism,"* *(Ephesians 4:5)*

Matthew recorded the words of John The Baptist:

*"I indeed baptize you with **water** unto repentance: but he that cometh after me is mightier than I, whose shoes I am not worthy to bear: he shall baptize you with the **Holy Ghost**, and with **fire**:"*

(Matthew 3:11)

In the order in which they are listed, these representations are-The Conversion Process of **The Will of Humanity** (Water); followed by The Regenerative Process by **The Will of God** (Holy Spirit); and concluded in The Developing Process by **The Work of The Holy Spirit** (Fire).[1]

JOHN BAPTIZES JESUS

John The Baptist went about preaching and baptizing in water. A close look at his ministry undoubtably places him in the company of Jews. He petitioned them to acknowledge Jesus as their Lord in the hope of Eternal Life. He would baptize all who consented in the hope of them being Saved. Yet, the baptism that he administered did not save, proven by the fact that the inaugural New Birth did not occur until Pentecost.

> *"And John also was baptizing in Ænon near to Salim, because there was much water there: and they came, and were baptized. For John was not yet cast into prison. Then there arose a question between some of John's disciples and the Jews about purifying. And they came unto John, and said unto him, Rabbi, he that was with thee beyond Jordan, to whom thou barest witness, behold, the same baptizeth, and all men come to him. John answered and said, A man can receive nothing, except it be given him from heaven. Ye yourselves bear me witness, that I said, I am not the Christ, but that I am sent before him. He that hath the bride is the bridegroom: but the*

---

[1] The basin contained water sufficient for 150 ritual baths (mikveh). According to the Talmud the laver was not entirely round, as might be inferred from Scripture; the upper two-fifths were round, but the lower three were square (Talmud. Eruvin 14a, b) The symbolism of the brazen sea is described in detail in the Midrash Tadshe. The sea represented the world; the ten ells of diameter corresponded to the ten Sefirot; and it was round at the top (according to the Talmud passage above cited) as the heavens are round. The depth of the sea was five ells, corresponding to the distance of five hundred years' journey between heaven and earth (compare Chagigah 13a). The band of thirty ells around it corresponded to the Ten Commandments, to the ten words of God at the creation of the world, and to the ten Sefirot: for the world can exist only when the Ten Commandments are observed, and the ten Sefirot as well as the ten words of God were the instruments of the Creation. The two rows of colocynths (knops) below the rim were symbolic of the sun and the moon, while the twelve oxen on which the sea rested represented the zodiac ("mazzalot"). It contained 2,000 baths (cubic measures), for the world will sustain him who keeps the Torah, which was created 2,000 years before the world. From Wikipedia, the free encyclopedia

friend of the bridegroom, which standeth and heareth him, rejoiceth greatly because of the bridegroom's voice: this my joy therefore is fulfilled. He must increase, but I must decrease.

(John 3:23-30)

John was by office a Priest and a Prophet. As a Priest, he was The Intercessor for the people. As a Prophet, he was The Messenger of God. His duties were that of going before The Lord and preparing all who would listen to The Truth of The Gospel of Christ. The Believers were commanded to be water baptized in a public setting to acknowledge to all that they had surrendered to Jesus as God. To do so was a bold act in a community where such conduct would certainly lead to excommunication or death.

Then cometh Jesus from Galilee to Jordan unto John, to be baptized of him. But John forbad him, saying, I have need to be baptized of thee, and comest thou to me?

(Matthew 3:13, 14)

It is often interpreted that John's remarks concerning his need for baptism infers water, since it was water that John was using. But John is really stating his understanding of the inability of his (water) baptism to make one Saved. At the same time, he is acknowledging the necessity of The Lord's (Spiritual) Baptism for one to be Saved. *(he shall baptize you with the Holy Ghost, and with fire) (Matthew 3:11)*

"And Jesus answering said unto him, Suffer it to be so now: for thus it becometh us to fulfil all righteousness. Then he suffered him."

(Matthew 3:15)

Jesus' response to John both acknowledges John's logic and infers a truth that John would know all too well about that which Jesus had come to do. When Jesus replied, *"for thus it becometh us"* He identified Himself and John as Jews, therefore inferring the conditions that were necessary for the preparation of The Sacrifice. The ritual was to be applied for the fulfillment of the conditions required by Jewish Law.

"To fulfil all righteousness" speaks to the need to carry out the plan of God flawlessly. Every Priest was instructed to wash himself and The Sacrifice before carrying out the duty of Intercessor.

> *"He made also ten lavers, and put five on the right hand, and five on the left, to wash in them: such things as they offered for the burnt offering they washed in them; but the sea was for the priests to wash in."*
>
> (2 Chronicles 4:6) [1]

Baptism is so important to The Jewish Rituals that a Mikveh (bath used for the purpose of Ritual Immersion-Baptism in Judaism), even to this day, must be built before the construction of The Synagogue that will house it. Although water, as a substance, is sufficient for The Ritual of Immersion, running water, as that of the sea, is believed to have a more purifying affect. Such may be the implication of John's choice of "… *baptizing in Ænon near to Salim, because there was much water there . . .*" The Mikveh, due to its tapping into a flowing water source, suffices the representation of a sea or fountain as in the name "Aenon."

Many Christians associate the act of Jesus' water baptism to be synonymous with the act of The Believer's water baptism. However, there are several notable differences. First, we shall consider the differences preceding Jesus' baptism.

The events following His baptism also reveal as much in Matthew 3:16. However, one must first consider the things that preceded Jesus' baptism:

- *The Believer's Baptism is preceded by Repentance from sin.*
- *Jesus had no need to repent for He was and is sinless.*
- *The Believer is also baptized in the hope of Salvation by faith in The "Word of God."*
- *Jesus did not need to be saved for He is "The Word of God."*
- *The candidate is instructed to follow the command of the minister.*
- *The minister (John) is commanded to follow the instructions of The Candidate (Jesus).*

---

[1]   Web-Site–Bible Study Tools

Therefore, one must focus on the fact that Jesus surrendered Himself to the testimony of a water baptism that pointed to Spiritual Truths otherwise unseen.

Secondly, Jesus' baptism concluded with a literal phenomenon of a dove-like rendering of The Spirit of God. Never has such occurred at the baptism of a Believer.

> *"And Jesus, when he was baptized, went up straightway out of the water: and, lo, the heavens were opened unto him, and he saw the Spirit of God descending like a dove, and lighting upon him:"*
>
> *(Matthew 3:16)*

The fact that John and Jesus were in the water together speaks loudly of the fact that the place where the baptism was to be administered had to be able to fully immerse both The Priest and The Sacrifice. There must be a reference to a watery grave and a lifeguard or Savior.

As John occupied two roles-Priest and Prophet-Jesus also had two roles-Sacrifice and Savior. It was necessary, for the fulfillment of prophecy, that He would first be The Sacrifice and then The Savior.

> *"And I beheld, and, lo, in the midst of the throne and of the four beasts, and in the midst of the elders, stood a Lamb as it had been slain, having seven horns and seven eyes, which are the seven Spirits of God sent forth into all the earth."*
> *(Revelation 5:6)*

> *"How much more shall the blood of Christ, who through the eternal Spirit offered himself without spot to God, purge your conscience from dead works to serve the living God?"*
>
> *(Hebrews 9:14)*

Lastly, unlike any before Him, Jesus is The High Priest. He is not only The Intercessor, but also The Intermediary that assures, like His Sacrifice, one's Salvation eternal in The Heavens.

"But Christ being come an high priest of good things to come, by a greater and more perfect tabernacle, not made with hands, that is to say, not of this building; Neither by the blood of goats and calves, but by his own blood he entered in once into the holy place, having obtained eternal redemption for us."
(Hebrews 9:11, 12)

The water represents a place of peril. To be buried in water results in death. The image, therefore, that is being projected is that of the death of Christ for The Salvation of the world.

After being dipped in the water, Jesus came up out of the river. His Ascension projected the image of The Resurrection. The Resurrection is The Power of Salvation which occurs at The Hand of The Holy Ghost.

To this point, The Scripture reports *". . . and he saw the Spirit of God descending like a dove, and lighting upon him . . ."*

This is the work of The Holy Ghost:

"Whereof the Holy Ghost also is a witness to us: for after that he had said before, This is the covenant that I will make with them after those days, saith the Lord, I will put my laws into their hearts, and in their minds will I write them; And their sins and iniquities will I remember no more.
(Hebrews 10:15-17)

"And lo a voice from heaven, saying, This is my beloved Son, in whom I am well pleased."
(Matthew 3:17)

Do we listen for or expect to hear a voice from Heaven at the baptism of our brothers and sisters?

The Bat Kol, or God's audible voice, was a well-known indicator of the presence of Jehovah. However, for those who were present, it was not a voice that had been heard in Judaism for over 400 years. God previously ceased to speak with The Jews as a means of helping them to understand a message that they had previously refused to heed too many times:

> *"But your iniquities have separated between you and your God, and your sins have hid his face from you, that he will not hear."*
>
> *(Isaiah 59:2)*

Jesus' obedience in a sinless posture prepares Him to make possible the union of sinful man and sinless God. Therefore, God's manifestation (1 Timothy 3:16) is the key to His perfection not being contaminated by the imperfection of His Fallen Creation. Through The Advent of Jesus, He is:

> *"To declare, I say, at this time his righteousness: that he might be just, and the justifier of him which believeth in Jesus."*
>
> *(Romans 3:26)*

> *"Seeing then that we have a great high priest, that is passed into the heavens, Jesus the Son of God, let us hold fast our profession."*
>
> *(Hebrews 4:14)*

As we can see, the message of Jesus's baptism is not the same message as that of which John administered. They agree that righteousness is accomplished at a level beyond the flesh which is represented in the death, burial, and resurrection. However, where John's message centers around water, and is therefore powerless for Salvation (albeit necessary for the fulfillment of righteous obedience to the commands of The Father), Jesus' message centers around The Spirit; therefore, is essential to Salvation.

THE COMMISSION

Much has been written and said about the administering of the baptism. It has almost taken on a cultish flavor. Some not only believe that a certain and timely baptism is essential to Salvation, but the exact use of specific words is also necessary. The error is in the lack of the understanding of The Spirit of The Law when it comes to "interpretation." To imply The Spirit of The Law, one must be well versed in The Letter of said Law. It is for that reason that God has given to The Believer The Old with The New Testament. Before one may safely proceed through an intersection bearing a stop-sign, one must first have a perfect "understanding" of the purpose of the sign.

One must answer the question, "Why Am I Instructed to Do So?" The correct answer will render one's focus entirely upon one's purpose as to their personal Savior. Although it is common language to associate the words, "This do in remembrance of me," with The Lord's Supper or Communion, the same may be applied to the "understanding" of The Baptism, albeit done only once Scripturally.

Matthew 28:19, 20 speaks of the purpose of The Christian Community and its' need to be taught the full meaning of The Message that it is to herald:

> "Go ye therefore, and teach all nations, baptizing them in the name of the Father, and of the Son, and of the Holy Ghost: Teaching them to observe all things whatsoever I have commanded you: and, lo, I am with you alway, even unto the end of the world. Amen."
>
> *(Matthew 28:19, 20)*

Many have considered the act of Immersion and the repeating of the words, "I baptize you in the name of The Father, in the name of The Son, and in the name of The Holy Ghost," as satisfying The Commission.

Yes, the literal "application" for the witness of The Saints may be performed as such. However, the 20th verse reveals the purpose of this baptism: *"Teaching them to observe all things whatsoever I have commanded you . . ."*

Therefore, the use of the word "baptism" implies the need to be totally immersed in the teaching of The Triune Persona of God. Each of The Persons of The Godhead speaks to different, but essential needs of humanity; without which, Salvation would not be efficient. It is also due to the lack of one's "understanding" of the essential nature of The Godhead-Father, Son, and Holy Ghost-that some deny "OSAS" (Once Saved Always Saved).

To this point, Matthew also recorded the outline to prayer which Jesus rendered to His disciples as the model of all prayers:

> *"Our Father which art in heaven, Hallowed be thy name. Thy kingdom come. Thy will be done in earth, as it is in heaven. Give us this day our daily bread. And forgive us our debts, as we forgive our debtors. And lead us not into temptation, but deliver us from evil: For thine is the kingdom, and the power, and the glory, for ever. Amen."*
>
> *(Matthew 6:9-13)*

In this prayer, we are instructed of the three provisions that ensure our Salvation. We are:

1. *Provided for in our present (Father)*
2. *Pardoned from our past (Jesus); and*
3. *Protected from the future (Holy Ghost)*

Such are the provisions of The Father Who gives us daily; The Son Who forgives us of our past; and The Holy Ghost Who delivers us from The Evil One-our future. To be baptized, totally indoctrinated (immersed), in the teachings of The Lord is The Mission.

A slight deviation from the point of Baptism as an Ordinance may help to solidify one's "understanding" of the essential nature of The Trinity. For emphasis, let's look at an often-misunderstood phenomenon of The Trinity, "El Shaddai."

EL SHADDAI

"Among Christians, the most common interpretation of *Shaddai* today is "Mighty," and *El Shaddai* would translate to "God Almighty." Coinciding with this, one suggested root meaning for *El Shaddai* is "The Overpowerer," meaning God will do what He purposes to do, overpowering all opposition."[1]

Anytime you see the use of the words, "power" or "might," or any Godly reference to the supernatural being applied, it will be with "El Shaddai" or "God Almighty" in mind. It is apparent that The Holy Spirit, El Shaddai, has been present from the beginning, and such fact is noted when John wrote:

> "But as many as received him, to them gave he **power** to become the sons of God, even to them that believe on his name:"
>
> (John 1:12).

By simple definition, "El Shaddai" means "Elohim Almighty." As one of The Personages of God, The Holy Spirit is The Person responsible for the execution of the unexplainable occurrences most often referred to as miracles. He is seldom regarded as A Personage, except when briefly mentioned, such as in "I am filled with The Spirit," or the like. It is certainly The "El Shaddai" that was represented by Jehovah when He spoke to Abram:

> "And when Abram was ninety years old and nine, the Lord appeared to Abram, and said unto him, **I am the Almighty God**; walk before me, and be thou perfect. And **I will** make my covenant between me and thee, and **will** multiply thee exceedingly."
>
> (Genesis 17:1, 2)

---

[1] In this the children of God are manifest, and the children of the devil: whosoever doeth not righteousness is not of God, neither he that loveth not his brother. (1 John 3:10)

In the above Scripture, note the words, *"the Lord appeared to Abram"*. The word "Lord" is translated Jehovah. Although Jehovah is The Lord, He speaks of a condition that would allow the future generations of Abram to multiply exceedingly. He qualifies the feat by announcing, *"I am the Almighty God"-El Shaddai.* The Father, at this junction, is giving the present condition of Abram that which The Persona of The Father gives: *Give us this day our daily bread. (Matthew 6:11)* However, for the future to be assured by The Word of The Father, there must be an assurance. That assurance is The El Shaddai or Holy Spirit: *"And lead us not into temptation, but **deliver** us from evil:" (Matthew 6:13)* It is the power/might of The Holy Spirit/El Shaddai that has kept Israel until this day. And shall keep them until The Lord has completed His mission.

The use of the term "Power-Might" denotes an act of The Holy Spirit or El Shaddai. During The Creation, El Shaddai is noted for the act of moving over the face of the waters.

> *And the earth was without form, and void; and darkness was upon the face of the deep. And the **Spirit of God moved** upon the face of the waters.*
>
> *(Genesis 1:2)*

Following the act of God in The Persona of The Holy Spirit, the word **"let"** became efficacious to the supernatural performances that followed. We have studied the presence of The Holy Spirit in the context of His being in The Kingdom of God. We referred to Him as The "Seven Spirits." Of course, we understand the reference to seven to be that of The "All Mighty." Look closely at the description given by Isaiah:

> *And the spirit of the Lord shall rest upon him, the spirit of wisdom and understanding, the spirit of counsel and **might**, the spirit of knowledge and of the fear of the Lord;*
>
> *(Isaiah 11:2)*

How does one explain any reference to any part of The Godhead without the references of Omnipresent, Omniscient, or Omnipotent?

Let me, in the probability of confusing the matter, try to explain: To say that God is not each of the references in question, would be like saying that God is not God. Therefore, one must assign each of the aforementioned attributes to The Father, The Son, and The Holy Ghost. However, if one was so inclined to take a deep dive into God's representation of Himself in The Personas of The Trinity, then, one might intellectually make logical distinctions in The Personas. So, let's say that The Father is Omnipresent. Everywhere His people went He was already there to direct them.

> *"If I ascend up into heaven, thou art there: if I make my bed in hell, behold, thou art there (Psalm 139:8)*

At The Earthily Coronation of Jesus, Jehovah confirmed the Personage of The New Testament; He says to the disciples of *Jesus,*

> *While he yet spake, behold, a bright cloud overshadowed them: and behold a voice out of the cloud, which said, This is my beloved Son, in whom I am well pleased;* **hear ye him**. *(Matthew 17:5)*

Jesus' character is noted for knowing all things: *"Come, see a man, which told me all things that ever I did: is not this the Christ?" (John 4:29)* Like the woman from Samaria, many of those who encountered Jesus were amazed by His omniscience. A logical assumption of The Personage of Christ is that He was not everywhere at the same time. However, one may not assume that He didn't know everything.

So, The Ever-Present-Father hands the baton to The-All-Knowing-Son. But the race isn't over until the final leg crosses the finish line. Jesus gives way to the next and most essential reference to The Mission-The Power to affect The Purpose.

> *Nevertheless I tell you the truth; It is expedient for you that I go away: for if I go not away,* **the Comforter** *will not come unto you; but if I depart, I will send him unto you. (John 16:7)*

The Personage of The Comforter/Paraclete, when represented, is never questioned. He is The Holy Spirit; He is The Spirit of Council; He is The Governor of The Hearts of the people. Without Him, regardless to the perceived relationship that one may have with the other Personas of God, one cannot be saved. (John 3:3, 5)

> *"Wherefore I say unto you, All manner of sin and blasphemy shall be forgiven unto men: but the blasphemy against the Holy Ghost shall not be forgiven unto men. And whosoever speaketh a word against the Son of man, it shall be forgiven him: but whosoever speaketh against the Holy Ghost, it shall not be forgiven him, neither in this world, neither in the world to come."*
>
> *(Matthew 12:31, 32)*

Jehovah gave Abram a condition when He said, *"walk before me, and be thou perfect."* He *was not* saying to Abram "IF" you walk and be perfect; He *was* establishing a need to conform to The Will of God. How would such an act occur? By The Power of The Holy Spirit-El Shaddai.

If there is to be a consummation of the attributes of Elohim (God), then it must be in The Personage of The Holy Spirit. For it is known that the time is coming when there must be an abdication.

> *Then cometh the end, when he shall have delivered up the kingdom to God,* **even the Father;** *when he shall have put down all rule and all authority and power.*
>
> *(1 Corinthians 15:24)*

> *And when all things shall be subdued unto him,* **then shall the Son also himself be subject unto him that put all things under him,** *that God may be all in all.*
>
> *(1 Corinthians 15:28)*

Despite all that Jesus did to affect The Salvation of His disciples, He still admonished them to refrain from any attempts to take on the wiles of The Enemy, Satan, until they had been endowed with El Shaddai.

In The Great Commission, recorded by Luke, we can see The Trinity at work together:

> And, behold, **I** send the promise of my **Father** upon you: but tarry ye in the city of Jerusalem, until ye be endued with **power from on high**.
>
> *(Luke 24:49)*

Jesus was speaking of **The Father** and **The Holy Ghost** (Power from on High). Just as Jesus was announced or coronated by Jehovah, He is now doing the same for The Holy Spirit/El Shaddai.

Ok, let's get a closer look at The Power (El Shaddai) of which Jesus spoke:

> And, being assembled together with them, commanded them that they should not depart from Jerusalem, **but wait for the promise of the Father**, which, saith he, ye have heard of me. For John truly baptized with water; but **ye shall be baptized with the Holy Ghost** not many days hence. *(Acts 1:4-5)*

> And when the day of Pentecost was fully come, they were all with one accord in one place. And suddenly there came a sound from heaven as of a rushing **mighty wind**, and it filled all the house where they were sitting. And there appeared unto them **cloven tongues** like as of **fire**, and it sat upon each of them. And they were **all filled with the Holy Ghost**, and began to speak with other tongues, as **the Spirit** gave them utterance.
>
> *(Acts 2:1-4)*

Therefore, as elusive as The Holy Spirit is, there is no question of which of The Personas is responsible for the assurance of *"Lead us not into temptation, but deliver us from evil"*; that would logically resolve to be the work of El Shaddai, "The Almighty God." *"God is a Spirit: and they that worship him must worship him in spirit and in truth."* *(John 4:24)*

The Holy Ghost is always defined as The Shaddai "of" Elohim. He is never defined as "the power" of Jehovah or Jesus. He is "the power" that Jehovah or Jesus yields. To understand that The Holy Ghost is The

Third Person in The Trinity is the beginning of one's "knowledge" of Him as being unique, but essential to the fulness of The Godhead. His uniqueness is the omnipotence that He displays.

First, when attempting to distinguish which member of The Trinity is responsible for a specific deed, one must carefully relate the matter to The Testament.

Secondly, one must examine the action that occurs.

When associating A Personage of The Trinity, we easily associate Him with The Testament. However, in either Testament, one must carefully consider the action before disregarding The El Shaddai or Power of God.

Our Jewish brothers easily acknowledge that Jehovah is God alone. They refer to The Holy Spirit as Ruach Hakodesh ("The Spirit of The Holy One"). The Jews do not acknowledge The Trinity. Therefore, they cannot relate to Shaddai as a distinct reference to A Personage. Even the term "Testament" is foreign to them as a distinction to a part of history or The Bible.

As a rule, if one would rather err on the side of caution, then one must never rule out El Shaddai in any act of The Father or Son; but may certainly rule out The Father and The Son when the act is solely that of The Holy Ghost/El Shaddai. Remember, "God Is One." Jesus clearly establishes that He and The Father are One. However, They would, by reason, need to depart from the people so that The Comforter/Holy Spirit/God's Power may come to them.

> *"And I will pray the Father, and he shall give you another*
> *Comforter, that he may abide with you for ever; Even the Spirit*
> *of truth; whom the world cannot receive, because it seeth him*
> *not, neither knoweth him: but ye know him; for he dwelleth*
> *with you, and shall be in you."*
>
> *(John 14:16, 17)*

Therefore, given a choice between Father, Son or El Shaddai, the logical answer for the act of assuring the future can only be El Shaddai/ Holy Ghost/Spirit. The "Our Father" Prayer (Matthew 6:9...) includes The Three Personas, just as does The Commission of The Ordinance of

Baptism (Matthew 28:19, 20): Jehovah-Father-*Give us this day*/**Present**; Jesus-Son-*Forgive us our Debts*/**Past**; El Shaddai-Holy Ghost-*Lead us not into temptation* and **"Deliver Us/Future."**

I hope this helped to shed light about The Trinity; most assuredly that of The Holy Ghost. Remember that the reason that He-El Shaddai-is as elusive as He is, is because He does not teach of Himself.

> *"Howbeit when he, the Spirit of truth, is come, he will guide you into all truth: for he shall not speak of himself; but whatsoever he shall hear, that shall he speak: and he will shew you things to come. He shall glorify me: for he shall receive of mine, and shall shew it unto you."*
>
> *(John 16:13, 14)*

El Jehovah   **Father**
El Jesus   **Son**
El Shaddai   **Holy Ghost**

JEWS FIRST

First, there was a baptism that was to be administered in the name of Jesus Christ. To do so, places emphases on Jesus without diminishing the importance of The Father and The Holy Ghost. Jesus is the name of The Man that they had crucified. Having presented Himself as The Christ is the reason for their justification of His Crucifixion (John 10:33).

The Jews were awaiting the arrival of The Messiah (Christ) who would occupy the role of The High Priest and restore unto them their freedom and control of the world. In their opinion, Jesus did neither. Therefore, He was not only a fake, but also an insult to their religion.

God (Jehovah-Father) and The Holy Ghost (God-Spirit) are present always in the mind of The Jew. However, Salvation may come by none other than Jesus: *"Neither is there salvation in any other: for there is none other name under heaven given among men, whereby we must be saved." (Acts 4:12)*

"But ye shall receive power, after that the Holy Ghost is come upon you: and ye shall be witnesses unto me both in Jerusalem, and in all Judæa, and in Samaria, and unto the uttermost part of the earth." (Acts 1:8)

Although The Great Commission speaks God's Word to the world, it began with Jews. Remember, Jews are God's "chosen people" and they are subject to the teachings that were provided them.

"For the wrath of God is revealed from heaven against all ungodliness and unrighteousness of men, who hold the truth in unrighteousness; Because that which may be known of God is manifest in them; for God hath shewed it unto them. For the invisible things of him from the creation of the world are clearly seen, being understood by the things that are made, even his eternal power and Godhead; so that they are without excuse: Because that, when they knew God, they glorified him not as God, neither were thankful; but became vain in their imaginations, and their foolish heart was darkened."

(Romans 1:18-21)

The pronouns "them-they" in the above passage speaks of The "House of Israel." There was and is no excuse for those whom God have enlightened to deny His Deity. However, neither you nor I can determine what a man knows in his heart. But The Lord knows. The separation that exists today between The "House of Israel" and "The Church" is a definite part of God's plan:

"For I would not, brethren, that ye should be ignorant of this mystery, lest ye should be wise in your own conceits; that blindness in part is happened to Israel, until the fulness of the Gentiles be come in."

(Romans 11:25)

Therefore, for the believing segment of The Jewish Faith, there was a need to repent of the denial of Jesus as Lord:

*"Therefore let all the house of Israel know assuredly, that **God** hath made that same **Jesus**, whom ye have crucified, both Lord and Christ. Now when they heard this, they were pricked in their heart, and said unto Peter and to the rest of the apostles, Men and brethren, what shall we do? Then Peter said unto them, Repent, and be baptized every one of you in the name of Jesus Christ for the remission of sins, and ye shall receive the gift of the **Holy Ghost**."*

(Acts 2:36-38)

Why is it appropriate to speak different words in The Commission of The Jewish Convert? First, is their familiarity with God. *". . . **that God hath made . . .**"* suggests that the one to whom those words were spoken had a correct "understanding" of God. Such is certainly not the case with those that are either Atheist or one of the other known religions. *". . . **whom ye have crucified . . . .**"* identifies the one to whom these words are spoken as one who had such a belief in the existence of Jehovah God that they felt that to crucify The One *proclaiming* to be God was a positive act:

"The Jews answered him, saying, For a good work we stone thee not; but for blasphemy; and because that thou, being a man, makest thyself God."

(John 10:33)

So much so that they cried for the relief of a very bad man over the release of Jesus:

"And they cried out all at once, saying, Away with this man, and release unto us Barabbas: (Who for a certain sedition made in the city, and for murder, was cast into prison.)

(Luke 23:18, 19)

So convinced were they of Jesus not being God, and therefore blaspheming, they subjected the consequences, if they were wrong, to be carried onto their children: *"...His blood be on us, and on our children."* *(Matthew 27:25)*

The conviction of The Holy Spirit, which allows them to see the light of their transgressions is rendered: ***"Now when they heard this, they were pricked in their heart . . ."***. They were made aware of their transgressions by The Holy Spirit. It is at the moment that they recognize the knock on the door of their heart as being Jesus/God requesting permission to enter (Revelation 3:20), that Conversion may follow the true act of Repentance: "*. . . and said unto Peter and to the rest of the apostles, Men and brethren, what shall we do?"*

Now, the next part will require careful consideration as it shall reveal two separate baptisms; the one with water and the other with The Holy Ghost. Which comes first is a matter of necessity and not a matter of standard. Peter said: "*. . . Repent, and be baptized every one of you in the name of Jesus Christ for the remission of sins . . ."* This is the water baptism. It is to be administered in the faithful expectation of the saving grace of The Holy Spirit. (To be baptized "in the name of" is a sure reference to the Water Baptism. More will be explained on that point later.)

To know this is to search further in the account of Jewish practice and their acts of convictions. We shall later discuss Gentiles who responded to the power of The New Birth and were then commanded to be baptized. But for now, staying with Jews as a people, we see that a public confession of their faith in Jesus, which recants their prior position of Him as a criminal, was required before they received The New Birth: "*. . . and **ye shall** receive the gift of the Holy Ghost."*

The gift of The Holy Ghost is The New Birth or Spiritual Baptism. For the religious Jew, there is no need to teach of God The Father or The Holy Ghost, as They are well known in Judaism. It is, mistakenly so, the reason that they reject Jesus. Peter, when speaking to them, relied on their knowledge of **God** by the simple inference: ***"Therefore let all the house of Israel know assuredly, that God** hath made that same **Jesus . . ."*** He did likewise with the simple statement: "*. . . and ye shall receive **the gift of the Holy Ghost**."* Therefore, there was no need to use in their Commission the words "Father" or "Holy Ghost," as they are well aware and familiar with both representations, as is inferred by the words of Peter.

SUBMISSION/OBEDIENCE

When one presents oneself for the ritual of Water Baptism, one is making a public testimony. Yes, The Convert may simply say to whomever, "I am Saved." As a matter of fact, to be Saved, one does not need to say anything to anyone except to Christ. Therefore, one should know that The Water Baptism is a type of initiation wherein one displays one's faith in an act of humble submission and obedience before The Body of Believers. The Water Baptism is the link that binds Believers in the physical body of The Lord. It is the threshold of brotherhood. Whereas the Spiritual Baptism is the act of Holiness; The Water Baptism is the act of Righteousness.

The testimony must provide sufficient verbal and optical messages so that the testimony may be clearly understood. The Lord instituted a "New Life" with The Advent of Christianity. "Death" is the appropriate term that speaks of the past life of The Believer moving forward in Salvation. That the message to Jews might not be confused as an extension to the already rituals of baptism to which they were subject, The Lord required them to recant their plea to crucify Him by publicly acknowledging through The Water Baptism that He is in Truth, Jesus The Christ.

Consistent to their religious principles of being inundated, they were to present themselves at a place and time where they could be bodily dipped in recognition of their surrender to The Power of The Holy Ghost to create in them a New Being. But, to repeat a very important aspect of The Jewish Water Baptism, they had to recant Judaism as a part of their Conversion by accepting The Truth of Jesus as The Christ: ". . . *and ye shall receive the gift of the Holy Ghost.*" *(Spiritual Baptism)*

GENTILE PROSELYTE OF JUDAISM

Scripture records the events of an Ethiopian Eunuch who was a proselyte of Judaism. He was treasurer to Candice, Queen of Ethiopia. He had traveled the dusty roads and deserts to Jerusalem so that he could be a part of The Temple Worship. On his way home, he was reading The Book of Isaiah and got hung up on:

> "He was oppressed, and he was afflicted, yet he opened not his mouth: he is brought as a lamb to the slaughter, and as a sheep before her shearers is dumb, so he openeth not his mouth."
>
> (Isaiah 53:7)
> (Acts 8:32)

The Eunuch invited Philip to join him in the chariot. As they rode, he inquired as to the meaning of The Scripture. Philip, from the passage of The Old Testament, taught The Eunuch about Jesus The Christ. Now remember, even though The Eunuch was a Gentile by nationality, he was a Jew religiously (Romans 2:28). If we are to apply the same methodology spoken by Peter, The Eunuch would need to repent and be baptized in water as a testimony to all that he had recanted Judaism and accepted Jesus as his God.

> "And as they went on their way, they came unto a certain water: and the eunuch said, See, here is water; what doth hinder me to be baptized?"
>
> (Acts 8:36)

Note the words that Philip spoke:

> "And Philip said, If thou believest with all thine heart, thou mayest. And he answered and said, **I believe that Jesus Christ is the Son of God.**"
>
> (Acts 8:37)

The importance of The Water Baptism of The Eunuch is seen in the fact that God made provisions for such in a desert.

> "And he commanded the chariot to stand still: and they went down both into the water, both Philip and the eunuch; and he baptized him. And when they were come up out of the water,

the Spirit of the Lord caught away Philip, that the eunuch saw
him no more: and he went on his way rejoicing."

(Acts 8:38, 39)

The Eunuch came up out of the water rejoicing because he had
received The Gift of The Holy Ghost.

GENTILES LAST

Consistent with The Order of The Acts of The Apostles, Jews and
their Conversions are mentioned almost predominately in the first 10
chapters. It is there that we may observe the prejudice of The Jewish
Culture and their perceived superiority over The Gentiles. Although
The Commission was clearly to be expanded *"unto the uttermost part of*
the earth" (Acts 1:8), the average Jewish Believer would not cross the
street to save a Gentile. (Luke 10:30–32)

Therefore, The Lord initiated the movement by sending an angel
to a Gentile commander with instructions to seek out Peter, the leader
of Jewish opposition to Gentile equality.

> *"He saw in a vision evidently about the ninth hour of the*
> *day an angel of God coming in to him, and saying unto him,*
> *Cornelius. And when he looked on him, he was afraid, and*
> *said, What is it, Lord? And he said unto him, Thy prayers*
> *and thine alms are come up for a memorial before God. And*
> *now send men to Joppa, and call for one Simon, whose surname*
> *is Peter:"*
>
> *(Acts 10:3-5)*

The Lord required Peter to take self-inventory before sending him
to The House of Cornelius. During Peter's years of preparation, he was
often on the wrong side with respect to his opinion. There were also
moments of frustration exhibited by Peter's perception of The Lord's
displeasure with him. Peter was once asked of The Lord if he loved
Him. Peter immediately replied "yes." The Lord then told Peter "feed

my sheep." That line of question was repeated three times. After the third time, Peter was displaying a bit of frustration:

> *"He saith unto him the third time, Simon, son of Jonas, lovest thou me? Peter was grieved because he said unto him the third time, Lovest thou me? And he said unto him, Lord, thou knowest all things; thou knowest that I love thee. Jesus saith unto him, Feed my sheep."*
>
> *(John 21:17)*

This is the same Peter who boldly proclaimed that he would willingly die for The Lord. But The Lord (*"thou knowest all things"*) told Peter that he would deny Him thrice before the cock crowed:

> *"Then began he to curse and to swear, saying, I know not the man. And immediately the cock crew. And Peter remembered the word of Jesus, which said unto him, Before the cock crow, thou shalt deny me thrice. And he went out, and wept bitterly."*
>
> *(Matthew 26:74, 75)*

Again, in The Mission to speak The Gospel to Cornelius, Peter undergoes three (3) renderings of God's words before concluding that that which God has cleansed, "let no man put asunder." Peter was being indoctrinated into the full meaning of that which reveals one's love of God:[1]

> *"But Peter said, Not so, Lord; for I have never eaten any thing that is common or unclean. And the voice spake unto him again the second time, What God hath cleansed, that call not thou common. This was done thrice: and the vessel was received up again into heaven."*
>
> *(Acts 10:14-16)*

---

[1]   By Chong Singsit The author is a US-based Research Scientist (Biotechnologist) and an Advisory Board Member of the Kuki International Forum.

"While Peter thought on the vision, the Spirit said unto him,
Behold, three men seek thee."

(Acts 10:19)

Peter went to The House of Cornelius where there was a large
gathering of Gentiles who were eager to hear The Gospel. Peter
expounded The Word perfectly. He told the people that God had
shown him that He is no respecter of persons. Although as a Jew, Peter
himself had been of a prior opinion that Jews were superior. But now,
those ideas and concepts were changed. He let the people know that
God loved them.

> *"While Peter yet spake these words, the Holy Ghost fell on*
> *all them which heard the word. And they of the circumcision*
> *which believed were astonished, as many as came with Peter,*
> *because that on the Gentiles also was poured out the gift of the*
> *Holy Ghost."*
>
> *(Acts 10:44, 45)*

"The gift of the Holy Ghost" is represented in the very acts that
occurred when The Apostles and the initial 120 were saved at Pentecost:

> *"For they heard them speak with tongues, and magnify God.*
> *Then answered Peter,"*
>
> *(Acts 10:46)*

For clarity, remember that the exact words, *"the gift of the Holy*
Ghost," were the same which The House of Israel would receive after the
baptism. (Acts 2:38) Now, Salvation has clearly preceded the baptism:
"Can any man forbid water, that these should not be baptized, which have
received the Holy Ghost as well as we?" (Acts 10:47) The Immersion that
one witnesses in The Water Baptism is the physical replica of The
Spiritual Baptism at Pentecost:

> *And suddenly there came a sound from heaven as of a rushing*
> *mighty wind, and **it filled all the house** where they were*
> *sitting. And there appeared unto them cloven tongues like as*

*of fire, and it sat upon each of them. And **they were all filled with the Holy Ghost**, and began to speak with other tongues, as the Spirit gave them utterance.*

(Acts 2:2-4)

Peter's response to that which he witnessed was simple:

"And he commanded them to be baptized in the name of the Lord. Then prayed they him to tarry certain days."

(Acts 10:48)

The baptism that ushered The Gentiles into God's fold is synonymous with The Commission that Jesus made to His disciples relative to the world.

"Go ye therefore, and teach all nations, baptizing them in the name of the Father, and of the Son, and of the Holy Ghost:"

(Matthew 28:19)

All Nations would certainly include Gentiles, and therefore the need to announce the *"Father, Son, and Holy Ghost."*

What is the difference between "The Name of The Lord" and "The Name of Jesus Christ?" The full name of The Lord must reveal The Three Personas of God. The Name of "Jesus Christ" is the name that God chose for His manifestation, which alone is The Second Person in The Godhead. Gentiles are from a prior culture that has no religious roots in Judaism or Christianity. Therefore, a Gentile needs the teachings and commandments that cover the whole of God's Personas. For The Gentile, it must be Father, Son and Holy Ghost. Why? God's personal introduction of Himself as recorded in the following words may not be disregarded or taken for granted:

I am Alpha and Omega, *the beginning and the ending,* **saith the Lord**, *which is, and which was, and which is to come, the Almighty.*

(Revelation 1:8)

The Name of The Lord according to The Lord Is: "I AM Alpha and Omega"!

I Am, The First Person in The Trinity-I Am is the name that Jehovah told Moses to use when referring to Him: *"...Thus shalt thou say unto the children of Israel, I AM hath sent me unto you." (Exodus 3:14)* Therefore, we have the reference to The Father (Present-*Which is*).

Alpha, The Second Person in The Trinity-The name represents the beginning, which, for man, is provided by "The Word"-Jesus The Christ: *"In the beginning was the Word, and the Word was with God, and the Word was God." (John 1:1)* Therefore, we have the reference to The Son (Past-*Which was*).

Omega, The Third Person in The Trinity-Referred to as "El Shaddai" (God Almighty). He was said to be necessary for the crowning of humanity in the name of Jesus: *"Nevertheless I tell you the truth; It is expedient for you that I go away: for if I go not away, the Comforter will not come unto you; but if I depart, I will send him unto you." (John 16:7)* Therefore, we have the reference to The Holy Spirit (Future-*Which is to come*).

The conclusion of the matter in reference to the name of The Lord is "ALMIGHTY." As much was said by Jesus as He prepared to return to Heaven after The Resurrection:

> *And Jesus came and spake unto them, saying, **All power** is given unto me in heaven and in earth.*
>
> *(Matthew 28:18)*

As previously mentioned, the nature of The "Father, Son and Holy Ghost" speaks to the human need for being saved from its Present, Past, and Future. So, at the baptism of a Gentile, you should hear a true facsimile of, "I baptize you in the name of **The Father, The Son, and The Holy Ghost."**

The exception, as previously written, is a baptism of a Jewish brother or sister whereby the words, "I baptize you in **The Name of Jesus Christ**" are to be used; and that only because they (Jews) are already familiar with The "Father and Holy Ghost." Although Peter expressly spoke The Commission in The Name of Jesus Christ, he inferred The

Holy Spirit with the words, "... *ye shall receive the gift of the <u>Holy Ghost</u>;* and The Father with the words, "*... even as many as <u>the Lord</u> our God shall call.*"

Peter continued to carry out his Commission just as it was stated by Jesus:

> *"Teaching them to observe all things whatsoever I have commanded you: and, lo, I am with you alway, even unto the end of the world." (Matthew 28:20)*

The people desired of Peter that he would remain with them certain days: "*... Then prayed they him to tarry certain days." (Acts 10:48)*

Certainly, it was during that time that Peter taught them to ". . . *observe all things whatsoever I have commanded you . . ." (Matthew 28:20)* The first commandment was to be baptized!

IN THE NAME OF

To The Jews Peter said, be baptized in the name of Jesus Christ; to The Gentiles Peter said, be baptized in the name of The Lord. In either case, the reward was the gift of The Holy Ghost (Acts 2:38, 10:45)

After reading the following six verses, take a moment and try to determine what is the constant in each of them:

1. *"Then Peter said unto them, Repent, and be baptized every one of you **in the name of** Jesus Christ for the remission of sins, and ye shall receive the gift of the Holy Ghost."*
   (Acts 2:38)

2. *"But when they believed Philip preaching the things concerning the kingdom of God, and **the name of** Jesus Christ, they were baptized, both men and women."*
   (Acts 8:12)

3. *"(For as yet he was fallen upon none of them: only they were baptized **in the name of** the Lord Jesus.)"*

(Acts 8:16)

4. *"And he commanded them to be baptized **in the name of** the Lord. Then prayed they him to tarry certain days."*
   (Acts 10:48)

5. *"When they heard this, they were baptized **in the name of** the Lord Jesus." (Acts 19:5)*

6. *"Is Christ divided? Was Paul crucified for you? Or were ye baptized **in the name of** Paul?"*
   (1 Corinthians 1:13)

In each of the above references, the words *"the name of"* are announced to indicate that The Water Baptism associated is administered by man under orders (Ordinance) of Christ. There is no baptism of man that brings with it the act of being Born-Again. There is, however, many today who would refute those words believing themselves to be able, by God's Word, to baptize people into Salvation. They are preceded by a host of heretics of whom Paul inferred with his findings in Corinth:

> *"For it hath been declared unto me of you, my brethren, by them which are of the house of Chloe, that there are contentions among you. Now this I say, that every one of you saith, I am of Paul; and I of Apollos; and I of Cephas; and I of Christ. Is Christ divided? Was Paul crucified for you? Or were ye baptized in the name of Paul?"*
>
> *(1 Corinthians 1:11-13)*

Paul was inferring to them that Salvation comes only by the baptism of The Holy Ghost. Although he had, on occasion, administered The Believers' Water-Baptism, it was not that which God had sent him to do:

"For Christ sent me not to baptize, but to preach the gospel: not with wisdom of words, lest the cross of Christ should be made of none effect."

(1 Corinthians 1:17)

Could it have been that Paul, on the occasions mentioned where he baptized with water, did so because The Converts were Jewish? Although it is not entirely affirmed, it is worth considering.

"I thank God that I baptized none of you, but Crispus and Gaius; Lest any should say that I had baptized in mine own name. And I baptized also the household of Stephanas: besides, I know not whether I baptized any other."

(1 Corinthians 1:14-16)

Although Gaius was a popular Roman name-Gaius Julius Caesar, Gaius Octavius (Augustus) – The Gaius of which Paul spoke was probably one with whom Paul resided in Corinth (Romans 16:23) when he wrote The Book of Romans. A search of the name Gaius also appears in the 3rd Epistle of John as one who was worthy to be honored by John.

As for Crispus of Chalcedon, he was "the chief ruler of the Synagogue" at Corinth:

"And Crispus, the chief ruler of the synagogue, believed on the Lord with all his house; and many of the Corinthians hearing believed, and were baptized." (Acts 18:8)

According to the narrative involving the inquisition of Paul, before the Roman Governor/Senator Gallio and the events that followed, Crispus and Sosthenes are the same person, "the chief ruler of the synagogue".

"Then all the Greeks took Sosthenes, the chief ruler of the synagogue, and beat him before the judgment seat. And Gallio cared for none of those things."

(Acts 18:17)

Paul would have only ministered here and there to Jews: *"For I speak to you Gentiles, inasmuch as I am the apostle of the Gentiles, I magnify mine office:" (Romans 11:13)* However, on the few listed occasions when Paul did witness to a Jew, he apparently followed the instructions of Acts 2:38 which required Water-Baptism as the means of Conversion, which precedes "the gift of The Holy Ghost" (Spiritual Baptism-New Birth).

WAS SAUL/PAUL BAPTIZED IN WATER?

The words spoken by Ananias, *"And now why tarriest thou? arise, and be baptized, and wash away thy sins, calling on the name of the Lord." (Acts 22:16)*

The Greek word "Apōlouō" is only used two times in The New Testament. It is translated "wash" and "washed," respectively, in Acts 22:16 and 1 Corinthians 6:11. Paul's explanation of his experience when called to the ministry was: *"And now why tarriest thou? arise, and be baptized, and wash away thy sins, calling on the name of the Lord." (Acts 22:16)* Did Saul wash away his sins? If we connect the act of Water Baptism with that which washes away sin, then Saul would have immediately, literally, become sinless. What this baptism accomplished for Saul was his Regeneration (Spiritual Baptism) by The Holy Ghost.

> *"But God, who is rich in mercy, for his great love wherewith he loved us, Even when we were dead in sins, hath quickened us together with Christ, (by grace ye are saved;) And hath raised us up together, and made us sit together in heavenly places in Christ Jesus: That in the ages to come he might shew the exceeding riches of his grace in his kindness toward us through Christ Jesus. For by grace are ye saved through faith; and that not of yourselves: **it is the gift of God**: Not of works, lest any man should boast."*
>
> *(Ephesians 2:4-9)*

Although some have published that Ananias baptized Saul, it must be an assumption since there is no Scriptural reference to the same. To the contrary, Ananias did lay hands on Saul, but that would not have been a baptism. Many assume that the order and the use of *"wash away thy sins"* must constitute a baptism; therefore, affirming that a Water Baptism is required or sufficient to remove sin.

Those who only received The Believer's Baptism (John's Baptism) without The Holy Spirit's Baptism were powerless: *"He said unto them, Have ye received the Holy Ghost since ye believed? And they said unto him, We have not so much as heard whether there be any Holy Ghost. And he said unto them, Unto what then were ye baptized? And they said, Unto John's baptism."* (Acts 19:2, 3)

Going back to the events that occurred as Ananias carried out The Lord's instructions, there were two things that were to occur: *"... that thou mightest **receive thy sight**, and **be filled with the Holy Ghost**." (Acts 9:17)* The two are confirmed in the very next verse: *"And immediately there fell from his eyes as it had been scales: and **he received sight** forthwith, and arose, and **was baptized**. (Acts 9:18)* The baptism spoken of here is the *". . . and be **filled with the Holy Ghost." (v.17)**

Back to the "wash" as a product of Water Baptism-how was Saul to wash away his sins? The answer is in his public confession of Salvation and his anointing by Jesus to The Apostleship. As an Apostle, Saul/Paul would be endowed with the ability to confirm his Conversion by not only his testimony, which is more than half The New Testament, but also using miracles. The use of the word "wash" is metaphorically Saul's instructions to show himself cleansed from The Sin Nature (Reborn) and advancing to The Kingdom of God through Christ Jesus.

If the baptism were water, and with-it Saul washed away his sins, then they (his sins) must have returned during his speech to The Romans: *"Now then it is no more I that do it, but sin that dwelleth in me."* (Romans 7:17)

The same is said of The Corinthian Saints of whom Paul spoke of their victories over a sundry of sinful natures: *"And such were some of you: **but ye are washed**, but ye are sanctified, but ye are justified in the name of the Lord Jesus, and by the Spirit of our God." (1 Corinthians 6:11)* Here the word "washed" is an indicator of a work that is essential to that which follows Sanctification – that being Justification, in the name of the Lord Jesus *"**by the Spirit of God.**"*

Jesus made perfectly clear in His own words the difference between Water Baptism and that of The Holy Ghost:

> *"And, being assembled together with them, commanded them that they should not depart from Jerusalem, but wait for the promise of the Father, which, saith he, ye have heard of me. For John truly baptized with water; but ye shall be baptized with the Holy Ghost not many days hence. When they therefore were come together, they asked of him, saying, Lord, wilt thou at this time restore again the kingdom to Israel? And he said unto them, It is not for you to know the times or the seasons, which the Father hath put in his own power. But ye shall receive power, after that the Holy Ghost is come upon you: and ye shall be witnesses unto me both in Jerusalem, and in all Judæa, and in Samaria, and unto the uttermost part of the earth."*
>
> *(Acts 1:4-8)*

There is not one Scriptural reference to The Water Baptism of any Apostle. The Apostles received the power of their New Birth at Pentecost with the 120 Saints (Acts 1:15) that formed The Inaugural Church. It must also be affirmed that none of The Inaugural Saints would have been baptized in water either unless they were Converts of the ministering of John the Baptist or the disciples of Christ. While some do assume that Jesus had to have baptized his disciples, since they were baptizing others, The Scripture says: *"Though Jesus himself baptized not, but his disciples,"* (John 4:2)

THE OPTICS OF BAPTISM

Without a doubt, the recipients of The Holy Ghost are Born-Again. Therefore, there is nothing to add to their Salvation. However, The Water Baptism is still required as a means of acknowledging their faith in God to all who would witness. The first act after becoming Saved is that of sharing one's Salvation with those who are near. It is for this reason that God chose the optics of baptism. The act itself is on one hand, humiliating and deadly; while on the other hand, glorifying and living.

While many will associate the water with washing, there is nothing from The Truth. As an example, there was an occasion where Naaman sought The Lord because of his leprosy: *"And Elisha sent a messenger unto him, saying, Go and wash in Jordan seven times, and thy flesh shall come again to thee, and thou shalt be clean."(2 Kings 5:10) "Are not Abana and Pharpar, rivers of Damascus, better than all the waters of Israel? may I not wash in them, and be clean? So he turned and went away in a rage." (2 Kings 5:12)* Naaman was made aware of the fact that God's Word is that which cleanses. However, Naaman thought it to be the water. His reasoning, if water were necessary, was logical. He knew that the waters of The Jordan were filthy compared to the clean waters of Abana and Pharpar.

The water represents a deeper meaning that begins with one's obedience to God despite one's opinion of the acts or the events that are to occur. After the created world for mankind was infected with the sin of a fallen culture and the contamination of a fallen angelic host, God chose to wash The Earth with a Flood that took the life of every breathing creature, except those that were allowed to enter The Ark of Safety. The story of Noah is an often-repeated narrative for students of The Bible. But while all who know of the story marvel at the devastation of the waters, few recognize the beauty of The Salvation of God afforded to Noah's family of eight humans, including himself. At the end of their journey, locked in The Ark, they walked out on dry land.

The place where one is to be baptized should be open to the view of all who may desire to observe the event. It should have sufficient water to ensure that the candidate is totally submerged. There must be an ordained member of The Church present to administer The Commission. With both parties in the water, the minister shall commence explaining the meaning of the physical testimony. Carefully read the following verses and try to picture what they represent concerning The New Birth.

(Romans 6:3-7)

3 "Know ye not, that so many of us as were baptized into Jesus Christ were baptized into his death?"

When we enter the water, we are stating by our submission and obedience that we believe that Jesus' death was the necessary Atonement for the sins of the world. It doesn't mean that we are requesting to die; but to the contrary, to live. The next time you observe someone standing in the baptismal pool, imagine their body as the vertical beam of The Cross and the water as the horizontal beam. Imagine the person saying, by the picture in your mind, that they have confidence in Jesus' power over death. Therefore, they stand willingly, by faith, in potential danger.

4 "Therefore we are buried with him by baptism into death: that like as Christ was raised up from the dead by the glory of the Father, even so we also should walk in newness of life."

This statement is not to be taken literally in the sense of physical death. We do not expect to die due to the baptismal process. However, The Word states clearly that we are buried with Him by baptism into death. The understanding is the fact that we have placed our faith in the saving power of God, through Jesus' blood, to give unto us Life Eternal: *"But now is Christ risen from the dead, and become the firstfruits of them that slept." (1 Corinthians 15:20)*

Eternal Life comes by means of the crucifixion of the flesh. *"And they that are Christ's have crucified the flesh with the affections and lusts." (Galatians 5:24)* For such a powerful transition to have occurred, there has to have been a Spiritual Baptism which changes the nature of the being from carnal (which is destined for damnation) to Spiritual (which is destined for eternal life): *"And these shall go away into everlasting punishment: but the righteous into life eternal." (Matthew 25:46)*

For such a magnificent event to occur in The Water Baptism, the transition would have to be from carnal life to physical death. Then it would be the work of The Devil and not of Christ.

As powerful and meaningful as was the death of Christ, it was not by death alone that we have cast upon Him our faith. There are countless accounts of men and women who have died for the cause of God. It is The Truth of His resurrection that glorifies His Deity and brings comfort to all who trust Him. Now, as sure as one may be of the reality of death, Life Eternal has become an even more assuring Truth. Verse 4 represents The Spiritual assurance of The New Birth.

> 5 "For if we have been planted together in the likeness of his death, we shall be also in the likeness of his resurrection:"

Now imagine the moment when The Convert is dipped bodily under the water. Let's suspend the thought and take a long look at that which occurs in a fraction of a second. The human anatomy is positioned under water in the presence of all who may witness. Verse 5 said that we have been planted with The Lord. The thought of planting something is followed by the desire to see it grow. The seed goes through a process whereas it dies. A publication by a scientist about germination stated:

> "The amazing complexity of each plant is composed in millions of specialized cells, developed from a single cell, the fertilized egg. The exact mechanisms as to how a single fertilized egg turns into a seed and then how the seed turns into a reproducing plant is yet to be fully understood. In germination, we observe a seed (diploid) turn into a gamete (haploid) producing plant."[1]

While scientists struggle with trying to understand "how," The Christian has all the understanding required in the "knowledge" of "Who." Jesus said: *"Verily, verily, I say unto you, Except a corn of wheat fall into the ground and die, it abideth alone: but if it die, it bringeth forth much fruit. He that loveth his life shall lose it; and he that hateth his life in this world shall keep it unto life eternal. (John 12:24, 25)*

How real and convincing is the display of such "knowledge" in the actual baptismal process? What would happen if we kept the candidate under the water for about 3 minutes? As stated in verse 4, we are

---

[1] Be ye followers of me, even as I also am of Christ. (1 Corinthians 11:1)

buried with Him in death; and here in verse 5, we are planted (from one existence of flesh to another existence of Spirit). To know that this transition into an acceptable fruit bearing vessel is real, Jesus said, *"I am the true vine, and my Father is the husbandman. Every branch in me that beareth not fruit he taketh away: and every branch that beareth fruit, he purgeth it, that it may bring forth more fruit."* (John 15:1-2) Jesus is saying that every branch worthy of keeping must be of Him or it shall be taken away and burned, *"If a man abide not in me, he is cast forth as a branch, and is withered; and men gather them, and cast them into the fire, and they are burned."* (John 15:6) So great an occurrence does not occur in the water, but in The Spirit wherein The Believer must remain for all of Eternity. Verse 5 closes with, *"we shall be also in the likeness of his resurrection:"*

> 6 *"Knowing this, that our old man is crucified with him, that the body of sin might be destroyed, that henceforth we should not serve sin."*

Verse 6 opens with that which every Believer should know: the "old man" is crucified and that the "new man" is free of The Penalty of Sin. Imagine coming up out of the water after having been dipped totally under. The first breath is a welcomed breath having come from a space where any attempt to breathe would result in strangling and even death. The joy of the experience is multiplied many times over for the obedient and faithful witness of The Truth concerning Jesus The Christ!

> 7 *"For he that is dead is freed from sin."*

The Spiritual Baptism is the act of saving one who asks Christ into one's life. The Penalty of Sin-Eternal Damnation-has been removed by the justification of Christ. There is but one place that God chooses to not enter without invitation. It is into the heart of humanity. Yes, the most valuable distinguisher of our individuality is our "Will." God gave it and "will" not take it back. You must surrender it. Does He really want it? Yes, He said: *"Behold, I stand at the door, and knock: if any man hear my voice, and open the door, I will come in to him, and will sup with him, and he with me."* (Revelation 3:20)

That you are Spiritually Baptized/Born Again/New Creature, then willingly allow your testimony, according to the conditions of your faith, to be boldly and publicly displayed in honor of our Lord's sacrifice and our victory. Were it not for the fact that there is, *"One Lord, one faith, one baptism," (Ephesians 4:5)* I would gladly present myself daily in recognition of so great a feat as that which our Lord has done!

"For the wages of sin is death; but the gift of God is eternal life through Jesus Christ our Lord."

(Romans 6:23)

"Buried with him in baptism, wherein also ye are risen with him through the faith of the operation of God, who hath raised him from the dead."

(Colossians 2:12)

QUESTIONS AND ANSWERS

QUESTION: WHAT IS THE MEANING OF BAPTISM?

ANSWER: BAPTISM IS THE CANDIDATE'S TESTIMONY OF HAVING PUT TO DEATH (CRUCIFIED) THE CARNAL PERSON AND BEING BROUGHT TO LIFE AS A NEW SPIRITUAL PERSON. THE WATER REPRESENTS THE GRAVE WHERE THE OLD PERSON IS BURIED AND THE NEW PERSON IS RESURRECTED.

QUESTION: WHAT IS THE BIBLICAL ADMINISTRATION OF BAPTISM?

ANSWER: TO BE TOTALLY DIPPED IN A BODY OF WATER IN THE PRESENCE OF THE SAINTS.

QUESTION: AT WHAT AGE MAY ONE BE SCRIPTURALLY (WATER) BAPTIZED?

ANSWER: ONE SHOULD SEEK TO FULFILL THE COMMAND TO BE WATER BAPTIZED ONLY AFTER HAVING SURRENDERED THEIR WILL TO CHRIST BY FAITH IN HIS SAVING GRACE. SUCH IS THE ACT OF CONVERTING AFTER HAVING TRULY REPENTED OF THE SINFUL NATURE. THE SPIRITUAL BAPTISM SHALL BE ADMINISTERED ACCORDING TO GOD'S DECREE. ONE MUST BE OF "THE AGE OF ACCOUNTABILITY" AND THEREFORE, MINDFUL OF GOD'S WORD CONCERNING THEIR SALVATION.

QUESTION: DOES THE ACT OF BEING BAPTIZED IN WATER SAVE?

ANSWER: NO! IF THE WATER ALONE IS THAT WHICH IS ADMINISTERED AND THE PERSON ENTERS UNSAVED, THEY WILL SURELY EXIT UNSAVED. GO IN DRY DEVIL, COME OUT WET DEVIL.

QUESTION: HOW MANY TIMES SHOULD I BE BAPTIZED?

ANSWER: ONE TIME! REMEMBER THAT THE SCRIPTURAL (WATER) BAPTISM IS APPLIED ONLY ONCE. SCRIPTURAL MEANS THAT THE BAPTISM WAS ADMINISTERED ACCORDING TO THE DIRECTION OF THE BIBLE WHICH FITS PERFECTLY THE CANDIDATE REGARDLESS OF BEING JEW OR GENTILE. THE ONE-TIME WATER BAPTISM IS THE MIRROR IMAGE OF THE ONE SPIRITUAL BAPTISM OR NEW BIRTH. **"ONE LORD, ONE FAITH, ONE BAPTISM," (EPHESIANS 4:5)**

QUESTION: CAN I BE SAVED WITHOUT BEING BAPTIZED IN WATER?

ANSWER: YES! HOWEVER, IF YOU ARE SAVED, YOUR FIRST DUTY TO YOUR SAVIOR IS (IF ABLE) TO MAKE A PUBLIC CONFESSION, BE BAPTIZED, AND SUBMIT TO THE DIRECTION OF THE CHURCH. **"PRAISING GOD, AND HAVING FAVOUR WITH ALL THE PEOPLE. AND THE LORD ADDED TO THE CHURCH DAILY SUCH AS SHOULD BE SAVED." (ACTS 2:47)**

QUESTION: DOES THE CHURCH I ATTEND DECIDE THE MEANS AND WORDS OF THE BAPTISM?

Answer: Yes and No! Although the church has assumed the power to determine the method and commission, she has often done so without regard to the Scripture. It goes without saying, that we are all subject to being led incorrectly. However, if the Lord, in His infinite wisdom, should allow us to reach a full understanding of His truth, then we should be governed accordingly: **"Wherefore, my beloved, as ye have always obeyed, not as in my presence only, but now much more in my absence, work out your own salvation with fear and trembling." (Philippians 2:12)** Ultimately, you should reason, according to Scripture, that the means and words are correctly representing your confession and faith! The church will not answer for you in the judgment![1]

Question: What if I WERE baptized wrong, may I get baptized again?

Answer: For the believer, there is no Scriptural baptism if the baptism is wrong. Therefore, one should not question baptism as an act that can be considered as "again." You should be Scripturally baptized and that can only be once. If you were wrongfully baptized, then being Scripturally baptized recants the wrong doctrine and satisfies the LORD'S COMMAND.

Question: If my church does not immerse the candidate in water, may I get baptized someplace else and continue at my church?

Answer: YES, but would you consider yourself to be acting in the best interest of all considering the apparent incorrect doctrine being taught? What else are you

---

BEING FED THAT MAY HAVE UNDESIRABLE CONSEQUENCES IN THE JUDGEMENT? "THEREFORE TO HIM THAT KNOWETH TO DO GOOD, AND DOETH IT NOT, TO HIM IT IS SIN." (JAMES 4:17)

QUESTION: IF I WITNESS TO SOMEONE AND THEY ACCEPT JESUS AS THEIR SAVIOR, SHOULD I BAPTIZE THEM WITH URGENCY (LIKE IN A PERSONAL POOL OR BATHTUB)?

ANSWER: NO! PLANNING THE BAPTISM TO BE A PERSONAL TESTIMONY FOR FAMILY, FRIENDS, AND SAINTS AT A CHURCH OF THE NEW SAINTS CHOICE IS THE BEST PLAN.

HE THAT BELIEVETH AND IS BAPTIZED SHALL BE SAVED; BUT HE THAT BELIEVETH NOT SHALL BE DAMNED.

(MARK 16:16)

CHAPTER 12

BIBLE-KISS

KEEP IT SIMPLE STUDY–5 STEP PLAN

Having engaged in and completed this analysis of how to study, you are ready to take on the exciting, emotional, and rewarding discoveries of God's Love Letter to mankind, The Bible. Add to the process this easy to remember "5-Step" Method and you are well on your way: C X C= C+ C.

FIVE STEP METHOD
C = Context
X = Cross Reference
C = Culture
C = Conclusion
C = Commentary/Corroboration

Every Bible Teacher is a Bible Student. But every Bible Student is not a Bible Teacher. You should always endeavor to engage children in Bible Study. But never endeavor to teach children to study The Bible. Even our Lord was questioned concerning His "knowledge" at such a young age, *"And all that heard him were astonished at his understanding and answers." (Luke 2:47)* It is at "the age of accountability" that the mind of the student may begin to take on the responsibility of teaching. Christ noted this fact by simply replying, *"And he said unto them, How is it that ye sought me? wist ye not that I must be about my Father's business?" (Luke 2:49)* The disciples, and even The Apostle Paul, spent three years learning to correctly interpret The Scriptures before being commissioned to teach. Unprepared teachers are the primary reason for many of the unfounded doctrines so prevalent in Christianity today. Many of them became teachers long before having received the appropriate guidance as students.

> *Let them alone: they be blind leaders of the blind. And if the blind lead the blind, both shall fall into the ditch.*
> *(Matthew 15:14)*

It is imperative that one understands his/her station when attempting to explicate The Scriptures. There is a succor for the men whom God has called to Pastoral Ministry. It is The Anointing; and even then, it is accompanied by the necessity of study.

> *My brethren, be not many masters, knowing that we shall receive the greater condemnation. For in many things we offend all. If any man offend not in word, the same is a perfect man, and able also to bridle the whole body.*
> *(James 3:1, 2)*

The above acronym (C X C = C + C) may be used to remember the sequence that a Bible Teacher should follow. The last "C" represents Commentary, and mistakenly too many Bible Scholars are more inclined to begin there, rather than end there. Understandably, those who admit their weakness in biblical growth are correct at following the annotations of reputable teachers and authors. However, even the neophyte has an opinion. Every student should prayerfully attempt to gain understanding of the passage before researching the opinions of others. Deviating from this path may cause mental mapping, which hinders the ability to reach a fresh personal understanding.

CONTEXT:

Does the initial "observation" conflict with your doctrinal stance? Take the following verse as an example:

O daughter of Babylon, who art to be destroyed; happy shall
he be, that rewardeth thee as thou hast served us. Happy shall
he be, that taketh and dasheth thy little ones against the stones.
(Psalm 137:8, 9)

At face value, the above Scripture not only approves the slamming of the infants of Babylon against a wall, but also applauds those who do so. Regardless to one's personal "interpretation," such considerations are inherently wrong.

For when the Gentiles, which have not the law, do by nature
the things contained in the law, these, having not the law, are
a law unto themselves: Which shew the work of the law written
in their hearts, their conscience also bearing witness, and their
thoughts the mean while accusing or else excusing one another;
(Romans 2:14, 15)

And if such is inherently wrong, then there is a deeper "understanding" that must be reached before correctly interpreting that Scripture.

CROSS REFERENCE:

Are there any other Scriptures that jump out to you that might shed some light on the Context of Psalm 137:8, 9? When I think of the sin of culpable negligence to children, I am reminded of the following:

But Jesus called them unto him, and said, Suffer little children
to come unto me, and forbid them not: for of such is the
kingdom of God. Verily I say unto you, Whosoever shall not
receive the kingdom of God as a little child shall in no wise
enter therein.
(Luke 18:16, 17)

Jesus clearly likened The Kingdom of God to little children. Not some children, but all. Therefore, the infants of Babylon are no exception.

"O Daughter of Babylon" brings to mind The Book of Revelation where John penned these words:

> *And upon her forehead was a name written, MYSTERY, BABYLON THE GREAT, THE MOTHER OF HARLOTS AND ABOMINATIONS OF THE EARTH. And I saw the woman drunken with the blood of the saints, and with the blood of the martyrs of Jesus: and when I saw her, I wondered with great admiration.*
>
> *(Revelation 17:5, 6)*

So, Babylon is clearly a reference to The Satanic System that eats at the souls of all living until God Himself brings it to an end. The retribution that is inferred in Psalms, "*Happy shall he be, that taketh and dasheth thy little ones against the stones*" is speaking prophetically of the day that God will conquer Evil off of the face of The Earth.

> *And the devil that deceived them was cast into the lake of fire and brimstone, where the beast and the false prophet are, and shall be tormented day and night for ever and ever.*
>
> *(Revelation 20:10)*

The Allegorical Application of the little ones tends to bring to mind adults rather than children. They are the offspring of an evil, vicious human clan. Where might I find a Biblical reference to such?

> *Ye are of your father the devil, and the lusts of your father ye will do. He was a murderer from the beginning, and abode not in the truth, because there is no truth in him. When he speaketh a lie, he speaketh of his own: for he is a liar, and the father of it.*
>
> *(John 8:44)*

The appropriate Theological Process will ensure the keeping in Context ones' "interpretation."

CULTURE/HISTORICAL:

Babylon has a very long history of being a mighty city, often in conflict with God's people. The city of Babylon is spoken of around 265 times by name and countless other inferences. Once the reader confirms The Allegorical Babylon, then the "interpretation" of Psalms 137 begins to make sense.

CONCLUSION:

Having reached a Conclusion that speaks to the "interpretation" of Psalms 137, one must advance their "understanding" to an acceptable and appropriate act. No sane person will find approval to harm any person, let alone children.

Upon reaching a Biblically correct Conclusion, the reader will hopefully receive an overwhelming approval from The Spirit of The Lord. This Conclusion is the matter from which the proverbial "Amen" speaks.

COMMENTARY:

When The Spirit of Agreement reaches your mind and soul, then it is appropriate to compare notes. Read the comments of other scholars on the same subject or text that was considered. How much in agreement are you? Do not forget that a lack of agreement does not mean that you are wrong, and equally an agreement does not mean that you are right. However, at the end of the day, one must hold him/herself responsible for their actions or lack of the same.

> *For it is written, As I live, saith the Lord, every knee shall bow to me, and every tongue shall confess to God. So then every one of us shall give account of himself to God.*
> *(Romans 14:11, 12)*

EXAMINING COMMENTARY

Using those skills that you have developed in this study, consider the conflicting commentaries relating to the appropriate "interpretation" of the term "son(s) of God." Think critically of the information provided by each contributor. Conclude with a decision of your own based on comparative notes, comments, and your personal conclusion.

Does the reference "son(s) of God" imply a Being who exist by the unassisted act of God alone?

C. I. Schofield:

"For over 90 years people have relied on this reference work in their daily study of God's Word. Written originally in 1909, C. I. Scofield's intent was to provide a concise but complete tool that would meet the need of someone just beginning to read the Bible."

The above words are associated with most outlets advertising The Schofield Study Bible. The following commentary was taken from a more comprehensive collection of references composed from the study of The Bible by C. I. Schofield. Note that his comments concerning the events of Genesis Chapter 6 refute any attempt to understand the Spiritual assault Satan levied against humanity. Further examination by Scofield references The Flood as a consequence of humanity's refusal to abstain from interfamily marriages and or consummations.

Genesis Chapter 6

6:4 There were giants in the earth in those days; and also after that, when the sons of God came in unto the daughters of men, and they bare children to them, the same became mighty men which were of old, men of renown.

"sons of God"

Some hold that these "sons of God" were the "angels which kept not their first estate". (Jude 1:6) It is asserted that the title is in the O.T. exclusively used of angels. But this is an error. (Isaiah 43:6) Angels are spoken of in a sexless way. No female angels are mentioned in Scripture, and we are expressly told that marriage is unknown among angels. (Matthew 22:30)

The uniform Hebrew and Christian interpretation has been that verse Genesis 6:2 marks the breaking down of the separation between the godly line of Seth and the godless line of Cain, and so the failure of the testimony to Jehovah committed to the line of Seth Genesis 4:26. For apostasy there is no remedy but judgment; Isaiah 1:2-7, Isaiah 1:24, Isaiah 1:25; Hebrews 6:4-8;10:26-31. Noah, "a preacher of righteousness," is given 120 years, but he won no convert, and the judgment predicted by his great-grandfather fell; Jude 1:14 Jude 1:15; Genesis 7:11.

Culture and character coupled with conditions often prove to make one complicit. Mr. Schofield was raised at a time when civil unrest had a profound impact on Bible "interpretation." His audience strived for answers that would satisfy the general and popular premise of their political era (August 19, 1843 – July 24, 1921). One must remember that although The Bible speaks to all times, it is not affected by anytime. Too often, scholars attempt to construct their own opinions with a calculated attempt to make The Bible conform to their personal situations.

Scofield's attestation that it is the "uniform Hebrew and Christian interpretation" to assume that the events relating to the "sons of God" is about the sons of Seth is incorrect. Several centuries before Christ, Jews embraced Enoch's apocrypha, which survived as a midrash on Deuteronomy 33:2. That removes any doubt of the widespread belief that angels compromised humans.

N. J. McClain, Sr.

In the book Spiritual Ménage a Trois, McClain[1] contradicts the teachings of C. I. Schofield and the renowned Matthew Henry (18 October 1662 – 22 June 1714) about the "sons of God." While comparing the following excerpt with that of these authors, be mindful of the need to either disagree or agree, depending on the persuasion exhibited by Scriptural Analysis and Context.

Schofield's proclamation stated:

> … It is asserted that the title is in the O.T. exclusively used of angels. But this is an error. (<u>Isaiah 43:6</u>)

> *I will say to the north, Give up; and to the south, Keep not back: bring my sons from far, and my daughters from the ends of the earth;*
>
> *(Isaiah 43:6)*

The words "sons of God" and "my sons" are clearly two completely different expressions. Yes, without a doubt, each use of the term "my sons," in The Old Testament was a reference to human beings, while "*sons of God*" were exclusively angels.

Note below that keeping the term "my sons" in Context renders an indication of not only sons but also daughters. Isaiah's use of the term "my sons" includes all the people of Israel.

> *Thus saith the Lord, the Holy One of Israel, and his Maker, Ask me of things to come concerning my sons, and concerning the work of my hands command ye me. I have made the earth, and created man upon it: I, even my hands, have stretched out the heavens, and all their host have I commanded. I have raised him up in righteousness, and I will direct all his ways: he shall*

---

[1]   Matthew Henry Commentary © 2004-2014 by Biblos.com

build my city, and he shall let go my captives, not for price nor
reward, saith the Lord of hosts.

(Isiah 45:11-13)

We are all God's children by Creation. However, except He personally empowers our being exclusive of any other, we are not "of God." Without exception, the five times that the term "sons of God" is used in The Old Testament, each relates to heavenly beings. In the following text, God admonishes Job with rhetorical questions concerning Job's whereabouts before and during The Creation of the world. Note the inference of the absence of humanity, yet the presence of the "sons of God."

Where wast thou when I laid the foundations of the earth?
declare, if thou hast understanding. Who hath laid the measures
thereof, if thou knowest? or who hath stretched the line upon it?
Whereupon are the foundations thereof fastened? or who laid
the corner stone thereof; When the morning stars sang together,
and all the sons of God shouted for joy?

(Job 38:4-7)

MATTHEW HENRY, a predecessor of Scofield, also taught that the "sons of God" were of the godly line of Seth, rather than angels. However, in Henry's Commentary of Job 38:4-11, he never once mentioned the inclusion of the "sons of God." But he does reference the fact that this Scripture speaks of God's creative works. Therefore, the "sons of God" had to precede The Creation of humanity.

"Job 38:4-11 For the humbling of Job, God here shows
him his ignorance, even concerning the earth and the
sea. As we cannot find fault with God's work, so we need
not fear concerning it. The works of his providence, as
well as the work of creation, never can be broken; and
the work of redemption is no less firm, of which Christ
himself is both the Foundation and the Cornerstone.
The church stands as firm as the earth."

Matthew Henry Commentary
© 2004-2014 by Biblos.com

Do you think that Henry simply overlooked any mention of the "sons of God" in his comments? Any reference that Henry could have made of the "sons of God" in Job 38 would have clearly brought the presence of angels to the scene. The following is a portion of Henry's commentary on Genesis 6:1-7. There is no reference to the Spiritual attack suffered by the people of The Antediluvian Era. The emphasis is clearly on human marriage and segregation.

> 1-7 The most remarkable thing concerning the old world, is the destroying of it by the deluge, or flood. We are told of the abounding iniquity of that wicked world: God's just wrath, and his holy resolution to punish it. In all ages there has been a peculiar curse of God upon marriages between professors of true religion and its avowed enemies. The evil example of the ungodly party corrupts or greatly hurts the other. Family religion is put an end to, and the children are trained up according to the worldly maxims of that parent who is without the fear of God. If we profess to be the sons and daughters of the Lord Almighty, we must not marry without his consent. He will never give his blessing, if we prefer beauty, wit, wealth, or worldly honours, to faith and holiness.[1]

If we are to interpret Henry's words to mean that one's godliness should be the first consideration when contemplating marriage, then it is correct. However, if we are to consider these words to represent racial distinction, then it would be entirely wrong, seeing as how there was no race distinction at that time.

In a word, Henry, Scofield, and others bought into the deception that God destroyed the world because members of differing families

---

[1] Genesis 5:3 And Adam lived an hundred and thirty years, and begat a son in his own likeness, after his image; and called his name Seth:

united in marriage. If that is true, justification for segregation is of God. But was it not God who said, "Be fruitful and multiply"? If the human family dynamic was a real concern for that era (Dispensation), one might concentrate on when incest became immoral. Commentators who see the events following the exodus from Eden as sexual perversions are overlooking the apparent incest that occurred. Since Eve is "The Mother of All Living," her sons had to marry their sisters. God was not concerned about the relationships that humans were having with humans. At which generation were siblings not to marry each other? Was it the 120 years that God gave humanity to discontinue its path away from His Will?

> And the Lord said, My spirit shall not always strive with man, for that he also is flesh: yet his days shall be an hundred and twenty years.
>
> *(Genesis 6:3)*

No! As will be explained later, the above Scripture relates to the strife between Spirit Beings and Human Beings. God's intervention was due to the attack of a formidable foe. The magnificence of The Deluge is but another example of how far God will go to erase the effects of sin.

As Moses penned the first paragraph in Genesis 6, he clearly establishes The Context and The Culture in which Satan's genetic influence flooded the DNA of humanity.

> And it came to pass, when men began to multiply on the face of the earth, and daughters were born unto them, That the sons of God saw the daughters of men that they were fair; and they took them wives of all which they chose.
>
> *(Genesis 6:1, 2)*

It was at the moment that "men began to multiply on the face of the earth," that the "sons of God" took interest in the "daughters of men." According to The Bible, Cain's descendants preceded the descendants of Seth. Therefore neither Seth nor his descendants were present at the beginning of human multiplication on Earth. As a matter of fact,

The Bible references Seth's heritage to be the beginning of those that worshiped The Lord. Now, since Seth was born one hundred and thirty years after men began to multiply on The Earth, how could he or his generations qualify for the title "sons of God"?[1]

> *And to Seth, to him also there was born a son; and he called his name Enos: then began men to call upon the name of the Lord.*
> *(Genesis 4:26)*

This fact alone should be enough to secure an agreement that refutes the teachings of mainline Christian scholars to the contrary. Yet, there are numerous other literal matters that logically agree that the "sons of God" were angels. Genesis 6:1-2 includes two contrasting subjects: one relates to the human condition and the other to angels. A point made earlier by Scofield is that there has never been a biblical mention of a female angel. Since there were no female angels, then a reference to "sons and daughters" would in such case render the reference to "angels" as impossible. The pairing of "sons" with "daughters" is undoubtedly referring to humans. The union of "sons and daughters" will produce a pure offspring of humankind. In Isaiah 43, the "sons" were accompanied by "daughters" —thus the inference can only be human. Not so in the reference to "sons of God" and "daughters of men." The word "God" references The Spirit and "men" the physical. Moses wrote that they "took them wives of all which they chose." Since The Scripture is representing a Spiritual intrusion into the physical realm, one would have to expect an abnormal result.

> *And the Lord said, My spirit shall not always strive with man, for that he also is flesh: yet his days shall be an hundred and twenty years. There were giants in the earth in those days; and also after that, when the sons of God came in unto the*

---

[1] Brandt "Die mandäische Religion" 1889 pp. 197, 198; Norberg's "Onomasticon," p. 31; Adriaan Reland's "De Religione Mohammedanarum," p. 89; Kamus, s.v. "Azazel" [demon identical with Satan]; Delitzsch, "Zeitsch. f. Kirchl. Wissensch. u. Leben," 1880, p. 182

daughters of men, and they bare children to them, the same
became mighty men which were of old, men of renown.

(Genesis 6:3, 4)

Next is the contrast of sons vs. daughters; the former not being able to bear children, but the latter can. If the problem were exclusively among humans, could there have been some women from Seth's family (daughters of God) becoming involved with the men of Cain's family (sons of man)? It is highly improbable that only the sons of Seth would have found only the daughters of Cain to be beautiful and desirable. Surely the daughters of Seth were fair and desirable. As such, the sons of Cain would stop at nothing to have them. Cain's sons had already established a precedent that led to the taking of more than one wife. It stands to reason that if a particular family were to be blamed for the taking of the women of the other family, the likeliest suspect would have been Cain, and not Seth. If the problem were truly with the worshipping family being contaminated by the heathens, The Scripture most probably would have read, "The sons of Satan saw the daughters of Seth that they were fair; and they took them wives of all which they chose."

The early translators were careful with their translation. However, many of the more current translations have lost the beauty of the words that describe the events surrounding the interaction of angels and humans. The Authorized Version-AV (King James Version-KJV) demonstrates the importance of maintaining a word for word, inclusive of every syntactic in the translation. In the case of Genesis 6:1, 2, most of the early translations kept the same punctuation as the AV. However, they changed the first letter "T," beginning at verse 2, from a capital type to a small type. The "observation" is important because the capital "T" begins a comparative contrast to the subject matter of Genesis 6:1 with the subject matter of Genesis 6:2. To add to that fact, the early translators split the sentence into two separate verses. The first verse references human conditions. The second verse references angelic intrusion.

The very next verse (3) opens with another contrast, spirit and flesh. Both are products of the creative authority of God, yet different. God said that the one, spirit/angel, would not always strive with the other, flesh/man. To strive is to struggle or fight vigorously. If the *"sons of God"* were men and the *"daughters of men"* were women, would there have been a need to fight? However, if the *"sons of God"* were angels operating out of their habitat, such invasion would constitute strife. Since angels are powerful beyond our imagination, I think it is safe to say that an eventful offspring would be abnormal.

> *And GOD saw that the wickedness of man was great in the earth, and that every imagination of the thoughts of his heart was only evil continually.*
>
> *(Genesis 6:5)*

The condition of humanity above differed greatly from the original condition at Creation. *"And God saw every thing that he had made, and, behold, it was very good. And the evening and the morning were the sixth day."* Genesis 1:31 How did every imagination of the thoughts of man's heart become evil? Angels that were serving Satan's cause infected humanity.

> *And it repented the LORD that he had made man on the earth, and it grieved him at his heart.*
>
> *(Genesis 6:6)*

It was said that those of us who accept the fact that the "sons of God" were angels reference Jude verses 6 and 7 as proof.

> *And the angels which kept not their first estate, but left their own habitation, he hath reserved in everlasting chains under darkness unto the judgment of the great day. Even as Sodom and Gomorrha, and the cities about them in like manner, giving themselves over to fornication, and going after strange flesh, are set forth for an example, suffering the vengeance of eternal fire.*
>
> *(Jude 1:6, 7)*

In the above Scripture, there is evidence that there are angels who are reserved in everlasting chains due to having left their First Estate.

What does it mean to have left their Estate? The Estate in question is Heaven versus Earth. Although angels minister in Earth, they are heavenly beings. Jesus made this distinction this way: *"And he said unto them, Ye are from beneath; I am from above: ye are of this world; I am not of this world."* (John 8:23) Note also that Jesus represented Satan's Fall as having left Heaven:

> *And he said unto them, I beheld Satan as lightning fall from heaven. Behold, I give unto you power to tread on serpents and scorpions, and over all the power of the enemy: and nothing shall by any means hurt you.*
>
> *(Luke 10:18, 19)*

Scofield represented the impossibility of human and angelic relationship by offering Matthew 22: 30 as proof. To the contrary, I will show that it is proof that it can occur.

> *For in the resurrection they neither marry, nor are given in marriage, but are as the angels of God in heaven.*
>
> *(Matthew 22:30)*

Jesus was speaking to The Sadducees, who challenged the fact of The Resurrection and denied the existence of Angels. The Sadducees questioned Christ on the matter of seven brothers who each had the same wife during their life. Which of the seven could claim her in Heaven? Jesus told them, *"Ye do err, not knowing the scriptures, nor the power of God."* (Matthew 22:29) Then He followed with the above explanation of the difference in matters in Earth and Heaven. The above Scripture places humans and angels on equal footing sexually by the designation *"in heaven."* So, if humans in Heaven are like the angels (asexual), then angels in The Earth, who have left their first habitat, are as humans (sexual.) The angels that left their habitat are destined to Eternal Fire. What could they have done that would lead to such a damnable Eternity? They dared to move against The Will of God by attempting to overthrow His Kingdom and all that is in it. They followed the lead of Satan and subtly intruded in the genetics of earthly beings, people.

WIKIPEDIA-AZAZEL

The following excerpt taken from Wikipedia sheds light on the subject of Genesis 6: 1-4):

> According to the Book of Enoch, Azazel (here spelled 'ăzā'zyēl) was one of the chief Grigori, a group of fallen angels who married women. Many believe that this same story (without any mention of Azazel) is told in the book of Genesis 6:2–4: "That the sons of God (בְּנֵי הָאֱלֹהִים: benê'ĕlō·hîm) saw the daughters of men that they were fair; and they took them wives of all which they chose. [...] There were giants in the earth in those days; and also afterward, when the sons of God came in unto the daughters of men, and they bore children to them, the same became mighty men which were of old, men of renown."
>
> Some believe, however, that the reference to "sons of God" in this passage is referring to men in that God formed man from the ground, and woman from men. Genesis 2:7, 23. They cite nine other places that refer to men as "sons of God": Deuteronomy 14:1, 32:5, Psalm 73:15, Isaiah 43:6, 7, Hosea 1:10, 11:1, Luke 3:38, 1 John 3:1, 2, 10. They also claim that Hebrews 1:5 *"For unto which of the angels said he at any time, Thou art my Son, this day have I begotten thee?"* argues that God never referred to angels as his sons. Because of these things they see the "sons of God" as merely men.
>
> But the nine passages referred to above are all based on simple English translation comparison and not an actual Hebrew textual comparison with Genesis 6:1-4, which

contextually places the daughters of men into one group representing humanity (Gen 6:1 "And it happened that, when humankind began to multiply on the face of the ground, daughters were born to them"), and the "sons of God" (בְּנֵי הָאֱלֹהִים: benê'ĕlō·hîm) into a second group. None of those nine passages refer to the benê'ĕlō·hîm, but only to English translation references to Israel, Judah, and as God's children.

The six Old Testament passages cited do not support the claim that "sons of God" is referring to all humanity, but only that God did refer to Israel and Judah as his children. Though the end of Luke 3:38 is translated into English as "son of God", it simply says "of God" in the Greek. In 1 John 3, the author, who refers to his audience as "my little children", does, indeed, proclaim that those who are in Christ (1 John 1:28) are God's children, but this has nothing to do with the benê'ĕlō·hîm of Gen 6 because they existed thousands of years before any Christians. And since Israel also did not exist until thousands of years after the events of Gen 6, the benê'ĕlō·hîm cannot be referring to them either. The only other usage of benê'ĕlō·hîm in the Hebrew Bible is found in Job 1:6, and Job 2:1, both of which refer to supernatural beings. These three verses are the only benê'ĕlō·hîm verses in all of the Hebrew Masoretic Text, which was finalized around 1000 a.d. But the ancient understanding of benê˚ĕlō·hîm as supernatural beings was so firmly established over the history of Israel and Judah that in the Septuagint, which was completed some time between the 3rd and 1st century b.c.,[1][2] the term "sons of God" is replaced with "angels of God" in all three of these verses.[3] Thus demonstrating that the translators of the Septuagint did not consider benê˚ĕlō·hîm a matter of question, but rather a matter of fact: they were supernatural beings.

The Jewish Bible Community has several noted "interpretations" of Genesis 6. The following three are the most prevalent:

Explanation 1: Angels fell (were corrupted) with women

Explanation 2: Corrupt Authorities

Explanation 3: Fallen Humans

The beauty of the mind is its ability to approach any given precept from every possible angle. Therefore, one must not stop with their first "interpretation." Are there any other logical explanations? Before reaching a final "conclusion," examine each of the perceivable "interpretations" by explaining why yours is more desirable.

In Closing:

Every person must accept his/her personal responsibility for the things that are done here in the flesh. As a matter of personal consideration, examine the doctrines you hold to be true; and hopefully,

[1] Ralph D. Levy The symbolism of the Azazel goat 1998 "the midrash is less elaborate than in 1 Enoch, and, notably, makes no mention of Azazel or Asa' el at all."

[2] Enoch xiii.; compare Brandt, "Die mandäische Religion", 1889, p. 38

[3]

confirm and conclude that you are on the right side (God's Love – Grace) of "interpretation" and "application."

> *Whosoever transgresseth, and abideth not in the doctrine of Christ, hath not God. He that abideth in the doctrine of Christ, he hath both the Father and the Son. If there come any unto you, and bring not this doctrine, receive him not into your house, neither bid him God speed: For he that biddeth him God speed is partaker of his evil deeds.*
>
> *(2 John 1:9-11)*

The joy of feeling comfortable with The Greatest Book ever written is the gift of God to all who will, through faith, trust Him and seek His aid for Spiritual growth. The Enemy hates your due diligence in applying God's Word to your every endeavor. Therefore, you should oblige his weakness with the strength of an anointed Bible Study. Remember not to forget that The Bible is "Basic Instructions Before Leaving Earth" (B. I. B. L. E.) Take joy in the fact that there is more to be discovered in the depths of The Bible than that which all men together could ever reveal. Such is proof that there are many epiphanies awaiting your diligent search.

JUDE 1:24, 25

> **Now unto him that is able to keep you from falling, and to present you faultless before the presence of his glory with exceeding joy, To the only wise God our Saviour, be glory and majesty, dominion and power, both now and ever.**

AMEN.

CPSIA information can be obtained
at www.ICGtesting.com
Printed in the USA
BVHW071638060422
633551BV00006B/120